# FREE BLACK COMMUNITIES AND THE UNDERGROUND RAILROAD

# FREE BLACK COMMUNITIES AND THE UNDERGROUND RAILROAD

## The Geography of Resistance

CHERYL JANIFER LaROCHE

UNIVERSITY OF ILLINOIS PRESS
Urbana, Chicago, and Springfield

Manufactured in the United States of America
1 2 3 4 5 C P 5 4

∞ This book is printed on acid-free paper.

Library of Congress Cataloging-in-Publication Data
LaRoche, Cheryl Janifer.
Free Black Communities and the Underground Railroad : the Geography of Resistance / Cheryl Janifer LaRoche.
pages cm
Includes bibliographical references and index.
ISBN 978-0-252-03804-4 (hardback)
ISBN 978-0-252-07954-2 (paper)
ISBN 978-0-252-09589-4 (ebook)
1. Underground Railroad—Indiana. 2. Underground Railroad—Illinois. 3. Underground Railroad—Ohio. 4. Fugitive slaves—United States—History. 5. African Americans—History—19th century—Sources. 6. Antislavery movements—United States—History. 7. frican Americans—Antiquities. 8. Excavations (Archaeology)—United States.
I. Title.
F450.L37 2013
973.7'115—dc23 2013024073

# CONTENTS

# LIST OF FIGURES

# PREFACE

This book presents a place-based study of free Black communities in Illinois, Indiana, and Ohio. The humble settlements of Rocky Fork, Miller Grove, Lick Creek, and Poke Patch highlight Underground Railroad activities using vital elements of what I term the "geography of resistance." By using the land as a document and relying on archaeology and community and church histories, in addition to traditional Underground Railroad stories, the lives of the people forming church and community finally connected. From there I began to look for broader examples.

Near the end of my research, Pamela Tilley, historiographer for the lay organization of the African Methodist Episcopal (AME) Church, assured me that Reading, Pennsylvania, had everything I was looking for. She arranged a meeting with local historian Frank Gilyard Jr., sadly, now deceased, and his dynamic wife, Mildred, who took me on a tour of their marvelous Central Pennsylvania African American Museum housed in the Old Bethel AME church. It was here in Reading that the pieces of my research came together. The town had it all: the Black church, the ever present William Paul Quinn, documented Underground Railroad escapes, iron forges, waterways and caves for hiding, a cemetery with Civil War graves—all components I had come to recognize as elements essential to how Blacks operated along the Underground Railroad as part of the geography of resistance.

I was grateful that Tilley had traveled east from Texas to help me solve the last parts of a vexing puzzle. She and I spent hours talking about the importance of the AME church beyond its religious functions. We both agree that the magnitude of the influence of the denomination during the historic period of the Underground Railroad has yet to be fully appreciated. I hope this study moves the church beyond the realm of religion and catapults it to a stature equal to its historic importance for the Underground Railroad.

By the time of Tilley's visit, I had been studying African American involvement in the Underground Railroad for more than ten years. I had come to understand a story quite different from the usual fare of frightened fugitives and their benevolent abolitionist accomplices. As I learned the mechanisms behind the stories, I began finding names of Black abolitionists and Underground Railroad operatives, such as New York's Charles B. Ray, Illinois's John Jones, and Pennsylvania's Lewis Woodson, turning up across several states, Black organizations, and social networks. At times, they were members of the Free Masons or attended colored conventions together. They assembled at the Phoenix Society, emigration conventions, and general conferences. Many had been ministers in the rural black churches or independent denominations that animate this study.

This book is divided into three parts. Part I focuses on four specific sites: Rocky Fork and Miller Grove in Illinois, Lick Creek in Indiana, and Poke Patch in Ohio. Part II defines and explores each of the components of the geography of resistance. Part III combines family stories and individual narratives with Black community and church histories and the activism of the Prince Hall Masons to place African American families inside these institutional structures.

Combining history and geography fosters an expanded understanding useful for recognizing and recovering African American participation beyond sites normally associated with the Underground Railroad. Redrawing historic maps of Underground Railroad routes to include Black settlements and churches makes visible unrecognized parallel connections between free Black communities and larger better-known abolitionist centers (see map 1). Where the historical record was thin, I relied on archaeology and studied the cultural landscape. It may well come to pass that the archaeological signature of the Underground Railroad will be the footprint of the Black church rather than the underground tunnels and concealed passageways that first attracted the narrow focus of the discipline.[1]

Concentrating on the landscape, Black communities, and Black churches emphasizes the self-determination of free Blacks. Community and church histories bundled with well-worn narratives and brief biographical accounts tie together the lives of seemingly unrelated operators, both Black and White. Within the Black community, an alternative oral, local, and family history was handed from parent to child, from family to family, and from Black historians to the reading public. Each passed along a powerful narrative of Blacks ensuring their own liberation in the midst of constant economic, social, judicial, and educational hardships.

Through this work, my understanding of the Black community expanded from the small rural pre–Civil War midwestern clusters I had spent a dozen years studying, to include Underground Railroad operatives who were openly meeting with one another at convention, conference, church, and society gatherings convened for worthy and respectable causes. At each of the historic settlements I visited, a community of Black families had once come together, initially meeting in one another's homes, to lay the foundations for the Black church. Most frequently AME churches, but AME Zion and Baptist churches as well, were magnets binding families to one another, connecting the settlements to the larger world. Beyond the official minutes and newspaper accounts, I began to see that family members, Black institutions, and Black churches, particularly their ministers, were in league with one another.

Throughout my travels, I repeatedly ran across one name, William Paul Quinn, one of the first seven itinerant preachers appointed by the AME Church. Quinn later rose to prominence as its fourth bishop. When I first arrived at Rocky Fork in Illinois, he was listed as the organizer of the small congregation. When I traveled to Lick Creek in Indiana, his name was on the deed for the church. When I came back to Maryland, I found Quinn Chapel less than an hour from my home; Quinn had been active in Frederick, Maryland. Now Tilley was taking me to Pennsylvania to visit Old Bethel AME, which Quinn had helped organize in 1821.

Each one of these churches has a local Underground Railroad story behind it. In the countryside sanctuaries, tucked away on remote land, beyond the ready reach of the outside world, Quinn and other itinerant preachers were sanctioned to move from place to place spreading the word of God and the gospel of liberation.

When archaeologist Paul Shackel first suggested I travel to Illinois to determine whether a small town started by Frank McWorter, a free Black man in New Philadelphia, Illinois, was a viable archaeological site, I could not have anticipated the rich reward that the journey would yield. Over the span of years, my journey has taken me from the African Meeting House in Nantucket, Massachusetts, to the grave of Moses Dickson in St. Louis, Missouri, to an early AME church and settlement in San Francisco, California, looking for historic Black communities, their organizations, and their churches.

* * *

As originally defined, the Underground Railroad was a movement that began in the 1830s as an outgrowth of the unrelenting actions of self-liberators' and abolitionists' efforts to aid those escaping slavery. In contrast to persistent misperceptions of the Underground Railroad, Blacks were positioned on the edge of freedom, on what historian Keith Griffler calls "the front line of freedom."[2] Now defined as a mode of operation rather than as a structured organization, the Underground Railroad was a movement—a political position—defined by a philosophical relationship with freedom for all who were involved.

While abolitionism has received considerable attention, academic historians tended to ignore the Underground Railroad, particularly throughout the twentieth century. Involvement of African Americans beyond the actions of those escaping slavery was difficult to recover. Graham Russell Hodges laid out the various reasons that gave historians pause in ascribing importance to it.[3] Denied the traditional interpretative approaches historians provide, the topic was allowed to lie fallow, prompting Congress, in 1990, to direct the National Park Service (NPS) to determine the most appropriate ways to interpret and commemorate the widespread national and international work of the Underground Railroad in ways commensurate with its importance. It is as though the movement needed an organized cohesive interpretative plan so that the disparate components could resonate.

For centuries, escaping Blacks found sanctuary in a wide range of places representing freedom both at home and abroad and Congress emphasized the importance of approximate escape routes. As a result, NPS expanded the scope of the Underground Railroad beyond the original nineteenth-century meaning and beyond popular understanding. The "retrospective" use of the term by NPS now includes "incidents which have all the characteristics of Underground Railroad activity, but which occurred before 1820."[4] The National Historic Landmark Archaeological Initiative defines the Underground Railroad as "every attempt the enslaved made to escape from the 1600s to 1865."[5]

Throughout this book, when referring to the Underground Railroad as broadly defined by NPS, I refer to the "Underground Railroad movement," which includes unassisted escapes and events occurring prior to 1830. I use the term "Underground Railroad" to refer to the traditional definition of escapes, assisted or not, which originated after 1830 where escapees either used known routes or accepted aid once they crossed into the border states.

Underground Railroad lore frequently defies logic; one part of a long cherished story may prove false and misremembered, yet the remaining elements of the story may hold historical truths. Contrary to conventional wisdom, I am cautious about disregarding lore and longstanding legends without research supporting refutation. Often we are less rigorous in denial of fact than we are in corroboration and acceptance. I use oral testimony as a starting point or research thread and urge reevaluation of oral histories. I advocate preserving stories despite apparently implausible, anachronistic, or temporally and geographically inaccurate data. These same errors can and do occur in the written record as well. Rather than dismiss inaccurate oral histories, we should begin to think of that instability as an expected component. I am wary of completely accurate narrations. I think legends offer clues which exist in a pre-verifiable form; in that way stories can be maintained as research questions rather than assigned to oblivion.

I refer to African American people using the terms "Black" and "people of color" interchangeably, "colored," or "Negro" as historic terms or within direct quotes. Nineteenth-century African American history is a particularly racialized subject, requiring a racialized language. Black abolitionist Henry Highland Garnet traveled over this same linguistic terrain more than two and a half centuries ago. "How unprofitable it is for us to spend our golden moments in long and solemn debate upon the question whether we shall be called 'Africans,' 'Colored Americans,' or 'Africo Americans,' or 'Blacks.' The question should be, my friends, *shall we arise and act like men, and cast off this terrible yoke*?"[6] Throughout this book, in recognition that Blacks often intermarried or had relations with Native Americans and with Whites, I also employ the nineteenth-century term "free people of color" to indicate the range of Black people within a racially diverse population. When possible, I minimize the use of terms such as "slave," "runaway," "fugitive slave," or "fugitive from justice." These terms dehumanize and criminalize those escaping the multiple oppressions of slavery and define freedom-seeking behavior from the enslavers' legal vantage point.

Again, following the lead of Henry Highland Garnet, I avoid general use of the word "slave," substituting whenever possible the term "enslaved" or "captive." In understanding the power of language to sway opinion, either positively or negatively, and in realizing how language codified racialized oppression, Garnet was already using "enslaved" rather than "slave" four years before the start of the Civil War.[7]

# ACKNOWLEDGMENTS

Gladys Marie Fry set me on this path years ago by opening my eyes and my ears to the power of one's story. Through her, I became a better listener, and I am deeply appreciative of all who listened as I spoke or who critiqued aspects of this work. I am grateful to venerable bibliophile and collector Charles Blockson, the modern father of Underground Railroad research.

In the course of my first year in Illinois, the Center for American Archaeology in Kampsville funded my research as a "Women in Archaeology" intern and Monticello Scholar. I was fortunate to meet Charlotte Johnson, who was passionate about preserving the Underground Railroad history of Rocky Fork, in the middle of Illinois. Charlotte's husband, Cyrus, is a descendant of the Johnson family, who founded a farm in Wood River in the 1840s. The homestead stands as the oldest African American family farm in Illinois.

Charlotte was adamant that I study Rocky Fork, a small Black settlement outside Alton, in addition to my original destination of New Philadelphia, for the real story of the Underground Railroad. She wanted me to understand how Blacks had worked to free themselves from slavery even as they worked and lived among Quakers and other Whites. In her quest to have the story told, she introduced me to Charles Benjamin Townsend, Clementine Kennedy, Rich Edwards, John Matlock, and the members of the New Bethel AME Church at Rocky Fork, all of whom shared their family histories, records, and photographs. As Clementine Kennedy fed me, I experienced the delicious foods made from family recipes that had been passed down through the generations and that were mentioned in historical accounts. Aunt Clem, as I came to know her, sheltered me and treated me like family. It was a pleasure to attend church services with her as I learned firsthand about the historical legacy of centuries-old Black churches. The Green-Hawkins family, of which she is a member, warmly received me at their family reunion in 2002. Rocky Fork descendants shared the richness of their African American family legacy and their sense of place. Their family history informed my research and deeply influenced my understanding of the inseparable relationship among free Black communities, Black organizations, the Black church, and the Underground Railroad.

The Committee on Black Pioneers of the Alton Museum of History and Art, in recognition of the importance of the local story, preserved the heritage of Rocky Fork settlement through an oral and family history project. As a committee member, Charlotte Johnson brought me out to walk the rocky terrain. As a local historian, she was seeking help in commemorating and documenting Rocky Fork and its Underground Railroad legacy. Through oral interviews, local histories, and newspaper accounts that Charlotte provided privately and using the Black Pioneer resources at the museum, I gained insight into the preserved memory of the small historic community. The Underground Railroad figured prominently but was not well-known beyond the region. Voids in documentary history, particularly around clandestine African American sites operating as Underground Railroad stations, dictated that I do something different. Unlike New Philadelphia and Miller Grove—two Illinois sites that I studied that summer—existing historical resources for Rocky Fork were limited.

I spent three summers excavating and researching Miller Grove, where I worked closely with Mary McCorvie, heritage officer and forest archaeologist in the Shawnee National Forest at Murphysboro, Illinois. Through efforts of National Forest Service employees Elizabeth Fuller, Marlene Rivero, and Vickie Davenport, I received extensive research support. Their efforts led me to other descendants of the Miller Grove community, James Crimm and Jessie McClure. I was able to conduct a telephone interview with Wilbur McClure before his death. McCorvie drove me from Illinois to Indiana and then to Ohio so that I could meet and work with heritage officers and forest archaeologists Angie Krieger of the Hoosier National Forest and Ann Cramer of the Wayne National Forest. Under their guidance, I continued to collect necessary archaeological information. Through their Underground Railroad work and their associations with Historically Black Colleges and Universities, the three women exhibited a commitment to making the most of African American historical resources located within their jurisdictions on National Forest Service properties.

Once I returned home, I spent hours with my research partner, Ambassador Ronald D. Palmer, debating what I had learned about William Paul Quinn's maddeningly elusive life. With Palmer's assistance, I built upon the work of Hannah Gefert, Hillary Russell, and others whose research helped to expose Black institutional ties to the Underground Railroad by linking the activities of the Free Masons, many of them ministers. Fellow Quinn researcher and colleague Donna Stokes-Lucas generously shared her extensive research on Quinn's ministry in Indiana and provided a critical list and map of Black churches in Indiana drawn by Indiana researcher Coy Robbins. Stokes-Lucas was invaluable in helping me decipher the churches and settlements in Indiana for the revised Underground Railroad map of Indiana (map 5).

A word about Coy Robbins. He died just as I was beginning my research in Indiana. So much of the clarity I have been able to bring to the subject of free Blacks and the Underground Railroad is because of his extensive work on Black settlements in Indiana. I am truly grateful for his historic legacy.

As I extended my research into Canada, Karolyn Smartz Frost became an important ally. She and Bryan Prince have a mindboggling grasp of their subject matter, which they most graciously shared with me in my quest to form new arguments about Blacks and the Underground Railroad. Frost introduced me to community descendants who embraced me and treated me like family as we toured communities at Chatham, Buxton, and Dresden. Through Frost, I met Bryan Newby, his wife, Alice, and their wonderful daughters, Quinn and Blair. The circle was complete when I met Bryan, a descendant of Civil War veteran James Newby. Newby had lived in Lick Creek, Indiana, one of the sites investigated for this study and from which Blacks migrated to Buxton. I am grateful I was able to meet Bryan before his premature death in 2006.

Sheri Jackson, while she was the Northeast regional coordinator for the National Underground Railroad Network to Freedom program of the National Park Service, was a gracious ally, answering my every request. She and Park Service regional program coordinators Barbara Taggar, James Hill, Guy Washington, and Diane Miller work tirelessly to promote the Network to Freedom program.

When I returned east, visits with Museum Director Beverly Morgan Welch and her staff, L'Merchie Frazier, Chandra Harrington, and Tracy Gibbs, at the Museum of African American History in Boston broadened my perspective. I first began to connect the larger work of free Black communities through the African Meeting Houses in both Boston and Nantucket. Likewise, John Creighton, Pat Lewis, Kate Clifford Larson, and Barbara Taggar generously shared information about Harriet Tubman and Blacks on the Eastern Shore of Maryland that complicated the role of Blacks, both free and enslaved, who indirectly facilitated escapes or worked directly on the Underground Railroad. A word of thanks also to archaeologist Chris Barton, who invited me to the Timbuctoo site in New Jersey. Barton's sharing of an Underground Railroad map of New Jersey helped me confirm my argument.

My work benefited from the steady hand of Paul Shackel and guidance from Ira Berlin, Lynn Bolles, Elsa Barkley Brown, John Caughey, Mary

Sies, and Roy Finkenbine. Chris Fennell's careful reading of the manuscript strengthened this work as did Shelby Shapiro's review. Susan Winfield's organizational skills added logic and flow to the manuscript.

Prize-winning author and *Washington Post* journalist Wil Haygood led a nonfiction workshop for the Hurston Wright Writer's Workshop that completely altered my relationship to writing and to story telling. The organizers, novelist Marita Goldman and bibliophile Clyde McElvene, warrant all the praise I have to offer. My gratitude runs deep, and Sonja Williams from Howard University's School of Communication deserves a special word of thanks for convincing me to apply. Fellow participants Oya Johnson, Carroll Blue, Imani Perry, Stephanie Boddie, Amanda Lockett, Amelia Reid, Edra Chandler, and I formed a sisterhood of "Literary Lionesses" during that magical week.

Throughout the writing phase, I was supported by the women of The Connection Writer's Congress, Gina LaRoche, Kim Hunley, and Stacy Blake-Beard. Thank you too to my sufficiency partners, Brij Masand, Susan Varn, Shareda Hosein, and Malik Williams.

The Bethesda Writer's Center in Maryland became my haven and my laboratory as I completed the manuscript while working with authors Ken Ackerman and David Stewart. Again, I bonded with my fellow workshop members, Bonny Miller, Diana Parsell, Stephanie Boddie, Michael Kirkland, Sonja Williams, Nancy Derr, Michael Scadron, and Judi Moore Latta, who critiqued, and at times endured, various sections of the manuscript.

Of course, a special thanks to my family, Gina LaRoche and Alan Price, Renee LaRoche-Morris and Ralston Morris, Danielle LaRoche, Dan King, Elizabeth and James Janifer, and Vicki Wilson, who have supported me in ways too numerous to mention. Repeatedly, I have depended on Cherise Wilson, who has been my tireless ally in organizing and preparing all the graphics for this work. I appreciate the efforts of Russell Campbell who read and critiqued an early version of this manuscript and am very thankful for the constant support and encouragement of my colleague Joshua Woodfork.

I am grateful to all who generously shared research data and exchanged thoughtful ideas. Without their help, elucidating the history of the Black community's involvement with the Underground Railroad would have required countless more years in pursuit of elusive evidence. Through it all, I learned to both respect and appreciate the power of memory and oral traditions in shaping and sustaining the history of African American families and communities. I drink from the fountain of an untapped historical reservoir.

# FREE BLACK COMMUNITIES AND THE UNDERGROUND RAILROAD

*Map 1.* Map of eastern United States and Canada showing free Black communities in Illinois, Indiana, and Ohio and six Underground Railroad sites, which are underlined.

# INTRODUCTION

The Underground Railroad movement secretly operated in conjunction with free Black communities and their historic Black churches. Peering at these sites through a cultural landscape lens allows a new perspective for understanding the relationship between free Black communities, the Black church, and the Underground Railroad. Blacks, enslaved and free, operated as the main actors in the central drama that was the Underground Railroad. Extended families populated Black communities and filled the Black churches at the heart of the movement. Ministers, such as William Paul Quinn, and their wives, in addition to congregations of interrelated families, acted as major forces for social change.

The Underground Railroad dwells in national imagination as a well-known yet poorly understood icon of American lore. Once etched in the national memory as the solitary work of Harriet Tubman and kindly Quakers from Ohio or misunderstood as an actual train complete with tracks, the Underground Railroad movement nags at the nation's psyche. Elastic, interconnected escape routes and networks merged with creative ruses, legal maneuverings, and bold confrontations by African Americans to sustain the contradictions of a movement that was at once clandestine and well-known.

Drawing from sources such as church histories, newspaper articles, and biographies, for example, informed by oral narratives, convention records, and church and organization minutes, this work provides an alternative account of the mechanisms of escape from slavery. Few histories connect the Underground Railroad with Black churches, Black communities, or fraternal societies such as Freemasonry.

Gone are the century-old definitions of the Underground Railroad dominated by images of shivering, frightened fugitive slaves. Fading away are the biased images of solitary men, criminalized for escaping slavery, usually on foot, and aided by sympathetic White abolitionists working within a loosely organized network dominated by kindly Quakers. Historian Larry Gara calls the Underground Railroad "America's favorite legend."[1]

Using these landscapes of freedom introduces methodological and theoretical approaches to preservation of the history and memory of free Black communities and their associations with the Underground Railroad. Until recently, African Americans were not part of the American collective identity and therefore required few or no preservation efforts.[2] The language of the landscape reveals evidence of daily activities of those who left few written records even though large parts of the evidence are missing from the landscape as well.[3]

Tracking escape routes through Black communities and mountain passes and adding iron furnaces as an important new link in the Underground Railroad chain, this history charts poorly understood African American pathways to freedom. Blacks participated in a movement thoroughly identified with routes and landscape, terrain, landforms and natural shelters, as well as settlements and houses, all of which define the landscape of the Underground Railroad and the geography of resistance.

Historically however, the Underground Railroad narrative has slanted away from the harrowing stories of free Blacks contending with the tyranny of slavery toward interactions with better-known and documented groups of Quaker families, White abolitionists, and other antislavery activists. Invariably these are the main focus of Underground Railroad literature.

Reexamining the romantic tales of heroism and moral drama exposes the risks African Americans endured in the cause of their own liberation. Free Blacks with their churches, literary societies, fraternal orders, and other institutions simultaneously ensured their own freedom and the liberty of family and friends as well as that of strangers

Small communities of Black families in rural and border regions acted as conduits for escape before the Civil War. As first points of entry into treacherous southern regions of Illinois, Indiana, and Ohio, Black communities in the southernmost counties bordering the Ohio and Mississippi Rivers were positioned to offer sanctuary to anyone able enough to escape slavery. Fleeing, however, was not the sole or most preferable alternative to slavery, nor was it the most common expression of the desire to be free. Purchasing oneself was the enslaved's legal path to freedom and deathbed manumissions the slaveholder's path to exoneration.

Federal law ensured that most of the millions of enslaved Africans would never be freed by their own hand. As Frederick Douglass observed, passage of "that legislative monster," the Fugitive Slave Law, in 1850 brought "some of the most repugnant features of slavery into the heart of Northern cities and towns" with ramifications for Black communities.[4]

In addition to small local settlements, large cities, Chicago, Philadelphia, and New York, for example, in addition to Boston and Pittsburgh, with strong Black communities and significant numbers of abolitionists, offered escapees sanctuary and anonymity. With and without the assistance and cooperation of White America, however, Blacks came together collectively and individually seeking freedom from servitude and an end to slavery. In the face of devastating racial oppression, people of color had been escaping bondage since the advent of New World slavery centuries before the rise of the Underground Railroad.

The small rural settlements and their churches, which are the subjects of this study, were not necessarily organized as traditionally conceived Underground Railroad "stations"—deliberate spaces, planned or appropriated, often with the aid of White abolitionists, to hide and then facilitate a steady flow of freedom seekers to specific destinations. In contrast, small rural African American communities functioned more as havens for individuals or family members determined to find freedom. These first stops out of slavery frequently consisted of internal, church-based paths to freedom and salvation.

## Escape from Slavery: The Law, Media, and Literature

Escape as a response to slavery predated the formation of the nation. Although the Underground Railroad began in the late 1830s, the first sign of the enslaved's opposition to slavery was apparent in the early laws of Virginia and New York. Legislation from the colonial period attempted to regulate two consistent responses to slavery—running away and harboring. In rulings too numerous to discuss, lawmakers struggled to regulate escapes and dissuade abettors in an effort to curb behavior sufficiently rampant to warrant legal intervention. The subject of "fleeing from service" first appeared in the colonial record in 1629. Numerous Fugitive Slave Bills enacted from then until 1854 attest to the extent to which escape from slavery plagued America's founders.

At the nation's founding in 1788, an anonymous freeman authored an early antislavery pamphlet, "An Essay on Slavery," believed to be the work of astronomer Benjamin Banneker. The scientist stood at the forefront of African American protest writing, paving the way for others to find a way out of slavery. By the end of the Revolutionary period, Black Loyalists escaping with the British to Nova Scotia in Canada and other destinations beyond the colonies fueled a long tradition of international sanctuary from slavery that widened freedom seekers' options. Black veterans returning from the War of 1812 brought with them news of Canada as a haven for freedom. Religious historian Charles Eric Lincoln also points to the War of 1812 as instrumental to the rise in consciousness of Canada as a site of freedom, leading to its pivotal position in the Underground Railroad movement.[5]

Seventeenth- and eighteenth-century runaway slave advertisements in addition to plantation and industrial record books are the documents that reckoned with escape. The combination of runaway slave ads and Fugitive Slave Laws during colonial times provides evidence of the magnitude of the problem of escape long before the advent of the formal period of the Underground Railroad in the 1830s.

Lawmakers learned that the pulse of liberty, the impulse toward freedom set in motion at the founding of the nation, could not be contained by word of law. Federal and state laws attempting to thwart escapes leave a powerful documentary record. Between the foundation of the Constitution in 1778 and 1860, legislators would enact thirty-eight national acts, propositions, bills, and Indian treaties, excluding Black Codes, in an effort to control escaping slaves.[6] Two of the most notorious among the thirty-eight had the greatest impact on Black displacement and disruption of the Black community.

The much hated law of 1793 allowed slaveholders and other claimants to seize escapees without a warrant. Yet to the utter consternation of President George Washington and his wife, Martha, the first lady's enslaved personal maid, Oney Judge, escaped three years after the law passed after learning that she was to be a wedding gift to Mrs. Washington's granddaughter. Washington placed a runaway slave advertisement, seeking her return. In a newspaper interview granted years later from Judge's home near Portsmouth, New Hampshire, she was quick to state that she had been aided by the free Black community in Philadelphia at the time of her escape from the executive mansion. She told her interviewer, "I had friends among the colored people of Philadelphia, had my things carried there beforehand, and left Washington's house while they were eating dinner."[7]

The connection between runaway slave ads and Fugitive Slave Laws attest in print to the conflict between enslavers seeking control and determined escapees seeking freedom. Slaveholders paid for the printing of handbills and broadsides advertising for the return of those they held in slavery. Taken together, the notices narrate the slaveholders' frustrations and provide solid evidence for the movement before the 1830s and independent Black activism before the advent of abolitionism.

In the last sentence of the last section of the Missouri Compromise of 1820, Congress again turned its attention to the mounting problem of escape from slavery, and "provided always" that anyone escaping slavery could be lawfully seized and returned to bondage. With each law, responses and escape strategies changed with the times. Following the gradual abolition of slavery in the northern states, escape to northern destinations became a viable solution. The idea of free Black settlements in Canada and in the western states and territories took hold. Blacks had been escaping to Ohio as early as 1812.[8]

As knowledge of escape strategies grew, secrecy and ingenuity coexisted with public awareness of Underground Railroad activities, if not its specific operations. By 1843, newspapers such as *The Albany Patriot* made taunting reference to the operation: "**WE KNOW ALL ABOUT IT!** And we wish we could gratify our readers by detailing the history of escape of victims without endangering others."[9] Frederick Douglass's newspaper, *The North Star*, reported on a meeting of the New York State Vigilance Committee held at Zion Church in Lower Manhattan in 1848. "This Society," the paper indicated, "is composed mostly of colored people, instituted expressly for the management of the Underground Railroad."[10]

Historian Richard Newman acknowledges early Black activists' ability to quickly recognize "print as a most powerful political tool." Early Black newspapers such as *Freedom's Journal* and *The Colored American* and explosive pamphlets such David Walker's *Appeal* began the process of giving widespread "public voice" to Black protest. In its quest to present an authentic voice of Black Americans, *Freedom's Journal* proclaimed that others had "too long spoken for us," "we wish to plead our own cause." Frederick Douglass would carry forward that tradition as editor of *The North Star* and later in *Frederick Douglass's Paper*. Martin Delany, who became America's foremost advocate of Black Nationalism before the Civil War, wanted it "borne in mind that Anti-Slavery took its rise among *colored men*." *Frederick Douglass's Paper* printed blatant notices sketching the comings and goings on the Underground Railroad.

The spread of Black activism reached beyond newspapers and pamphlets to speeches, lectures, and firsthand accounts of the nightmare of slavery. During the 1840s, narratives of escape, as a distinctive form of the slave narrative, rose in popularity. "The moment when the slave made up his mind to put an end to his slavery, through purchase of himself or through flight," observed literary historian Marion Wilson Starling, "marked the end of the enslavement of his spirit, as we learn from narrative after narrative of fugitive or manumitted slave alike."[11] In 1845, Frederick Douglass penned one of the earliest and most influential narratives describing his escape in 1838. In the decade between 1845 and 1855, long before William Mitchell, William Still, or Wilbur Siebert produced their classic works of the Underground Railroad, freedom seekers narrated several of the most important and enduring works of the genre.[12] Moses Roper wrote two narratives, one in 1838, the other in 1848. In his second account written before passage of the infamous Fugitive Slave Act of 1850, Roper mentioned moving to Canada West with his family in 1844, "it being as near as I can get to my relations (who are still in bondage) without being again taken."[13]

In 1849 alone, one year before the Fugitive Slave Law destabilized Black communities, Blacks escaping slavery were responsible for three major narratives. Canada again emerged as a destination. Josiah Henson produced *The Life of Josiah Henson, Formerly a Slave, Now an Inhabitant of Canada, as Narrated by Himself*, the narrative now famed for its purported influence on Harriet Beecher Stowe's writing of *Uncle Tom's Cabin*. After multiple escape attempts, Henry Bibb wrote in his 1849 narrative, "all that I heard about liberty and freedom to the slaves, I never forgot. Among other good trades I learned the art of running away to perfection. I made a regular business of it, and never gave it up, until I had broken the bands of slavery, and landed myself safely in Canada, where I was regarded as a man, and not as a thing."[14] J. W. C. Pennington also penned an influential narrative that year describing his escape nearly twenty years earlier.[15] But Frederick Douglass maintained a critical view of narratives that divulged too much.

In June 1850, three months before passage of the Compromise of 1850 that contained the Fugitive Slave Law, Ohio statesman James Loudon considered using military might against the forces of the Underground Railroad. *The Ohio Statesmen* reported on "a large settlement of colored persons—a place of refuge for the runaways of the slave States—a sort of depot for the Underground Railroad. The time may come, when, in order to preserve the peace of the State among them, it may be necessary to call on the light troops in the vicinity, and even upon the militia."[16]

Compromise, counterbalanced by schism and secession, dominated the negotiating styles of the century with calamitous consequences for the rights and liberty of people of color. Demonstrating southern legislators' understanding of the acuteness of the problem of escape, the strengthened Fugitive Slave Law contained in the Compromise deputized the citizenry; a direct choice confronted citizens—serve either your country or your conscience, reflecting the split between personal, religious, and moral duty and civic responsibility.

Finally, the Kansas-Nebraska Act of 1854 specifically extended the reach of the Fugitive Slave Law over the Nebraska Territory and reaffirmed the preceding Fugitive Slave Laws.[17] Sitting at the decayed junction of religious principle and civil disobedience, the 1854 act drove a wedge deeper into the mounting sectional division. To add to this judicial and legislative nightmare for Blacks, one unjust law followed another. The Missouri Compromise was repealed by the Kansas-Nebraska Act only to be followed by the equally pernicious *Dred Scott* decision of 1857.[18]

As black abolitionist William Wells Brown observed, it was a contest between southerners' efforts "to make the institution of slavery national, and the equally powerful growing public sentiment at the North to make freedom universal."[19] The battle lines tightened in the contest between the enslaved's constant push toward freedom and the slaveholders' constant push toward legal control.

The 1856 publication of Benjamin Drew's *A North-side View of Slavery. The Refugee: or The Narratives of Fugitive Slaves in Canada. Related by Themselves, with an Account of the History and Condition of the Colored Population of Upper Canada* began the tradition of interviewing and collecting multiple narratives of escape as "direct and unimpeachable testimony" intent on exposing the true nature of slavery in contrast to the biographic works produced earlier. Drew provided an early view of Harriet Tubman, who was among those interviewed representing St. Catharine's, Canada.[20]

Hundreds of exposing newspaper articles referencing the Underground Railroad did not deter escapes. By 1860, when Rev. William M. Mitchell, a Black Baptist minister, wrote one of the first books on the subject, *The Underground Railroad: From Slavery to Freedom*, the war between slavery and freedom had been raging in the journalistic, legal, and literary arenas for two centuries. In both form and content, Mitchell's firsthand account ushered in a new era by explicitly naming and describing methods of escape. Narratives written by former slaves had been careful not to delve into betraying details.

Mitchell wrote from experience. He became a member of the Vigilance Committee in Ohio, "to aid fugitives from slavery in escaping to Canada."[21] In his trailblazing work, the author was quick to observe that free Blacks had been viewed as a constant threat because they "encouraged the slaves to improve their condition and to escape to the North."[22] Furthermore, he continued, free Blacks were known to voluntarily venture into the southern slave states to bring bondsmen out of captivity. Rev. Mitchell explained their motivations: "Some of these venturous men, having themselves been slaves," jeopardized their own liberty because they were "truly desirous their brethren should taste the sweets of freedom." Mitchell believed that "no class of men are better prepared for this perilous and dangerous occupation than the fugitives themselves," partly because they were better acquainted with their own neighborhood when rescuing their friends, family, and acquaintances.[23]

William Still's massive yet hardly comprehensive 1872 work, *The Underground Railroad*, recorded narrative accounts of escapes taken as freedom seekers passed through the Philadelphia office of the Vigilance Committee. Acting chairman of the committee and the "father of the Underground Railroad," Still penned the only chronicle or survey of the Underground Railroad written by an African American directly involved.[24]

In 1895, Wilbur Siebert, a Harvard-trained historian, contributed the first academic, comprehensive understanding and in-depth mapping in *The Underground Railroad from Slavery to Freedom*. Siebert's work detailing kindly Quakers and shivering, frightened "fugitives" dominated the literature for more than a century while Still's equally long-lived work gave voice to the enslaved's quest for freedom and their ordeals as they fled.

Each writer captured the last vestiges of eyewitness accounts, or stories from individuals who had interacted with conductors, station keepers, and workers along the antislavery line. Again, Siebert, positioned mainly outside and at a distance, retold the stories primarily of White abolitionists, although he did include African Americans. Most important for this study, he mapped, identified, and included the work of free Black communities. Understanding that Blacks in the border states continually found ways to help their fellow bondsmen, Siebert confirmed that "it was natural that Negro settlements in the free states should be resorted to by fugitive slaves."[25] Much of how subsequent writers approach the subject is shaped by these early works, along with the influential memoir of Quaker Levi Coffin, who is often designated the "president of the Underground Railroad." He, too, witnessed and participated in the clandestine work of African Americans on the frontline of freedom.[26]

Cautious resistance to slavery guaranteed limited local or regional understanding of the details about sanctuaries and routes, footpaths and rescue activities. Surveyors and map makers, itinerant preachers and circuit riders, tinkers and peddlers, geologists and book salesmen, all those whose occupations required them to freely move about the land were recruited. For the most part, knowledge circulated as seditious information within the Underground Railroad movement. The majority of participants' anonymous efforts resulted in an operation so successful that two centuries later researchers continue to experience great difficulty in unraveling the "riddle wrapped in a mystery inside an enigma."[27]

The Underground Railroad remained a popular, enthralling subject at the turn of the twentieth century before it became increasingly maligned as legend and lore as the decades unfolded. In referring to *History of the Underground Railroad in Chester and the Neighboring Counties of Pennsylvania,* the 1883 work by R. C. Smedley, historian Christopher Densmore notes that the work "has stood up very well" in the face of criticism and recent scholarship.[28] Although scholars of the Underground Railroad have taken Smedley to task for not paying adequate attention to the role and involvement of Blacks, enslaved and free, he, nevertheless, does mention the role of African Americans and free Black settlements such as Columbia, Pennsylvania. "The large number of colored people who settled in Columbia, made that place the goal of the fugitive to which he directed his anxious footsteps with the reasonable hope that when arriving there he would receive aid and directions on his way to freedom. His expectations were not disappointed." Referring to the northeastern portion of the borough, where "gradually all the colored people in the vicinity collected," Smedley continues, "[b]eing thus brought into one community it was quite natural that any strange colored persons going that way would seek shelter among them."[29]

In a full-page newspaper article in 1900 Moses Dickson, head of the Knights of Liberty, a vast armed and drilled Black militia he claimed had been prepared to go to battle over slavery, chose to break his silence and reveal the secret history of the Underground Railroad for the first time, "how its operation was systematized and the work of the colored people toward their liberation from bondage."[30]

The *History of the Underground Railroad as It Was Conducted by the Anti-Slavery League* written by Col. William Cockrum in 1915, relied on interviews with participants to describe his family's involvement with the work in Indiana. However, in explaining a popular escape route near Evansville, Cockrum noted that "there were free Blacks in the city among whom the refugees could be easily hidden."[31] Cockrum made numerous indirect references to the role of free Black communities along the Underground Railroad, describing antislavery pilots traveling "along different routes to places where the Negroes had friends who carried them farther north." Cockrum continues, "There were probably more Negroes crossed over the Ohio river at two or three places in front of Louisville than any place else from the mouth of the Wabash to Cincinnati. The reason for this was that the three good sized cities at the Falls furnished a good hiding place for the runaways among the colored people."[32]

The narrative tradition also continued into the twentieth century with interviews conducted in conjunction with the Works Projects Administration (WPA). The oral narrations, often in the words of the former captives, fall outside Underground Railroad operations and the traditional literature associated with it. *Homeless, Friendless, and Penniless*, which focuses on Indiana, is one among several collections of WPA narratives that are treasure-troves of reports of escapes or attempted escapes by individuals and their accomplices.[33]

Wilbur Siebert also revisited the topic of the Underground Railroad at midcentury, late in his life. Ohio was Siebert's home. Judging from the amount of documentation he included pertaining to African American participation in Ohio's Underground Railroad in *Mysteries of Ohio's Underground Railroad*, Siebert broadened his data collection strategies to include a greater number of Black informants. *Mysteries* contains images of Black participants, includes their names, and mentions several of the more than forty Black settlements scattered across the state. The inclusive nature of Siebert's latter work encouraged broader understanding of the relationships developed across racial and religious lines.

*The Liberty Line: The Legend of the Underground Railroad*, the more recent work of Larry Gara, in the second half of the twentieth century, although ground breaking, revealed no new sites. His critique, which advanced the study of African American involvement in the Underground Railroad, remains the major contribution of his work. His was a clarion call to place African American efforts at the center of the Underground Railroad story. Gara reiterated the active role of enslaved African Americans in initiating and facilitating escape from slavery, in contrast to "their passive roles in the legendary accounts."[34] Gara forcefully argued that African Americans had been written out of one of their most powerful historical moments. Gara wanted the Underground Railroad narrative of kindly Quakers and frightened slaves replaced with the story of African American escapes from slavery and their involvement in their own quest for freedom.[35] Historians and scholars had written African American agency out of one of the central episodes of their historical being.

The publication of bibliophile Charles Blockson's *National Geographic* article, "Escape from Slavery: The Underground Railroad," resurrected the topic in 1984 and rekindled national interest.[36] John Hope Franklin and Loren Schweninger's work at the dawn of the twenty-first century presaged a new era in the historiography of the Underground Railroad movement, one that rivals the end of the nineteenth century in importance. *Runaway Slaves: Rebels on the Plantation* documented a crucial piece of the puzzle, escapes out of the South, before escapees and abolitionists found one another. Runaways frequently planned and executed the initial phase of their escape on their own, or with the aid of friends and family in the South potentially providing food and shelter. Escapees often negotiated the most dangerous portion of the route through the South unassisted, particularly before origination of the Underground Railroad in the 1830s.[37]

The field of study now offers an integrated analysis of the Underground Railroad as well as a look at the role of women in abolitionism. Encyclopedias, compendia, and reference guides identify routes, people, and places associated with the Underground Railroad. From Kate Clifford Larson and Carolyn Smardz Frost, to Fergus Bordewich, Bryan Prince, and Bettye DeRamus and numerous other writers, author after author acknowledges the vital importance of African American participation.[38]

In *David Ruggles: A Radical Black Abolitionist and the Underground Railroad in New York City*, Graham Russell Hodges has followed the lead of other historians who have observed that the "renewed interest in social histories of northern black communities has led to a proliferation of biographies of prominent black abolitionists."[39] Richard Newman's important biography of AME bishop Richard Allen, *Freedom's Prophet: Bishop Richard Allen, the AME Church, and the Founding Black Fathers*, filled a forty-year void following the biography by eminent Black historian Charles Wesley in 1969. Similarly, Harriet Tubman's story had remained untold for nearly seventy-five years after publication of her original narrative until Black author Earl Conrad rescued her story and wrote her biography in 1943, only to suffer the same fate for an additional sixty years before Tubman again became the focus of recent biographies. My own work has benefited from the biographical outpouring that Hodges observed "has led to clearer understanding of how blacks created a new style of antislavery activity based on militant conduct and community mobilizing." Richard Newman also points out that activists realized they "must organize the black community just as a political party would mobilize a base of supporters."[40]

Oral and family histories represent the emerging genre of Underground Railroad scholarship written by lay or local historians. Emma Marie Trusty's *The Underground Railroad: Ties That Bound Unveiled* folds her family stories into the larger context of the Underground Railroad in southern New Jersey. This important book demonstrates how oral and family histories can support scholarship to yield a more complete story. Her work takes a careful look at the relationship between the AME Church and the Underground Railroad as well as the interpersonal relationships among African Americans in New Jersey. This study addresses many of the same topics.[41]

When Black community formation is understood through the landscape, contemporary writings consistently mention the Underground Railroad or escape from slavery. In *America's First Black Town: Brooklyn, Illinois 1830–1915*, Sundiata Keitha Cha-Jua found that "rarely were absconding slaves aided by abolitionists while still on the slaveocracy terrain."[42] Laurence Glasco indicated the same for Pittsburgh in southwestern Pennsylvania: "many struggled northward without the aid of the Underground organization."[43] In her article, "Escaping through a Black Landscape," Rebecca Ginsburg relied on firsthand accounts from African American autobiographies to reconstruct escape efforts.[44]

*Front Line of Freedom: African Americans and the Forging of the Underground Railroad in the Ohio Valley* by Keith Griffler distinguished the borderland region in the northern portions of slave states and the southern portions of free states as the front line "where African Americans . . . routinely engaged in the most hazardous, intensive, and effective work."[45] Griffler's findings mirror my own, particularly "the historical agency of oppressed peoples in their own liberation" and the critical importance of Black settlements. He, too, links the Underground Railroad with the struggles to establish African American communities.[46] My work diverges from Griffler's in distinct ways, however. Although *Front Line of Freedom* emphasizes the centrality of the Black church, the relationship between the Black church and the Underground Railroad remains unexplored.[47]

Without a depth of understanding focused on the land, conventional historical analysis using traditional sources may not yield the wider story of the Underground Railroad movement. *A Nation within a Nation: Organizing African-American Communities before the Civil War* examines self-determined African American community formation from the late eighteenth century to the Civil War. John Ernst and I adopt parallel themes: community organization, Freemasonry, the Black church, and education. His work ties Freemasonry, the Black church, and its preachers to radical activism that extended to the Underground Railroad. Ernst addressed each component separately, however, and did not entwine these elements with the Underground Railroad.[48]

As the Underground Railroad expanded and developed, the movement took on a decidedly religious quality. Often, routes were organized along denominational or sectarian lines. Siebert deemed the religious character of operators most important to the success of the enterprise. The activism of different denominations is an important component for landscape analysis. AME, Black Baptists, AME Zion, Quakers, Wesleyan Methodists, Presbyterians, Congregationalists, and Covenanters all participated and worked within their individual congregations and denominations that can be tracked and mapped. Interracial bonds were far more likely than interfaith ones.[49]

Several of the key Black abolitionists and Underground Railroad operatives served as ministers representing different denominations although historians generally do not connect their religious affiliations to their Underground Railroad activities (see the appendix). Syracuse's AME Zion minister Jermaine Loguen advertised himself as a prominent Underground Railroad agent, writing that the Underground Railroad "was never doing a better business than at this time." All who wished "to take stock in this valuable and mysterious Railroad" needed only to contact Loguen since "the stock [was] rising."[50] Loguen repeatedly made it clear in *Frederick Douglass's Paper* that he and his family could be found operating an Underground Railroad depot at their Syracuse, New York, home.[51]

The relationship between the Underground Railroad and the Black church reached across denominations and regions. Independent Black churches began as "protest institutions" and "dissenting movements."[52] In Delaware, where a small free Black population emerged very early, Peter Spencer led forty Africans out of Wilmington's Asbury Methodist Episcopal Church in 1805 in protest over discriminatory treatment by the White establishment. The Black congregants completely broke free in 1812 to form the Mother African Union Church, one of the early stations on the Underground Railroad. U.S. marshals, slave catchers, slaveholders, and constables viewed the church with much suspicion, particularly the August Big Quarterly meeting, which served as the starting point for many escapes.[53]

In a 1984 letter contained in *Peter Spencer and the African Union Methodist Tradition*, then Delaware senator Joseph Biden asserted, "the social and political history of black Americans is indistinguishable from the history of their religious faith and of the churches that have ministered to their spiritual and temporal needs." Senator Biden elaborated, ranking "black religious independence with the Emancipation Proclamation, the 1954 Supreme Court decision outlawing segregated public schools, and the Civil Rights Act of 1964."[54] By extension, Black families and communities, as the genesis of the Black church, must claim the identical lofty lineage. Historian Leonard Curry puts it this way: "No aspect of the Negro church was more important than its interrelationship with the black community." A sense of community had to be "called into existence before the separate black church could be brought into being."[55]

History of the AME church's involvement survives in centennial commemorations and local church programs. Early historians of the denomination include substantial references to the church's relationship with the Underground Railroad, particularly in the centennial histories written after it became safe to proclaim their role in the veiled work. By 1916, AME church historian Richard R. Wright reported that during the first fifty years of the church's existence "many of the ministers of this church were active in the anti-slavery movement and 'Underground Railroad.'" Most significantly, Wright indicates that "much of the actual work of receiving and transporting escaped slaves was done by them."[56] Bishop William Walls, historian for the AME Zion Church, offers identical testimony: "The Underground Railroad was practically a church movement."[57] Preachers were prime leaders and their churches unsuspected stations. African American ministers, their churches, and their denominations combined with free Black communities to form a distinctive network separate from, yet integrated with, White abolitionists and Underground Railroad workers.

In *The Negro Church* notable historian Carter G. Woodson distinguished Black ministers as "the then best developed leaders among their people." Woodson continues, "almost every Negro minister was otherwise engaged in spiriting away fugitives from the slaveholding States through the North into Canada. They were in touch with men in other centers, found out what was going on, learned what was the trend of things, and planned to act accordingly."[58] As was true of so many who settled the Black communities, several of the ministers had once been enslaved or had escaped from slavery.

Modern-day historians of the church connect the church and the Underground Railroad. Gayraud Wilmore locates the founding of the AME Zion Church inside the struggle against slavery in *Religion and Black Radicalism: An Interpretation of the Religious History of African Americans* and identifies the denomination's congregations along the Mason and Dixon Line as known stations on the Underground Railroad.[59] In *The Black Churches of Brooklyn,* for example, Clarence Taylor names Bridge Street African Wesleyan Methodist Episcopal and Concord Baptist Churches as sanctuaries for runaway slaves. Albert Raboteau, scholar of African and African religions, devotes several pages to the Underground Railroad and the antislavery position of the Black church and black communities in *Canaan Land: A Religious History of African Americans*. In *A Will to Choose: The Origins of African American Methodism*, J. Gordon Melton tightly binds Methodism and the Underground Railroad across several states.[60]

Beyond history, archaeology has a role in recovering African American Underground Railroad sources by identifying, locating, and mapping remnants of no longer existing historic black communities, their churches, and their churches' associated cemeteries. Depending on historical and textural evidence alone, unsupported by a cultural landscape methodology, exploits the obvious where a more subtle critique is necessary. Archaeologists now incorporate investigation of the Underground Railroad into their field of study. *The Archaeology of Antislavery Resistance,* the comprehensive text by archaeologist Terrance M. Weik, presents the contributions that major archaeological sites have made toward the subject and is a companion to this interdisciplinary study.[61]

Combining three strands, I weave together history, archaeology, and landscape studies to yield an untold story that transcends the limits of each discipline. Archaeology and landscape studies *undergird* oral traditions and church histories that expand and give nuance to the narrative. Archaeology, mapping of settlements, and relying on the landscape itself underpin my argument and fill out the skeleton from written documents, oral tradition, and institutions such as the Black church and Masonic fraternities.

* * *

This Underground Railroad study is divided into three parts. Part I focuses on four specific sites: Rocky Fork and Miller Grove in Illinois, Lick Creek in Indiana, and Poke Patch in Ohio. Part II defines and explores each of the components of the geography of resistance. Part III combines family stories and individual narratives with Black community and church histories and the activism of the Prince Hall Masons to place African American families inside these institutional structures.

The histories of four specific communities contain parts of the whole story. Each site highlights aspects of the geography of resistance. The first section of the book breathes life into anonymous historical actors—husbands, wives, and interrelated families. Previously enslaved workers formed the hidden hand of the Underground Railroad and played a central role in the establishment of the frontier settlements and the Black churches frequently associated with them. Each chapter emphasizes different points by relying on available family or oral history, regional differences, and levels of archaeological investigation.

Chapter 1 relies on oral sources to give voice to the Rocky Fork community, particularly its relationship to other nearby Black communities and to the Underground Railroad. Tucked away outside Alton, Illinois, this small enclave sitting among the boulders and sweeping hills of Central Illinois yielded evidence of cooperation between Black settlements on the frontlines of freedom and known abolitionist towns. Minister William Paul Quinn and the early influence of the AME Church embedded in the Underground Railroad history of the little settlement characterizes the geography of resistance. Rural sites such as Rocky Fork remain relatively pristine, evoking the traces of the original nineteenth-century landscape.

The histories of Miller Grove in Illinois and Lick Creek in Indiana, the focus of chapters 2 and 3, offer distinct details of community formation and interracial cooperation within regional Underground Railroad operations. One of the important findings and major contributions of this work is the addition of routes running through several iron regions as pathways critical to the Underground Railroad movement. The Underground Railroad network around Poke Patch, the subject of chapter 4, relied heavily on African American operators. Routes through iron furnace regions surrounding the community illuminate an overlooked Underground Railroad escape strategy.

Part II shifts the focus away from individual communities and slants toward understanding how the land was used in support of freedom. Chapter 5 explores Black escape routes, the churches, iron forges, and waterways that make up the pathways to freedom and "the geography of resistance." Chapter 6 analyzes the processes of community formation and the causes of migration that led Blacks to live where they did and to flee when they had to. This work rethinks African American migration by sifting through the range of ways in which people of color entered into and interacted with their surroundings. Forced and voluntary migration was at the core of African American community formation and the Underground Railroad. This section places the Underground Railroad along a migration continuum that began with the Middle Passage and ended after the Civil War.

The collective work of families united the Underground Railroad with free Black communities. The first chapter in part III connects generations of abolitionist families who passed on the tradition. Family networks populated Black communities and their churches and sustained an important family organizational structure that drove the Underground Railroad.

A number of the prominent leaders in nineteenth-century Black America whose names weave through Underground Railroad accounts maintained family connections and religious ties to free Black settlements. Pious ministers who attended denominational conferences and visited the homes of congregants were also steeped in Underground Railroad intrigue. The various African American organizations that fed into the Underground Railroad network, the Black churches, conferences, societies, and conventions, were the public, often urban, action arm of the Underground Railroad. Noted sociologist W. E. B. Du Bois charted the different types of cooperative organizations among African Americans that are the subject of this book (chart 1).

The final chapter revisits research strategies and looks toward future implications for reshaping modern interpretation of the Underground Railroad. Sitting at the crossroads of history and memory, landscape and archaeology, heritage and legend, what follows is a landscape-inspired narrative.

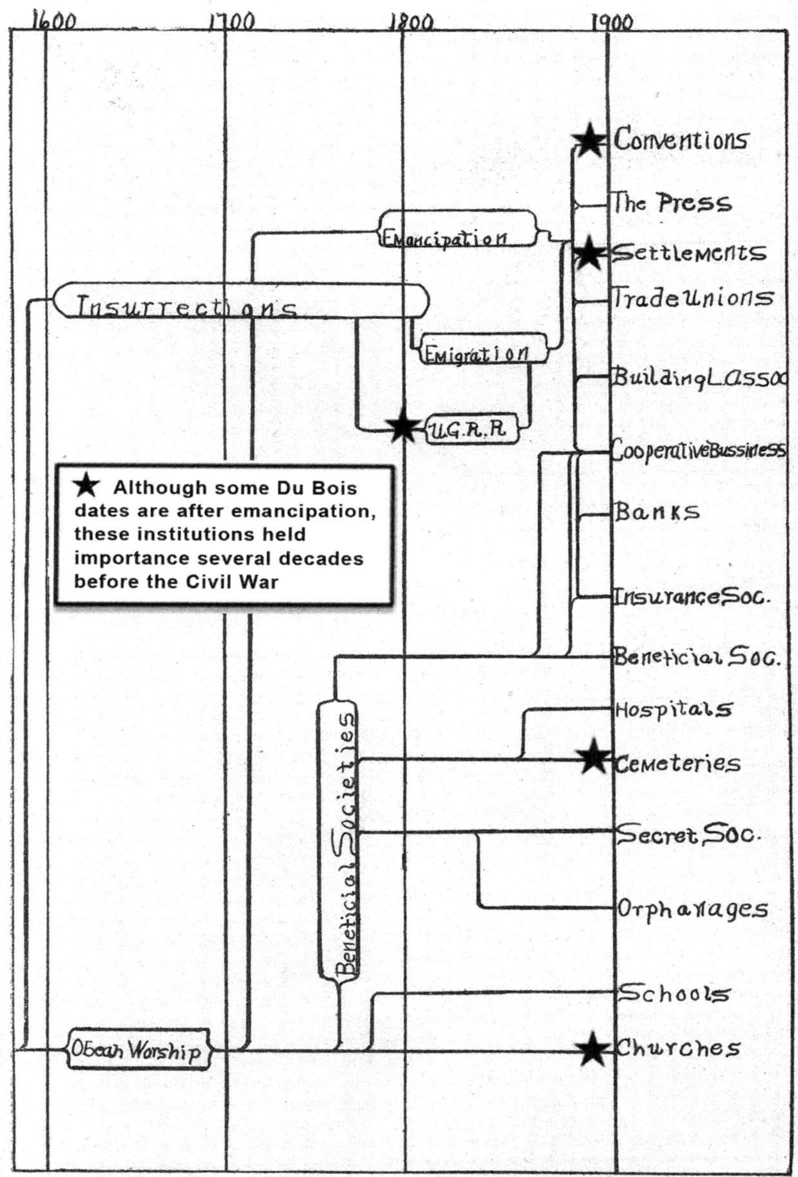


*Chart 1.* Du Bois's chart depicting the types of cooperative organization among African Americans. Du Bois's diagram of African American institutional development depicts the Black church in relationship to other Black organizations, including the Underground Railroad. Note that the Underground Railroad is a subgroup of emancipation, emigration, and insurrections. Equally as telling, Du Bois does not recognize Black settlements until 1900. Image courtesy of Documenting the American South, The University of North Carolina at Chapel Hill Libraries.

# PART I
# Free Black Communities

CHAPTER 1

# Rocky Fork, Illinois

## Oral Tradition as Memory

Communities as old as Rocky Fork carry a large measure of oral tradition and memory. Accounts of the settlement's activism survived through oral tradition, memory, and newspaper stories, as well as recollections of local families and communities. With much of their history standing outside traditional Underground Railroad narratives, residents were careful to preserve vital elements of the history of the Underground Railroad and of African American self-determination on the nineteenth-century midwestern frontier.

Remnants of the free Black settlement at Rocky Fork lie deep in the woods, rolling hills and pastures, and dramatic rock outcroppings of Godfrey, Illinois. Rocky Fork has an importance beyond its historical narrative. The humanity of the men and women shines through in a variety of sources, revealing names, physical descriptions, lifeways, family connections, and community bonds.

An early twentieth-century newspaper article captured the essence of the enclave just off Grafton Road, "set back and far away from habitation, just at the fork of two streams which give it its name." Rocky Fork's huge glacial boulders mark the rugged land, rendering much of the area unsuitable for farming, although by necessity, Black farmers tilled every usable acre.[1]

Four Black families purchased adjacent parcels in the heart of Rocky Fork drainage basin, marking the formal beginning of the Rocky Fork community (map 2). The loosely defined boundaries of the settlement shifted over time according to landownership and attendance at the small local AME church. The rebuilt Rocky Fork AME church, a few foundations, and the original terrain are all that survive of the small settlement situated approximately three miles west of Alton, a major Underground Railroad station and one of Illinois's main abolitionist centers (see map 1).[2]

*Map 2.* 1861 Plat map, Madison County, Illinois. 1861 Plat prior to construction of Rocky Fork Church showing names of G. Bell in Section 20, L. Parks in Section 28 and 29, P. Baker in Section 29, and D. A. Spaulding in Sections 28 and 33. 1861 Map of Madison County, Illinois. Holmes and Arnold, Civil Engineers and Map Publishers. Buffalo, NY.

Surrounding rivers and intersecting creeks soften the inhospitable contours of the land. Rocky Fork Creek, a small tributary accessible from the Big Piasa Creek, flows through the once thriving settlement. The creek empties into the legendary Mississippi River, affording anonymity and quiet accessibility to those escaping slavery along the border between the free state of Illinois, and Missouri, a slave state. In the years before the Civil War, the river and the Black workers who navigated it were vital partners on the Black pathway to freedom.[3]

Geography, politics, and location played major roles in populating the original settlement where the river and surrounding waterways facilitated escape from slavery. Rocky Fork's accessibility from the Mississippi River, to the Big Piasa Creek, to the Rocky Fork Creek, marked the area as a suitable stopping point for escapees from slavery—a secluded, safe refuge, a first stop in the North for those making their way out of slavery via the Kentucky route or crossing to freedom from Missouri. Escapees were in the Rocky Fork area as early as 1816, and free Blacks found the nearby town of Alton a tolerable place to live as early as the 1820s.

The abolitionist center and Underground Railroad town of Alton played a powerful role in the fight against slavery in the region. The town commanded an advantageous vantage point south of Rocky Fork on the Mississippi River across from St. Louis. Adding to the tensions of the region, large portions of Illinois maintained a strong proslavery stance, echoing sentiments in cities across the North. Those proslavery sentiments, however, did not stop escapees from making their way from either the Missouri or the Illinois side of the Mississippi River.[4]

## Family Histories

The rootedness of the originating families at Rocky Fork offsets the pervasive theme of African American migration. Families and communities and their churches had been wedded to the land for more than 170 years. Ann Bell, her mother, Tisch Garnet, and her uncle, Peter Baker, in addition to London Parks, were among the earliest settlers living amid their White neighbors. Land transactions of two prominent White antislavery families, the Spauldings and the Hawleys, shaped the evolution of Rocky Fork as an African American settlement. Don Alonzo Spaulding, a county surveyor from 1825 to 1835, engaged in one of the meandering professions that provided a convenient cover, above suspicion, of Underground Railroad business. He knew the land well and executed numerous land sales. Intermarriages between the two White and the several Black families further bound the residents to one another.[5]

Blacks and Whites lived among one another, and Spaulding seems to have held little concern about the close proximity to African Americans or the circumstances under which Blacks obtained their freedom. He supported their work clearing his land in exchange for eventual land ownership. Fifty-two of the ninety-seven Blacks residing in Godfrey in 1855 lived in direct proximity to Spaulding; many settled on his land.

Similar to patterns found by historian Stephen Vincent in Indiana, families intermarried and tied the community together "in a confusing array of marital alliances."[6] The extended Rocky Fork family tree reveals the interconnectedness of the residents. The families of the founders intermarried.

A. J. Hindman married Ann Bell's daughter, Lucinda. Church founders Erasmus and Jane Green were the great-great-great-grandparents of Benjamin Matlock; Peter Baker, Ann Bell's uncle, was the great-grandfather of ninety-eight-year-old Charles Townsend, whose oral testimony brought the community into focus.[7]

Erasmus Green, the son of his enslaver in Bolivar, Tennessee, is listed as a mulatto in the Illinois census. Both Green and Eliza Jane Duncan had been enslaved in Bolivar, where they married, before migrating to Rocky Fork upon obtaining their freedom. Green and his wife led the community in building its first church (figures 1.1 and 1.2). London Parks and his wife, Jane, important Rocky Fork landowners, also lived in the area during the first half of the century. Parks appears to have been a perceptive businessman who bought and sold several parcels of land in the community, the first of which he acquired in 1845. He and his wife stand out in the land transactions and establishment of two of the earliest AME churches in the area. In addition to Black landowners, African American farmers worked in the area.

The Spauldings and the Hawleys did choose to go against the prevailing racial attitudes existing in Illinois at that time. By 1829, the state of Illinois ruled that no Black or mulatto would be "permitted to come and reside in this State, until such person shall have given bond and security." The state further ruled that any person who brings into the state "any Black or mulatto person, in order to free him or her from slavery, or who aids or assists any person in bringing any such Black or mulatto person to settle or reside therein, shall be fined one hundred dollars on conviction, or indictment."[8]

The two families suffered no consequences from disobeying the law. According to Joseph Hindman, grandson of Rocky Fork co-founder A. J. Hindman, the Spauldings and the Hawleys gave out land to those who would clear it and pay over a period. Neither family appeared concerned about the source of freedom, whether appropriated, purchased, or granted, for the Blacks who came to them under the work-for-land exchange. Hindman continued, "the Spaulding and Hawley families set up a system of selling land to the one-time slaves, who availed themselves of the offer."[9] Local historian Charlotte Johnson reports, "When the escaped slaves came over [Spaulding and Hawley] gave them the ability to work . . . and as they worked for them they could move on or they could stay there and build their homes and buy property."[10] Oral accounts indicate laboring Blacks or their descendants eventually owned much of the district. Evidence of ownership was not borne

*Figure 1.1.* Erasmus Green, an early AME minister at Rocky Fork Church, in his Civil War uniform. Courtesy of the Black Pioneers Committee, Alton Museum of History and Art, Inc.

*Figure 1.2.* Jane Green, wife of Erasmus. Courtesy of the Black Pioneers Committee, Alton Museum of History and Art, Inc.

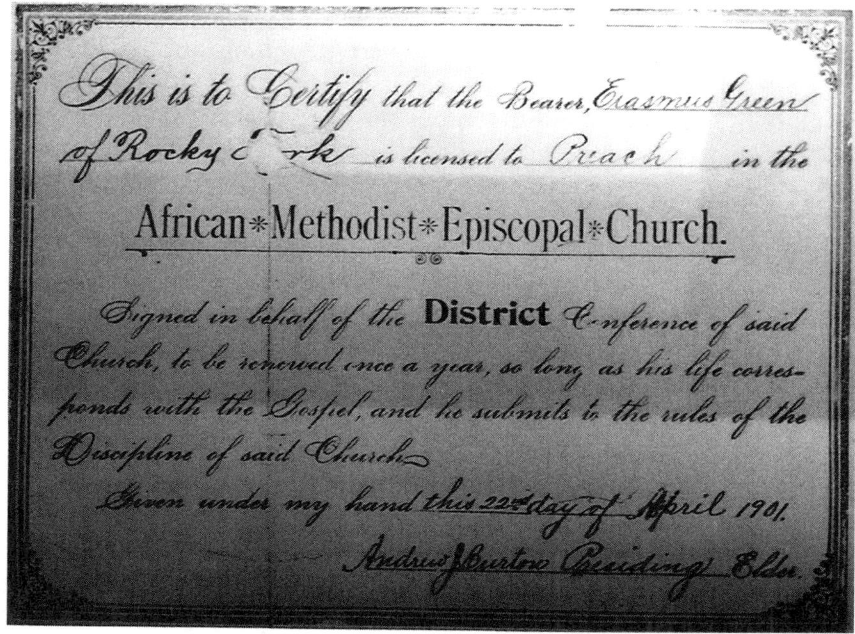

This is to Certify that the Bearer, Erasmus Green of Rocky Fork is licensed to Preach in the

African*Methodist*Episcopal*Church.

Signed in behalf of the District Conference of said Church, to be renewed once a year, so long as his life corresponds with the Gospel, and he submits to the rules of the Discipline of said Church.

Given under my hand this 22nd day of April 1901.

Andrew J Burton Presiding Elder.

*Figure 1.3.* Erasmus Green's AME preacher's license. Courtesy of the Black Pioneers Committee, Alton Museum of History and Art, Inc.

out in the documentary record, however. After the backbreaking work of clearing the land, land ownership was rarely formalized or legalized and therefore little documentation of the process remains.

Longtime resident Mr. Townsend asserts that Hawley "worked the folks pretty hard," suggesting that altruism was not a primary motivator. Charlotte Johnson found people worked for them for a year, "made a little bit of money, bought a house and a horse so that they could move a little bit farther up the line; came back and worked for them and earned a little bit more money; moved further up the line until they moved . . . to Springfield and to Peoria." [11] Often the workers did not take title to the land and therefore did not appear in official records, making this type of arrangement extremely difficult to track.

Ironically, and in contrast to prevailing local and family oral histories, London Parks, a free Black man, consistently appears in land transfer records. In 1856 Parks sold a parcel of land in Rocky Fork to one of the early settlers, Peter Baker, Ann Bell's uncle.[12] Land transfer records show the central role Parks played in the development of the community although his story does not occupy an important part of local historical and family narratives. Parks's descendants did not remain in the area. Consequently, memory of their contributions has not survived; their family history and connections to the church were not nurtured by the repeated acts of family recitation.

## The African Methodist Episcopal Church

In the early 1800s, self-emancipators, runaways, and Black freed men and women heeded the call to go west in pursuit of a better life, following the same impulses that drove White eastern and southern Americans. As these pioneers populated the western frontier, formal church buildings were not yet the norm. Weather permitting, early religious services took the form of outdoor group gatherings, camp meetings, and revivals. People traveled great distances, congregating for several days to receive the word of God from an itinerant minister or preacher. Such camp meetings were very popular in the Alton-Rocky Fork area. One elderly resident, Mrs. Florence Cannon, recalled stories of campground services on the property of Ben Matlock Sr., one of the early settlers, before the settlement built its place of worship.[13]

An active congregation must precede the building of any church. At Rocky Fork, in addition to holding campground meetings, the congregation met in the homes of members before forming the church. "We know the people met but I don't think they met as Baptist or Methodist until after Green became ordained," observed local resident and historian Charlotte Johnson, referring to its first pastor. "Rocky Fork [church] was already in existence and going but it was not a Methodist church; it was just a church. Folks got together and had church."[14] One of the oldest residents, Charles Townsend, also reported religious gatherings took place in the homes of different congregants.[15] Those who participated were free people of color, freed slaves, or enslaved persons, some of whom had reached "free territory via the Underground Railroad," as one church historian observed.[16]

Methodists required seven or so members for the beginnings of a Methodist society, which preceded formation of an officially sanctioned church. Oral accounts identify William Paul Quinn as the presiding AME elder who transformed the society into a congregation. Apparently, Elder Quinn mentioned visiting Rocky Fork and having religious services with the people there before 1840 (figure 1.4).[17]

*Figure 1.4* William Paul Quinn, fourth bishop of the AME Church. Courtesy of the African Methodist Episcopal Church.

Elaine Welch, Quinn's only biographer, describes him as standing six feet, three inches tall and weighing 250 pounds. The Black itinerant minister was a rugged man well suited for the "Herculean task of frontier preaching." Quinn was a traveling exhorter, or circuit rider, who "preferred half-wild horses and loved to come galloping up full tilt to places where he preached," dismounting just as the horse stopped. He routinely traveled from Pennsylvania and Maryland almost entirely on horseback to the banks of the Mississippi River, ministering to his far-flung flock, spreading the AME Church and the word of God at least three hundred miles beyond the Missouri line.[18] Quinn, who would become the fourth bishop of the AME Church in 1844, was a rough and ready man, not known for heeding the demands of racial protocol and hierarchy.

According to Welch, Quinn "helped many slaves to escape from their masters, and to find asylum in the north, away from the thralldom of the south." Welch continues, "being a man of resourcefulness, he was expert in smuggling slaves, and could on the spur of the moment form a ruse, by which the slave owner could be misled."[19] As research continues into Bishop Quinn's ministry, it may well be proven that everywhere he went and every church he established became an Underground Railroad stop. The AME churches at Brooklyn, Lower Alton, and Rocky Fork in Illinois count among that number.

The AME church, formed in Brooklyn, Illinois, forty miles south of Rocky Fork served as the first social institution and the earliest AME church built in Illinois. According to oral history, the first Brooklyn settlers were led by "Mother" Priscilla Baltimore, a remarkable biracial woman and former slave. Baltimore led eleven families composed of both free Blacks and escapees from Missouri across the Mississippi River in 1829. Baltimore, a Methodist preacher in her own right, established Mother Baltimore's Freedom Village, which folded into Brooklyn when the town was platted in 1837. Mother Baltimore influenced Brooklynites in establishing their Illinois town on the banks of the Mississippi River as a haven for anyone fleeing slavery. Baltimore had been sold in slavery several times before she finally managed to purchase her freedom. She understood from firsthand experience the costs of both slavery and freedom.[20]

Sometime in the late 1830s, Quinn organized the AME church there with the help of Baltimore. It is reported that the first AME church services in Illinois were held at Priscilla's Brooklyn home between 1838 and 1840 where she also gave refuge to Quinn. Brooklynites used Quinn Chapel AME Church and Antioch Baptist Church as Underground Railroad stops.

Because of her tireless work on the Underground Railroad, Priscilla Baltimore is known as the "the Moses of the West," in homage to her courageous work on behalf of escaping slaves paralleling the efforts of Harriet Tubman in the East.[21]

After William Paul Quinn's election as elder in 1838, he organized the Lower Alton AME Church in 1839. Better known as Campbell Chapel, the church stood halfway between Brooklyn and Rocky Fork. Quinn arrived in Alton during that harsh winter to find seven African Americans of the Methodist persuasion, who occasionally attended the Methodist Episcopal church. Together, they set about establishing one of the two earliest AME churches in the state of Illinois and arguably the first in Madison County. Quinn preached his initial sermon in William Barton's home, located between Alby and Easton Streets in Alton, which remained the preaching place for years. Alton's flourishing Black population supported the Union Baptist Church and Campbell Chapel AME Church, among the oldest Black churches in Illinois.[22]

Quinn also worked with the small religious group that congregated at Rocky Fork during that same winter of 1839. That would coincide with the oral history dating Quinn's formation of the church before 1840. Landowners London and Jane Parks were instrumental in granting the original charter for both the Rocky Fork and the Lower Alton AME churches. Parks and his wife would have known and worked with Quinn at both locations, which further ties Quinn to the Rocky Fork church. Parks is listed in the city directories as a businessman. Through his ability to donate the land for the church, Parks helped finance the early place of worship, leaving a powerful legacy for the independent Black church.

William Paul Quinn, Priscilla Baltimore, and London and Jane Parks are common to the churches at both the Rocky Fork and Brooklyn settlements. The AME Connection, or hierarchy, appointed Quinn bishop largely because of his strong work in planting the seeds of Methodism throughout the West. He reported to the 1844 AME General Conference that fifty Sunday schools with two hundred teachers and two thousand scholars had been established as a result of his efforts.[23]

Although Quinn helped to organize the churches, he rode through as a circuit rider, leaving the day-to-day ministering to local preachers. At Rocky Fork, Erasmus Green became the local minister to the tiny settlement, receiving his ordination in 1851 but probably not as a Methodist (see figure 1.3). He began the more formal, organized church between 1857 and 1859, but the congregation had to delay its plans until the end of the Civil War before erecting the church building that marks the "official" beginning of the "above ground" documented church history.

Oral and family histories tell the story of the African American presence at Rocky Fork. After serving in the Civil War for two years, Erasmus Green returned home with his friend and fellow war veteran, Andrew Jackson Hindman, to begin again and establish the AME Church at Rocky Fork. Green had served with Hindman in Company B56 of the U.S. Colored Infantry (USCI) in Helena, Arkansas, in 1863 and convinced his friend to come home with him to Rocky Fork after the war. Returning veterans such as Green and Hindman left an enduring legacy of Black towns and settlements organized after the sectional conflict.[24]

The two friends and their families co-founded the church, which they finally erected in 1863 on the land deeded for $1 by London and Jane Parks. The deed for the Rocky Fork AME church lists land donors among the first trustees and stewardesses. The couple was well established in the area and appears in the census records twenty years before the founding of the church.[25]

Local history remembers the church as active in the Underground Railroad. Congregants of what was to become the formal church actively used the area as a site of refuge before the church structure became a physical reality. Church members provided a haven for runaway slaves, some of whom stayed temporarily while working arrangements were made for them on farms in the area.[26] The church building may have been used to hide runaways between 1863 and 1865. Although Missouri remained in the Union as a border state throughout the war, the Emancipation Proclamation of 1863 did not grant freedom to those held in slavery there.

After the veterans returned from the war, the church preached that Rocky Fork should always be a place of refuge against trouble and strife—and it upholds that tradition today. The congregation has continually used the "Old Church" and its adjacent cemetery, the historical anchors of the community, ever since. Surveyors never failed to record the "Old Church" on Madison County plat maps (map 3). Oral history, cemetery inscriptions, and census data, however, indicate the settlement existed well before the officially documented origins of the church and that African American migration to Rocky Fork began at least forty years earlier than official records indicate. The Rocky Fork AME church anchored and centered religious and social activities. Members walked miles to receive the word of God. Consistent with the AME denomination's commitment to education, the Rocky Fork church also operated as the first school.

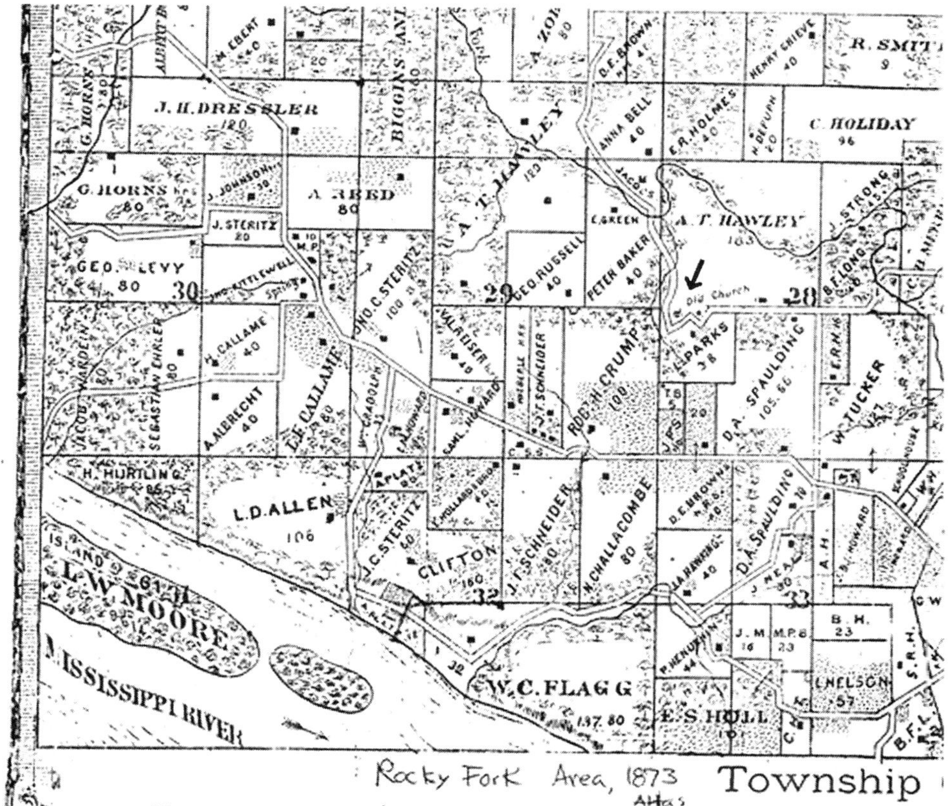


*Map 3.* 1873 Plat depicting "Old Church" at Rocky Fork. *Illustrated Encyclopedia and Atlas Map of Madison County, Ill.* Brink, McCormick & Company. St. Louis, 1873.

## Underground Railroad

### *Rocky Fork, Alton, and Brooklyn*

Oral histories gathered by the Black Pioneers, a local history group, explain how Andrew Hawley permitted use of his farm in Godfrey Township as a stopping place on the Underground Railroad. Family history remembers John Matlock Sr. as one of the early African American settlers who escaped slavery from Cuba, Missouri, and worked as a farm hand for the elder Hawley. After earning enough money, Matlock was able to purchase a substantial amount of acreage from landowner Don Alonso Spaulding.[27] Buffered by sympathetic neighbors in an otherwise hostile environment, Rocky Fork was ideally located, remote and not easily accessed. Homesteading deep in the woods helped discourage pursuers, who, fearing for their safety, would abandon the search for runaways.[28]

According to Spaulding's grandson, Spaulding helped establish Rocky Fork as "a refuge station for Negroes who had fled the terrors of slavery in the south." Following the example of other pre–Civil War Black communities across the country, escapees reached Rocky Fork in the first hours or days of freedom. The grandson continues, "when they got across the Mississippi River from Missouri, they knew the Underground Railroad that carried them out to Rocky Fork where they met a kindly reception." Wes Matlock, a fourth-generation Rocky Fork descendant of John Matlock, also reported that "hundreds of former slaves passed through the settlement on their way to Chicago or Canada in the years preceding the Civil War." Alton freelance writer John J. Dunphy reports that permanent residents of Rocky Fork served as conductors who helped guide escapees from Missouri.[29]

Oral narratives passed from generation to generation detail the escapees' flight from slavery. As early as 1830, runaways made their way up the Mississippi River to Piasa Creek, which they then followed to the Rocky Fork Creek. At that time, the Mississippi River would have looked quite different from its modern appearance, unaffected by the artificial intrusions that reshaped the landscape of the river, affecting its flow and breadth. Across the Mississippi, between St. Charles County, Missouri, and the mouth of the Big Piasa Creek lay two islands near enough to swim from one to the other. The Piasa Creek leading to the Rocky Fork Creek renders Rocky Fork, which is hard to get at by land, highly accessible by water.

According to the narrative of Mary Ann Clark, her great-grandmother swam across the Mississippi River, through the tunnel at what is now Enos Apartments, in Alton, where she was sheltered overnight before moving on to Rocky Fork. There has been some confusion about reference to the Enos Apartments in the oral sources, leading to implications that the story of the water crossing could not be true. Construction of the apartments began before the Civil War, was subsequently halted, and was not completed until after the war. Skeptics, believing the Enos Apartments were not built until after the war, therefore suggest that the story of Mary Ann Clark's grandmother could not be true.[30] Listeners should be aware, however, that modern landmarks frequently serve as reference points for oral historical narratives to orient the listener by framing details that rely on later existing recognizable landscape features for orientation.

From the Rocky Fork area, Blacks moved on to the Hamilton School in Otterville. From there the escapees traveled to Jacksonville and along the Illinois River to LaSalle and Ottawa, Illinois, and then on to Chicago. Possibly they found refuge in the home of former Alton resident and Underground Railroad activist John Jones. The Black abolitionist and his wife, Mary Richardson, gave shelter to many refugees before finally sending them to safety in Canada.[31]

Based on oral and documentary evidence, local historian Judy Hoffman concluded that Rocky Fork was a major Underground Railroad station. "In 1828," Hoffman observed, "Rocky Fork became a large-scale Underground Railroad station operated by both blacks and whites. The station drew fugitive slaves from southern Illinois and Missouri as far away as Kentucky and Tennessee, then transported them north to freedom." Hoffman believes "Rocky Fork's longevity and the hundreds of runaways who reportedly passed through the hidden settlement between 1828 and 1863 may make it the oldest and largest Underground Railroad operation in Illinois." She concludes that historians named Alton as the Underground Railroad hub and have overlooked Rocky Fork and Godfrey as "a major entry point in this elaborate secret system."[32]

The river port of Alton, strategically located ten miles downstream from Rocky Fork, doubled as a main point of entry for escapees from Missouri. Steep hills surrounding Alton provided a commanding view of the Mississippi; the city's location just below the Illinois River allowed the port town to control traffic on the waterway. Strategically, Alton sat between the tiny Black settlement of Rocky Fork to the west and Brooklyn, America's first Black town, to the south in St. Clair County. Most free Blacks worked in the river trade or at the brickworks; some of them conducted an Underground Railroad network running the length of the Mississippi River.[33]

One of the three major escape routes among the river towns originated in a series of caves in the bluffs around Alton, which received large numbers of runaways escaping slavery coming across the Mississippi. Wilbur Siebert dates the rise of the Underground Railroad in Alton to 1831 and stresses the role of the Presbyterian church where the first Illinois depot took root in Bond County. The line out of Alton converged in Springfield with the White Plains, Jerseyville, Waverley, Quincy, and Jacksonville lines.[34]

The first Underground Railroad escapee in Wisconsin history came through Alton. In the summer of 1842, sixteen-year-old Caroline Quarlls, "so White that she went openly by steamboat," found a way to secure passage to Alton after escaping enslavement in St. Louis. A local Black man, surmising the danger of her circumstances, urged her not to linger in Alton and had her whisked on to Milwaukee by stagecoach.[35]

Five recognized Underground Railroad stations operated within a seven-block radius in Upper Alton. Carl Spicer, one of Siebert's students, again referencing the internal network of African American friends and family, observed that once escapees were near Alton "they met friends who were generally expecting them." In 1854, a Black man driving a covered wagon passed through the county. He had fifteen men, women, and children concealed in the wagon. The driver-conductor was a free Black in Alton who transported his passengers from eastern Missouri, where they crossed the river in skiffs. He eventually sent them on to Chicago. After a series of group escapes in 1845, a St. Louis newspaper speculated that the runaways had been enticed by abolitionists who had helped them along "'the great underground railway' through Alton and Chicago to Canada."[36]

Brooklyn also connected to the riverfront economy and depended on the river trades for survival, but according to Brooklyn historian Sundiata Keitha Cha-Jua, "its growth was tied to its ability to attract runaways. The town was a city of refuge." Built as an expression of Priscilla Baltimore's dedication to freedom and inspired by the example of Paul Quinn, Brooklyn committed itself to the antislavery movement, providing refuge for escapees. The town organized itself as one big Vigilance Committee. At one point, a group of slave catchers descended on Brooklyn looking for an escapee. They rode into town and, upon finding the fugitive at the home of Brooklyn resident William Carper, they murdered Carper and recaptured the escaped slave. Despite Carper's martyrdom, Brooklynites continued their acts of civil disobedience.[37]

Freedom seekers such as William Wells Brown habitually escaped in anticipation of an impending sale or while being taken to auction in St. Louis. In 1833, Brown began one of his unsuccessful escape attempts with his mother. Leaving from St. Louis, Brown rowed a skiff across the Mississippi River using a board as his oar. Landing south of Alton, son and mother then headed along the main road toward the town, hiding in the woods during the day.[38] Brown made no mention in his *Narrative* of Brooklyn or of encountering any Blacks in the immediate vicinity. Brown would learn, however, that safety was not guaranteed merely because he was in a free state on northern soil.

Nowhere did proslavery convictions approach greater depth than in the Alton area, where a proslavery mob murdered editor and Presbyterian minister Elijah P. Lovejoy in 1837 for his stand for freedom of the press and his staunch position against slavery. For a brief time, William Wells Brown, who would go on to become one of the nation's great Black abolitionists, worked the press and received what little learning he would obtain while still held in slavery.[39] In retaliation for Lovejoy's defiant publication of radical works, angry mobs murdered him on the night of November 7. The martyrdom of the abolitionist newspaper editor mere miles from Rocky Fork announced the danger of the region.[40]

Notoriety also attached itself to Alton in the infamous Anderson Fugitive Slave case. After John Anderson had been sold away from his wife and child, he escaped in an attempt to rejoin them. When pursuers cornered Anderson, the escapee, while defending himself, stabbed and killed the slaveholder. Anderson then escaped from St. Louis to Alton before moving on to Canada via the Underground Railroad. The governor of Missouri and the U.S. government attempted to extradite Anderson from Canada, to no avail. His wife and child, however, remained in bondage in St. Louis. Fearing for his safety and his freedom, Anderson first migrated to England, where he was received by William Craft—himself a famous escapee, along with his wife, Ellen. Craft helped Anderson further his education and arranged his lecture tour in Britain before the escapee finally emigrated to Liberia.[41]

## Modern History

Time has taken its toll on three of the four primary sites that are the basis of this study; Rocky Fork alone has survived. Family member Joe Hindman remembered that during his childhood and that of his parents, there were many Black families along Rocky Fork Creek, "clustered together on small acreages." "The elder Hawleys permitted the families to acquire small parcels of the large farm in return for working at Lilac Lodge, the Hawley homeplace." Hindman continued, "Our forty-seven-acre farm, two miles west of the Alton city limits, and a short distance north of the Mississippi River, on bustling Old Grafton Road," was about a quarter mile from Hawley's Lilac Lodge farm.[42]

At the height of Rocky Fork's occupancy, as many as forty-five families called the settlement home. Blacks owned about two hundred acres.[43] By 1907, seven families remained, prompting a newspaper reporter to lament "the demise of the Black community in Rocky Fork," where the several hundred African American residents once placed great value in community entertainment and common background and aspirations.[44] Spaulding's grandson noted the exodus as early as 1921. "Many have moved away and what in the days of the Underground Railroad proved a good hiding place is today an out of the way place, with wild woods and wild life making it an ideal place for a Boy Scout camp."

In 1926, the "Old Church" succumbed to the forces of nature; erosion of the shallow foundation forced a move to its present site. Local builders, under the pastorate of Rev. Green Price, erected and remodeled the church using salvageable portions of the original church building, primarily the rough-hewn beam cut by community founders Erasmus Green and Andrew Jackson Hindman.[45] The second church built in 1926 was approximately ten feet longer and sat fifty yards south of the present church, which was rebuilt several times after numerous arson attacks. The 1926 structure, which rested on a stone foundation, had no cellar and a vaulted ceiling. The congregants christened the church the New Bethel AME Church at Rocky Fork.

For years, Charles Benjamin Townsend III (1908–2007) was the oldest descendant born in Rocky Fork. He was the community's "living library" (figure 1.5). Mr. Townsend's mother died when he was five, leaving his grandparents, Charles Robert and Augusta Darby Townsend, the responsibility of raising her son. Mr. Townsend's memories therefore skipped a generation and revealed the workings of intergenerational and communal memory. Townsend's oral narration of his life with his grandparents and his memories of the stories of his great-grandparents spanned five generations of family history. His lived experiences and the long reach of his memory, of his grandparents' memories, and of his great-grandparents' memories tied the contemporary directly to the nineteenth century.

Charles Townsend, Clementine Kennedy, and John Matlock Jr., who together represent several generations of descendants, fondly remembered the rosebush boundary markers meandering along property lines. Abundant lilac bushes planted along the Hawley and Matlock properties scented Rocky Fork homes. Traces of the beautiful original gardens cling to the Rocky Fork soil even today. Food was bountiful; children fished in the creek, catching enormous crayfish. Mushrooms abounded. The youngsters picked berries and damsel plums, and ate hickory nuts, walnuts, filberts and hazelnuts, delicious corn bread, and groundhog. The natural abundance sustained the community and helped it maintain self-sufficiency. The residents remember being treated to all manner of sumptuous cakes and pies baked from the produce of blackberry and blueberry bushes, wild strawberries, and peach,

*Figure 1.5.* Mr. Charles Benjamin Townsend III (1908–2007)

apple, plum, and cherry trees. "We had taffy-pulls; we coasted on the hills in the winter, swam and fished in the summer." Fishing was a large part of the Rocky Fork experience; in addition to the church, the Rocky Fork stream was a central feature in the landscape. John Matlock Jr. recounted many a fond memory of swimming in the swimming hole. In addition to the church and cemetery, small plots of land, farmsteads, and cabins loosely connected by a series of old internal pathways bound the Rocky Fork community together. A series of well-worn and intimate short cuts linked the community outward to surrounding neighbors. The undulating, craggy, natural park-like setting shrouds the settlement with the protection that once ensured the survival of its residents.

By 1962, only five or six families remained in the area.[46] The community repeatedly experienced the destructive physical and psychological effects of arson. The sheriff burned the remaining homes on New Year's Eve, 1976–77, in a fire training exercise, forcing the few residents out of their homes and effectively ending the residential history of Rocky Fork. The residents never recovered from the burning of their homes; most had no insurance and could not rebuild.

In the 1970s and 1980s, the church, too, was repeatedly vandalized, with racial slurs spray-painted on the walls. In 1974, homemade bombs damaged but did not destroy the interior of the church and the sanctuary was desecrated. Vandals burned hymnals, shattered windows, and stole a sacred painting. The tiny congregation rededicated the church in 1977, pledging to serve humanity in brotherhood and love just as they had done in the days of the Underground Railroad. Whites as well as Blacks joined forces in a grassroots campaign to renovate the church after the decimation. Hundreds of people gathered on church grounds to celebrate the rebirth of the church.[47]

Rocky Fork AME survives as one of the churches burned during the highly publicized period of terror against Black churches in the 1980s. Lifelong resident Clementine Kennedy was baptized at the church—the only church home she has ever known. From her honored position as the oldest member of the church and as its spokesperson, Kennedy vowed the congregation would not be driven from the beloved church that had provided sanctuary for so many for more than a century. Community effort and dedication rebuilt the church as a lasting modern legacy.[48]

The present place of worship in Rocky Fork is the third twentieth-century building; two other church buildings were burned in one six-month interval between April and October 1988. The congregation rebuilt the church after it was burned on April 16. Then, to the absolute horror of the worshipers and surrounding community, two weeks before its scheduled reopening, the church was burned to the ground on October 17. Miraculously, the hand-hewn beam originally cut by Hindman and salvaged from the original church "was not damaged by the fire, even though it directly supports the entire burnt out church building." The community held fast; the AME church survives and continues as a site of worship and spiritual sustenance.[49]

Black studies professor Clyde Woods indicated that this decades-old practice of bombing and burning rural Black churches re-emerged in the 1990s as a form of "social and political control over African-American communities through violence, fear, and out-migration." Arson and burning Black churches strike at the mother root of a society. The demise of Rocky Fork as a residential community was a direct result of the withering effects of arson and the bombing of the church, which devastated the physical and emotional resources of a settlement that had stood firm in the face of slavery. Fire breached the sanctity of place in ways that slavery and oppression could not, but the church community clung to their faith.[50]

Although the residences are gone, the small congregation remains in existence today because of the determination, fortitude, and bravery of its members. The New Bethel Rocky Fork AME Church stands as a testament to the resilience and endurance of the African American experience. The church and community symbolize the stamina, determination, and hardiness of not only of the Rocky Fork congregation but also of all African Americans who endured so much in the quest for freedom and equality.

The community stands in the face of a powerful legacy of forced migration among African Americans. The continual African American presence in the landscape started before the Civil War and extends to the present. While arson diminished their numbers, it has not obliterated their presence. The church congregation continues in direct descent from its founders. Countering the push toward further migration, families and their descendants remained in the community for more than a century, maintaining an uninterrupted association with the AME church at Rocky Fork.[51]

* * *

Considering its various components, the Underground Railroad emerges as a multi-pronged vehicle for Black resistance. The loosely organized subversive movement began with freedom seekers, supported first by Black community activities on southern plantations, then by free Black communities in the North, and finally by Black and White abolitionists. William Wells Brown, the escapee who had rowed himself and his mother across the Mississippi River in a skiff, learned from his repeated escapes. He endured recapture and arrest alongside his mother in Central Illinois, 150 miles from St. Louis. He learned that it was not the North that offered safety or refuge to escaping captives but rather communities and the support of moral-minded individuals, Black and White from the South as well as the North. Rocky Fork would have been one such sanctuary.

Until recently, preservation efforts and stewardship for the landscape resources at Rocky Fork were nonexistent although in the 1950s the Hawley family donated the remaining portion of their land in Rocky Fork to the Warren Levis Boy Scout Camp leaving large portions essentially undisturbed. In 2001, the camp was nominated and accepted as part of the National Park Service Underground Railroad Network to Freedom.[52] In 2003, the Center for American Archaeology and the Illinois Transportation Archaeological Research Program identified nine homestead sites, four of which correspond to homesteads owned by African Americans. Unprotected portions of the land fell into the hands of developers. Village and county officials proposed a cross-town highway that would meander through the heavily forested area to the north, forming a critical link to the future development of the town of Godfrey.[53] The mission of a recent preservation group, the Rocky Fork Historic District Project, is to save the land at Rocky Fork and rescue the history of a site believed to be one of the first stops on the Underground Railroad along the Mississippi River in Illinois.

With the passing of the oldest remaining members, the community is losing its connection to living memory. This book is an act of reclamation. Memory and tradition form an unbroken historical connection from the inception of Rocky Fork to the present. Rocky Fork and Brooklyn, Illinois, are among only a handful of nineteenth-century black towns that remain in existence.

CHAPTER 2

# Miller Grove, Illinois

## Linking a Free Black Community to the Underground Railroad

The stories of the free Black community at Miller Grove had no known historical connections to the Underground Railroad. The enclave was not included in the Underground Railroad legends of Illinois. Historical documents and letters supported by archaeological research gave shape to the experiences of the Miller Grove families. Ultimately, these documents led researchers to conclude that the Miller Grove area was an important antislavery location within a clandestine, poorly understood, broadly defined Underground Railroad. Freedom seekers often escaped from the South alone and passed through the area without benefit of organized assistance, relying instead on individuals of conscience.

The Miller Grove stories survive through four primary sources: the record of indentures and county recordings of the $1,000 bonds required of any free person of color entering the state of Illinois; marriage certificates, wills, and other official documents; the letters of two White abolitionist-minded Bible salesmen, James West and James Scott Davis; and landscape features, including a cemetery.

Foundations and wells, garden flowers and yucca plants, punctuate the landscape as visual reminders of the long abandoned settlement. National Forest Service archaeologist Mary McCorvie and her team have been piecing together the history of the small free Black community. The lives of Bedford and his wife, Abby Gill Miller, and the remains of the farmstead came to light through ongoing archaeological excavations in the Shawnee National Forest, in Southern Illinois.

Like so many other historic free Black communities in the North, the midwestern settlement began with the migration out of the South of newly freed African Americans, who often traveled with and settled alongside former slaveholders. Men and women, emancipated during the 1840s in

Hardeman, Marshall, and Henry Counties in south-central Tennessee, established the historic community in the Shawnee Hills, thirty miles north of Paducah, Kentucky (see map 1).[1]

Established in 1844, the cluster of rural farmsteads known as Miller Grove was named for Bedford Miller, the eldest son of founders Harrison and Lucinda Miller. The family stood among the sixty-eight people who received their freedom from one of four White families in south-central Tennessee. Bedford's father, Harrison, served as founder and patriarch. These freedmen and freedwomen, with Harrison and Lucinda among their guiding members, formed the nucleus of the Pope County community.[2] Bedford's parents had the wherewithal to deed the land for the Mt. Gilead AME Church, probably the settlement's central institution and first school.[3] The people recently freed by the four White emancipating slaveholding families from Tennessee settled near one another.

Upon his death, Peter Singleton, one of the four White family men, released forty-two people from bondage. Many intermarried and put the Miller Grove community on solid footing. An 1850 final decree filed in Shelbyville, Bedford County, Tennessee, named the persons who had "each and every one of them given bond," and "good and sufficient security in a sum equal to their respective values." The newly freed migrants paid these monies to the clerk and master of the court on the condition "that each and every one of them shall faithfully remove from this State." After meeting these conditions, Julia Singleton and forty-one others paid their way out of slavery and were "emancipated and set free."[4]

Primary archaeological excavations at Miller Grove took place at the farmstead of William Riley Williams, a free-born African American from Tennessee. Riley moved to Illinois in 1851 because of Tennessee's restrictive laws for Blacks during that period. He bought land near other African American farmers, recently arrived from Tennessee. Blacks carried a double burden, paying twice for their liberty, once to guarantee they would leave the state of Tennessee and again to Illinois to assure their worthiness upon entering the state. Taking on the costly task of purchasing their freedom, African Americans paid portions of the bonds required in Tennessee or in Illinois; former slaveholder Peter Singleton's estate may have provided part of the funds as well. The $42,000 cost of freedom did not include any additional bonds demanded by Tennessee to ensure their forced exodus. In all likelihood, the freed men and women combined their funds with Singleton's estate money in meeting the high cost that slaveholding states placed on freedom.[5]

Among the original migrants, former slaveholder Henry Sides and his wife lived among the freemen and freewomen at Miller Grove. Because of such high costs, Sides was known to keep large sums of cash on hand. Bible salesman James West mentions that he "spent the night with one who, a few years back, came to Illinois to liberate his slaves. And being Agent for some other liberated slaves, was robbed and injured."[6] West does not name the injured party. Apparently, however, he was referring to the well-documented robbery and beating of Henry Sides and his wife, Barbara. Sides was known to contribute substantial amounts of money helping migrating Blacks post their $1,000 bonds at the Golconda Courthouse as mandated by state law. From all indications, payment of the full $1,000 was demanded. Sides acted as a mediator for several of his former slaveholding Tennessee associates, including Joseph Dabbs. Sides posted bonds to warrant the emancipation of not only his own enslaved workers, but of the other migrants as well.

Presumably, Henry Sides migrated with the emancipated families. He used his land purchase near the freed families in Miller Grove to secure perpetual care for himself and his wife.[7] In his last will and testament, Sides bequeathed the land, all his farming utensils, and his young horse to "Abraham Sides a person of color . . . on the following conditions that he live with and take care of and do and perform all offices required of him as long as myself and my wife Barbara Sides shall live." The will further states that Henry and Barbara were to remain in possession of the land as long as either lived. If Abraham failed "to fulfill the requirements," then the portion of the will pertaining to Abraham would be null and void. Sides did not make his perpetual care a condition of emancipation, merely a condition of inheritance.[8]

Sides, in emancipating his enslaved workers, posting monies for their bonds, and living, dying, and being buried among the Blacks at Miller Grove, was true to his political or ethical beliefs. Although the Tennessee family associations are not clear, the ancestors of the migrating White families were Presbyterians who, similar to Quaker migrants, sold their holdings in the South and moved north with the newly freed.

The names of the Black families listed in the indentures and bonds suggest the Miller Grove community, which emerges from the pages of these records. Marriage certificates, grave markers, and tax documents combined with deeds, census records, and emancipation records further animate the relationships among the Black residents of Miller Grove. Community members adopted one another's children, widows and widowers married. Children of the different families intermarried and perpetuated the settlement.[9] They met in one another's homes for religious services before building the first of three AME churches.

Marriage records reveal the strong interrelationships among the Blacks who previously had been held in slavery by the various emancipating families. For example, Joseph Dabbs, head of one of the four White Tennessee families, moved to Miller Grove, "with my Black family," and then emancipated Ned or Edward Dabbs, his sister, Clarissa, and his brother, Charles. Whether Joseph Dabbs used the phrase literally, figuratively, or spiritually is unclear. Shortly after arriving in Miller Grove and receiving his freedom, Ned Dabbs married Dolly Sides in April 1848. Blacks at Miller Grove retained the names of the former slaveholding families.[10]

Ned Dabbs had been an active and central part of the settlement and, upon his death, left a sizable estate probably derived, in part, from his inheritance after the death of former slaveholder Joseph Dabbs. Joseph willed all of his estate "consisting of horses, open waggons . . . together with notes and vouchers for dues in the State of Tennessee be divided among my Black family whom I have freed in the State of Tennessee and with whom I have come to this state of Illinois." Ned's third of the estate included a mare, two beds, a shotgun, a cutting knife, and a wagon. When Ned Dabbs died in 1866, founder Harrison Miller served as executor of the estate, despite the fact that he could neither read nor write. Leaving a will not only protected assets, but also reduced Blacks' vulnerability in the face of marginalized legal status.

Ned Dabbs's probate inventory highlights his important standing within the community. In addition to numerous farm animals and implements, two clocks and several books, including law books and a U.S. history book, were itemized among his effects—unusual for the time, particularly for a Black man on the Illinois frontier. These items were among Ned's personal effects and not part of his inheritance.[11]

## The American Missionary Association as an Emerging Link to the Underground Railroad

Formed in 1846, the American Missionary Association (AMA), an eastern nonsectarian benevolent society, grew out of a merger of several organizations. Congregationalist minister and co-founder of the New York State Vigilance Society Charles B. Ray, Presbyterian minister Theodore S. Wright, and Samuel Ringgold Ward, also a Congregationalist minister, served alongside J. W. C. Pennington as the integrated association's first African American board members.[12] These same men weave in and out of the Underground Railroad effort as well.

The AMA advocated radical abolitionist principles and paid particular attention to work among people of color. At Miller Grove, Ned Dabbs maintained contact with local New School Presbyterian ministers and Bible salesmen James West and James Scott Davis, very active members of the AMA. West's letters and reports to AMA corresponding secretary Rev. Simeon Jocelyn in New York City, named Dabbs, Sheppard, and other African American residents of Miller Grove.[13]

Edward Dabbs and preacher Jeremiah Sheppard, important literate community leaders, subscribed to literature from the AMA exposing the readers to strong antislavery sentiments. The AMA maintained committed abolitionist principles and Underground Railroad ties. Jeremiah Sheppard also connected the work of the AMA to Miller Grove through his request for antislavery literature. Sheppard's role as an AME preacher brought the rural community, the AMA, and the larger world of the Black church in alignment with one another. His life reflected the interfaith, interracial cooperation that was the founding tenet of the association.[14]

Considering the volume and variety of books the AMA Bible salesmen sold, Dabbs may have obtained some of the books in his considerable collection from them. Dabbs's handwritten 1864 note to the AMA in New York requesting a subscription for antislavery literature reveals him as quite literate and directly connected to the AMA. Perhaps Dabbs made use of the law books in his possession to guard his freedom and that of other members of the Miller Grove community.

One might expect to find a Bible among Ned Dabbs's many books. Although Whites often based justifications for slavery on the Bible, for Blacks the holy book provided the path to godliness and moral uplift. Most importantly, it served as their first reader. Henry Bibb was convinced the Bible was a potent antislavery document to be widely distributed among the enslaved population. In 1849, he joined the AMA effort to distribute Bibles among southern bondsmen.[15]

Literacy and education were paramount concerns for the community and for the AMA. A writing slate was listed among the items in Ned Dabbs's estate, and archaeologists recovered slates from both the Riley Williams and Bedford and Lucinda Miller sites.[16] Julia Singleton, one of the forty-two persons emancipated by Peter Singleton, served as the community schoolteacher. Maps identify a schoolhouse in the Miller Grove community, although the foundation has not yet been located.[17]

West's letters link him to the Black community around Broad Oak and Miller Grove. He was particularly eloquent in his "purpose of enlightening the minds of the readers" and was dismayed to "look around and see the numbers that remain in the gaul of bitterness and bonds of iniquity." An 1856 letter indicates West experienced persecution and abuse for his views. One professed minister West encountered spoke of the propriety of running him off due to his "Abolition Principles."[18]

Author Edgar Raines concluded that generally White ministers, Bible salesmen, and missionaries had little contact with Blacks in the Southern Illinois area in the period leading to emancipation. Nevertheless, James West's letters demonstrate that, indeed, there was considerable contact and visiting among these three groups in their rural homes. West and Davis discuss their affiliation with the people of Miller Grove in their letters to Simeon Jocelyn back in New York. In 1859, West distributed eighteen Bibles and about ten small testaments "to the free Colored People" of Pope County "for which they were very thankful promised to read them for themselves and for others."[19]

## The Dissemination of Antislavery Literature

West and Davis brought this larger, radical world of the AMA to Miller Grove and to Southern Illinois through their correspondences. These Bible salesmen in league with their evangelical abolitionist sponsors understood the power of the press and the importance of literacy in effecting social change. The AMA list of titles available to the salesmen, also known as colporteurs, serves as a primer for antislavery thought and literature available at the time. The list of literature contained in Lewis Tappan's Antislavery Library included radical works such as *Uncle Tom's Cabin*, the possession of which among the enslaved in some states of the South meant certain imprisonment.[20] The AMA's position on education and literacy, and the efforts toward education by the residents of Miller Grove, stand in opposition to the antiliteracy laws enacted to perpetuate slavery by enslaving not only the bodies but also the minds of Blacks through legislated or forced illiteracy.[21]

It is no accident that the near-by Broad Oak post office was the colporteurs' main location for receiving mail. Historian Edgar Raines observed that "it required moral courage to receive a known abolition periodical through the mails and a greater commitment to the cause than a similar act in an area further north."[22] Federal law prohibited Blacks from carrying the U.S. mail. The postmaster general's 1802 objection to appointing African American mail carriers reveals post offices as important sites for the dissemination or suppression of seditious information or radical literature. As Leon Litwack observed, allowing Blacks employment in the postal service implied a level of literacy that constituted a peril to the nation's sense of security. Literate free Blacks epitomized an unacceptable and potentially threatening class of people. Employment in the postal service offered the potential opportunity to "co-ordinate insurrectionary activities, mix with other people, and acquire subversive information and ideas."[23] The widespread circulation of seditious literature, such as David Walker's *Appeal*, helped fuel the fires of fear of "the dangerous fringes of antebellum Black activism."[24] Post offices, therefore, were critical sites for control and dissemination of information. As the originator of an 1835 postal campaign that disseminated 175,000 copies of 4 antislavery pamphlets for the American Antislavery Society, Lewis Tappan understood the power derived from effective use of the postal system.[25]

Although West lived south of the Miller Grove area, he and Davis, for the short time he lived there, received their mail, including antislavery literature, at this location rather than in their own township. "Fred Douglass' Paper," formerly *The North Star*, was included among the antislavery literature introduced into the region by the colporteurs, "perhaps the first regular anti-slavery periodical that was ever mailed to any Office within the limits of the county."[26] The individual officers of the AMA contributed to Douglass's newspaper and served as subscription agents. Douglass's paper contained constant references to escapes on the Underground Railroad and was a radical publication in proslavery Southern Illinois.[27]

Through its missionary work, the AMA connected known Underground Railroad participants across the country. In the majority of the correspondence about Broad Oak between James West and Brother Jocelyn of New York City, West referred to southeastern Illinois as "Western Egypt." Clara Merritt De Boer describes Lewis Tappan and Jocelyn as "two great abolitionists with whom [Black abolitionist Charles B. Ray] was long associated in antislavery agitation and the more specific acts of aiding escaped slaves."[28] In total, by 1860, the AMA had expended an excess of $1 million on antislavery missions worldwide, including more than one hundred missions in North America. Their membership rolls contained the names of many, such as Pennington, Ray, Jocelyn, and Tappan, who were both the driving force and the hidden hand of the Underground Railroad.[29]

Abolitionist strategies involved disseminating antislavery literature among African Americans, particularly along the river counties in Southern Illinois.[30] West referred to the influence of disseminated literature as "silent, yet powerful messengers . . . exerting an influence for the last 12 months which my pen cannot portray to your mind."[31] West also mentioned selling a copy of Douglass's *My Bondage and Freedom* to a family that "seemed most pleased with it."[32]

Three months before he was forced to leave the state by an enraged mob, West sold a copy of Hinton Rowan Helper's *The Compendium of the Impending Crisis of the South* in September 1860.[33] In the years leading to the Civil War, he also mentioned in his monthly report to Rev. Jocelyn selling "Bro. Tappan's little tract, 'The War, Its Cause and Remedy.'" At the opening of the Civil War, Tappan's pamphlet along with his *Immediate Emancipation: The Only Wise and Safe Mode* was circulated by the thousands.[34]

This literature circulated among Ned Dabbs, Jeremiah Sheppard, and others in the Miller Grove community. Valued for his literacy skills, Dabbs served as a reader and disseminator of information for those in the community, such as Harrison, Bedford, and others, who had not been taught to read or write. In observing the popularity of one tract of the Christian press, West comments, "One individual . . . here told me that his 'Press' was read and loaned, until it was literally worn out."[35]

Fellow colporteur James Scott Davis came to Broad Oak, near Miller Grove, in 1860. His short stay in Broad Oak contrasts with West's extended commitment to the area. Davis had been driven out of "the Abolition" church in Lewis County, Kentucky, in December 1859, shortly after former AMA missionary Rev. John G. Fee and the antislavery colony at Berea had been expelled and the entire "Kentucky force" of the AMA exiled, victims of the aftermath of John Brown's raid on Harpers Ferry. Fee, who had been misquoted in the *Louisville Courier* as well as other Kentucky newspapers, paid dearly for the headline, "John G. Fee is in Beecher's church, calling for more John Browns."[36]

Davis had an impeccable antislavery pedigree with deep ties in the White antislavery community. In the fall of 1855, the year he arrived in Kentucky, "a colporteur traveling for the AMA in the same neighborhood was jailed on suspicion of aiding fugitive slaves." After his release, vigilantes forced him to leave the state. Of that incident, John Fee declared, "We had colporteurs in the field who were distributing Bibles, publications of the American Tract Society, and anti-slavery documents. One of these colporteurs was charged falsely with telling a slave how he might get into a Free State." Kentucky imposed serious retribution for those caught aiding freedom seekers. Oberlin's Calvin Fairbank, for example, was imprisoned for seventeen years for going south and helping escapees flee; he died in prison.[37]

Back in New York City, Lewis Tappan was well acquainted with Black members of the AMA, a number of whom had an impact on his thinking. In turn, Tappan's radiating influence affected AMA members such as Bro. Jocelyn, and George Whipple, with whom West and Davis regularly communicated. Working with people of color was central to the association and connected black abolitionists, many of whom were ministers, the Underground Railroad, and rural communities. Cooperation between the AME Church and the AMA, as indicated by the associations of AME bishops Morris Brown and Daniel Payne, was consistent with the interdenominational, interracial nature of AMA before the Civil War and with the stand of the AME Church working as a conduit for Black freedom through whatever channels necessary.

By 1860, the AMA-supported colporteurs in the home missions field discovered that the passing years did not diminish the dangers of the region.

West noted, "persecution is raging here to an alarming extent." However, violence had not erupted "but threats are freely made. Every issue of the *Golconda Weekly Herald* since March 9th has contained abuses, misrepresentations, and threats of the 'Martyr's Garment,' Tar and Feathers." By October, West's letters again contained continual references to threats of "tar and feathering," with reports of his persecutors active in slanderously attempting to injure his reputation.[38] Because of this incendiary press, "the contagion spreads with great rapidity."[39] In 1861, West's last alarming letter from Broad Oak described a mob threatening to lynch West and Davis, forcing them to flee Pope County while local authorities offered no assistance to the two abolitionists.[40] In his quarterly report to the AMA, West recounted, "if we are here at the expiration of the notice to leave, then I am to be hung," leaving him exposed and without protection from the "liabilities of an infuriated, drunk, lawless mob."[41] It was, by now, an experience with which he and Davis were no doubt familiar after suffering similar expulsion from Kentucky five years earlier. Work of AMA missionaries in the border states became increasingly hazardous, subject to mob action and expulsion, particularly after John Brown's raid at Harpers Ferry in 1859.[42]

Through their letters and AMA contacts, West and Davis exposed Miller Grove to the antislavery world. While principally serving as Bible salesmen, these two men were among seventeen other antislavery activists of various denominations in the Broad Oak area. The quiet manner in which Southern Illinois Black and White abolitionists conducted their work belies descriptions of the Underground Railroad as dramatic, glamorous, thrilling, or romantic. The deadly, unsafe, day-to-day labor of workers along the railroad frequently led to ruined health, financial hardship, imprisonment, or death. Blacks involved in the enterprise risked loss of freedom and the constant threat of reenslavement. Unlike the dramatic, flamboyant, well-known dealings of Harriet Tubman, William Still, Levi Coffin, and others, heroic deeds of the men and women in the small Black settlements received no exaggerated descriptions, no details of the confiding diarist, no glorified reminiscences. Furthermore, outlining the anonymous character of the Underground Railroad in southeastern Illinois, expert Wilbur Siebert failed to find evidence of routes in the southeastern portion of the state, owing, he surmised, to the extreme proslavery sentiment held by large portions of the area.[43]

By 1857, James West was writing to Jocelyn in New York that close proximity to the river and prospects for a railway passing through the region made the area "a favorable place for the second depot, near at hand." In the same report, West asked for a sufficient number of "our Eastern friends to form a nucleus, where we can make our influence to be felt. Why not engage in this enterprise, in sufficient numbers to build up a Town, put an engine into operation, and to build a church and such schools as may be needed?"[44] West's meaning is unclear; a railroad line already existed, there was no "first" depot in place to explain his reference to a favorable place for a second depot, and the passage referring to putting an engine in operation is cryptic considering the widespread use of railroad terms as part of the Underground Railroad. West also mentions making deposits in "the Golconda River Bank." Thus far, however, we have not been able to locate or identify such an institution, indicating that he may be speaking both literally and figuratively of Underground Railroad business. The word "depot," in particular, is language closely associated with the Underground Railroad, as are locations such as riverbanks. Metaphorically and ambiguously phrased messages commonly conveyed information about Underground Railroad activities. Through affiliations with outright stations on the Underground Railroad such as Oberlin, both West and Davis associated with known Underground Railroad operators.[45]

West's letters make frequent references to fugitive slaves. On August 24, 1859, he mentions a resident of Ohio he recently met who assured him that he gave a fugitive "some good advice." Presumably, that advice helped the escapee in the cause of his own freedom. In the same letter, however, West reports, "One man said, 'I would take up a fugitive, for the bribe that is offered,'" revealing the present danger of capture, kidnapping, and reenslavement as well as the polarity of opinions held by residents of Southern Illinois. In either case, fugitive slaves were passing through the Southern Illinois area and being actively pursued.[46]

## Building a Case for the Underground Railroad

Although Illinois is a free northern state, certain regions posed particular danger to those escaping slavery. The southeastern portion of Southern Illinois is one of the most misunderstood areas in the Underground Railroad network. Keith Griffler cites an 1854 survey of the region by eastern abolitionist Seth Concklin: "It is customary, when a strange Negro is seen, for any White man to seize him, and convey him through and out of the State of Illinois to Paducah [Kentucky]" thirty miles south of Miller Grove.[47] Overt and violent hostility of proslavery factions, the danger of kidnapping, and the activities at the saltworks at Shawneetown on the easternmost border of Illinois contributed to a dearth of activity.

Underground Railroad scholar J. Blaine Hudson explains: "While extreme southern Illinois would seem a natural escape route for fugitives from the Jackson Purchase region of far western Kentucky and from Tennessee, this section of the state also had a reputation for intense antagonism toward

African Americans and was home to relatively few free people of color." As late as 1861, Sarah Early reported that her husband, Rev. Jordan W. Early, later a bishop of the AME Church, was attacked by an angry White mob while riding through one of the six counties that comprised his Shawneetown circuit. She noted that this same mob had assailed and beaten many of the Blacks local to the area.[48] Such a dangerous region offered little support to anyone fleeing slavery.

Hudson does, however, identify a second route through Pope County. Escapees from Kentucky attempted to avoid or minimize the duration of their stay in Illinois by using Pope County, and possibly Miller Grove, as a corridor "that passed briefly through Illinois, skirting the Wabash River, then into Indiana." Hudson believes this second route out of Southern Illinois, following the course of the Wabash River into Indiana, was more important than the Cairo to Springfield route. Available records suggest Kentucky runaways frequently chose this second option or by-passed Illinois altogether, further characterizing the dangerous and hostile conditions threatening Miller Grove residents.

Evidence supporting Underground Railroad activity in or near Miller Grove comes together around a variety of factors: a free Black community, natural landscape features, the AME Church, and the missionary work of the AMA. Fugitive slave newspaper notices confirm nearby Golconda, the county seat of Pope County, as a destination and site of detention for escapees. Crow Knob and Sand Cave, which were in proximity to Miller Grove, fifteen miles west of Golconda, offered natural shelter and protection for freedom seekers. Local Pope County stories connect two geological features with the Miller Grove community. Sand Cave and Crow Knob purportedly served as hideouts and lookouts for the Underground Railroad. Crow Knob is a large sandstone bluff overlooking the Miller Grove community to the south. Known historically as "Nigger Knob," the pejorative term suggests how locals viewed this prominent landscape feature. Crow Knob served as both lookout and signal point, while Sand Cave, lying a few miles west and north of Miller Grove in the line of sight from Crow Knob, served as a hiding place. Local lore speaks of large bonfires lit on top of Crow Knob to guide escaping slaves toward the safety of the Miller Grove area. The view from atop Crow Knob extends for miles, a natural vantage point for anyone keeping a watchful eye for runaways or slave catchers. By contrast, the large, deep Sand Cave provided shelter and seclusion. Both features were located within the loosely defined boundaries of the Black settlement of Miller Grove.

Southern Illinois represented dangerous territory for abolitionists. Slave catchers infested the area, although both Eden and Sparta to the north of

Miller Grove deserved their reputations as stations on the Underground Railway.[49] Not only were slave catchers and kidnapping a problem, cash rewards offered for capturing escapees fostered betrayal. In Illinois, two escapees from slavery were arrested after they sought assistance from a free Black man more interested in the reward offered.[50] Pursuing runaways or unknown Blacks in the area and selling them South was a common practice, sanctioned by both the secular and religious leaders of the community.[51] James West's letters also confirmed this view. A minister in cahoots with another man pursued an escapee for forty miles and spent the night attempting to get ahead of him only to be denied "the pleasure of capturing him" and consequently missing the $150 reward.[52]

Not withstanding the unrest and risks involved, the Underground Railroad played a role in Southern Illinois. Historic documents indicate runaways passed through the area. Benjamin Drew, a Boston abolitionist acting in cooperation with officers of the Canadian Anti-Slavery Society, visited towns of Upper Canada around the mid-1850s, interviewing scores of refugees from the slave states, copying their words soon after they were spoken. One such informant was William Hall, whose route passed through Pope County and may have skirted Miller Grove. Blacks fed and clothed him along the way. Hall describes his lonely ordeal: "At night, I found a canoe, 12 feet long, and travelled down the river several days, to its mouth. There I got on an island, the river being low. I took my canoe across a tongue of land,—a sandbar—into the Ohio, which I crossed into Illinois. I travelled three nights, not daring to travel days, until I came to Golconda, which I recognized by a description I had [been] given on a previous attempt—for this last time when I got away was my fourth effort."[53]

From there, Hall lamented, he ventured too far west. Tired, lost, and sick, he attempted to reach Marion, Illinois, to the north. "At last I ventured, and asked the road—got the information—reached Marion: got bewildered, and went wrong again, and travelled back for Golconda—but I was set right by some children." Taking a route through Southern Illinois, he arrived at Frankfort at daybreak, after trekking "13 miles all night long." He went to Mt. Vernon, and after spending several days traveling, coping with illness, eluding captors, and back tracking, he tried to get to Springfield and then went on to Taylorville. He was eventually taken to Ottawa, Illinois, where he found an abolitionist who helped him get to Chicago. Hall eventually settled in Dresden and Dawn, Canada.[54]

In the narrative, William Hall clearly used Golconda as a major reference point in his escape route. This, according to his testimony, had been his fourth escape attempt. He specifically mentioned Golconda twice, first stating that he recognized Golconda from a previous description, and then, upon losing his way, began to head back to the town, presumably to reorient himself. Golconda is located approximately fifteen miles from the Miller Grove area. Hall's routes through the region transected somewhere in the vicinity of Miller Grove, indicting both an important escape route and Underground Railroad activity in the area.

Golconda was the site of the jail used to house captured runaways and from which they also escaped. That runaways were detained in the jail is evidence that freedom seekers passed through the area. According to an 1822 runaway notice, a sixty-year-old man named Adam, an unusually advanced age for the time, found himself trapped at the jail until his enslaver could claim him. Golconda's jail was also the place from which James Henry Jones, another runaway, escaped before the sheriff of White County recaptured him. Runaway advertisements attest to the longstanding hazards faced by escapees in this area of Pope County. Jones escaped from that same jail two months after his recapture. The $100 reward for his return posted in the *Illinois Gazette* confirms his success.[55]

Local tradition further suggests that Golconda was an active area for runaways. Local resident Bill Tanner stated that he grew up in Golconda and explored the area widely as a boy. He heard stories that the cellars he encountered along the bluff during his explorations were hiding places used by fugitive slaves. Connie Gibbs, the county clerk of Pope County, also repeated much the same story, adding that there were wine cellars in the side of the hill facing the Ohio River and that she was told that they were used to hide runaway slaves.[56] Although Shawneetown, or Cairo farther to the west, are the most frequently mentioned destinations of runaways coming through Southern Illinois, Golconda,[57] Crow Knob, Sand Cave, and the area surrounding the free Black community of Miller Grove were also likely destinations.

Southern Illinois, with its long borders along the Ohio and Mississippi Rivers, standing at the mouth of the Tennessee River, was an important entry point for escapees from Tennessee and Kentucky. Edgar Raines named 381 abolitionists and antislavery advocates in 20 of the 28 counties of Southern Illinois. During the period 1856 through 1860, the extreme southeastern portion of Southern Illinois was thoroughly covered by colporteur and fervent abolitionist James West working out of the Broad Oak post office, which serviced Miller Grove.[58] Taken together, the Miller Grove vicinity emerges as a critical site through which freedom-minded escapees from slavery passed. Although not formally organized, Southern Illinois occupied the borderland—the southern region of a northern border state that affected the choice of escape routes for Kentucky escapees and other runaways in the vicinity. At times, escapees were compelled to use this route despite the great risks involved. Attitudes toward slavery in Southern Illinois were more closely aligned with those of its southern neighbors than with the central and northern regions of the state. Proslavery forces in Kentucky, Tennessee, and Missouri bitterly complained about the antislavery activities within Illinois. Rigid borders demarcating the North, along the Ohio and Mississippi Rivers, were inconsistent with the fluid psychological and political proslavery boundaries characteristic of the southern region of the state. Noted Underground Railroad expert Wilbur Siebert identifies few Underground Railroad lines through Southern Illinois.[59] Miller Grove's position in the southeast portion of the state placed it squarely in "the enemy's country for the fugitive." Anyone willing to facilitate escapes in this section of Illinois faced bitter animosity. Southern Illinois was an extremely dangerous area for freedom seekers and abolitionists alike.[60]

* * *

The ultimate success of any clandestine operation is defined by avoidance of detection. Participants in the Underground Railroad struggled to maintain records and to cover their tracks. The illegal operation became more viable and grew more hazardous with the passage of the Fugitive Slave Bill of 1850. Conductors and beneficiaries were careful to leave few clues, particularly in the most successful cases, which for that reason never may come to light.

Although the settlement of Miller Grove no longer exists, headstones and scattered graves mark the lives of the freedom-minded Americans who comprised the community. The stones of the Miller family, as well as the "Woodsmen of the World" style marker for Henry Sides (Sydes), symbolize the Miller Grove community as a site of memory. Between 1830 and 1927, the rural farming community functioned as a place where African American families could worship, bury their dead, educate their children, and resist slavery and subsequent racial prejudice in relative isolation and inaccessibility. Throughout the period of its existence, an itinerant AME preacher, possibly Jeremiah Sheppard, ministered to the spiritual needs of the families and served the churches farther south and west at Elizabethtown and Golconda along the Ohio River.[61] According to oral accounts, the church building functioned as a church on Sunday and, during the remainder of the week, as a school. By 1927, Miller Grove was a dying settlement. With the exception of the cemetery, the community exists today solely as an archaeological resource. Few traces remain of Mt. Gilead, Miller Grove's pre–Civil War AME church.

CHAPTER 3

# Lick Creek, Indiana

## A Quaker Connection

A little graveyard is the only clue that the Lick Creek settlement once existed in the southeast corner of Paoli Township, Orange County, in southern Indiana (see map 1). The archaeological remains of the African American settlement once known as "Little Africa" are twenty miles north of the Kentucky border and forty-five miles northwest of Louisville. Chambersburg, the town recognized in local histories as an Underground Railroad station, lies farther north.[1] In 1817, freeborn African Americans came to the area and purchased land in what later became the Lick Creek settlement. Blacks also came accompanying Quakers fleeing persecution in North Carolina.

With the opening of frontier lands for settlement, free Blacks, encouraged by the antislavery provisions of the Northwest Ordinance, joined the country's westward passage to the Northwest Territory. As early as the 1740s, people of color had migrated to Indiana coming primarily from Kentucky and the eastern states of Maryland, Virginia, and North Carolina. Freedom seekers, driven to escape restrictive state laws mandating that newly freed men and women leave their slave states, usually within thirty days or face reenslavement, escaped and mixed among these early pioneers.

Lick Creek follows the pattern and landscape history of many early free Black communities, most of which were undefined by rigid boundaries. The settlers sunk their roots into Southeast and Stampers Creek Townships.[2] Archaeological findings indicate that scattered log houses formed the settlement where residents farmed or worked as tradesmen.[3]

Access to the hilly, remote area southeast of Paoli has always been difficult. Blacks in Indiana were often too poor to buy any land other than the least desirable—small, uncleared tracts, which men and women, mainly husbands and wives, purchased from White neighbors. The Black Codes of Indiana greatly restricted the liberty of African Americans after 1800.

Indiana's restrictive laws notwithstanding, Blacks found a haven in the state and many took refuge in the racially integrated Lick Creek settlement.[4] By 1820, more than a thousand free people of color made Indiana their home.[5]

Much of the substance of Black life in the area was extracted from freedom papers, an unfortunate source of information pertaining to residents of Lick Creek. Statements by White witnesses vouching for the registrants' free status and character attested that the persons in question comported themselves "civilly, honestly and industriously." Indiana law required that the County Register of 1853 record physical descriptions, often including distinguishing marks of people of color. Together, these documents defined the settlers of Lick Creek as objects of oppression if not slavery.

After the end of the Atlantic slave trade in 1808, kidnapping free Blacks and selling them into slavery in Kentucky became a prevalent practice. Whites routinely ignored papers confirming Blacks' status as free persons, leaving free Blacks little recourse to the law. Indiana law required that people of color file their freedom papers in the courthouse for inclusion in a Negro Register. The law reflects the grinding nature of slavery and semi-free legal status of Blacks in Indiana, leaving the historical record shaped by racist policies rather than by a rich, vibrant legacy of a people in control of their own destiny.

The Roberts family, a very prominent name in Indiana Black history, has ties to Lick Creek. The mixed-race, Native American ancestry of the family afforded the freeborn people of color an enduring relationship with independence. Ishmael Roberts, for example, a Revolutionary War veteran of Private Shepard's Company, Tenth North Carolina Regiment, received a government land grant for his war service.[6] In 1790, the family lived primarily in Northampton County, North Carolina, where they appeared in the first U.S. Census.

Quaker history marks 1811 as the year Jonathan Lindley brought eleven families from North Carolina to southern Indiana in a caravan of approximately two hundred people. Lindley and a group of antislavery Friends were on a quest for a new land that forbade slavery and offered racial tolerance. The group migrated from Cane Creek in Orange County, North Carolina, and settled in the area of Orange County, Indiana, five years before establishment of the county or the granting of statehood to Indiana.[7]

For those Blacks migrating with Quakers, traveling with them offered some protection on their journey and the promise of supportive neighbors upon their arrival. As former migrants or the offspring of migrants, most Quakers understood how to plan for long journeys into wilderness areas. "One participant even declared that the Quakers had developed migratory practices to the point of being a science."[8] North Carolina Quakers moving to the Northwest mostly followed well-established Indian routes or the paths of previous travelers.

Friends organize themselves around weekly, monthly, and quarterly meetings on regional, local, and communal levels culminating in yearly meetings. For several North Carolina Quaker communities, a major portion of the membership decided to make the journey westward together, leaving entire areas without the benefit of a monthly meeting.[9] After such a mass exodus, the meeting declined in membership, never to regain its former strength. Chatham County, North Carolina, Quakers belonged to the western quarterly meeting that encompassed the Cane Creek meeting attended by the Lindley family and included members from Centre in Guilford County.[10] Quakers migrating to Indiana from North Carolina specifically originated in Guilford, Chatham, and parts of Orange County and were members of the western quarterly meeting.

The Quaker exodus meant a boon for Indiana. As the late 1830s approached, the Indiana yearly meeting had swelled to one of the world's largest, growing steadily through new arrivals, particularly from North Carolina. This concentration of Quakers did not preclude Whites from actively barring any influx of people of color. Moreover, Blacks liberated by the Friends of North Carolina were generally not welcome in the Hoosier state. Sixty or seventy liberated Blacks arrived in 1818. Their presence fueled inhospitable reactions on the part of the White population.[11]

Black settlers continued to make Indiana their home, however. William Constant and Charles Goin together obtained a patent deed from the United States and purchased 160 acres in nearby Southeast Township. Eleven families made up of sixty-three people, most of them children, appeared in the 1820 census. Ninety-six Blacks lived in Orange County by then. Mathew Thomas became one of the first people of color to obtain land in the Lick Creek area in 1831. Thomas had been born free but his widowed mother indentured him in 1821, binding him to Zachariah Lindley. Once Thomas had fulfilled his apprenticeship, he was able to purchase eight acres. Two years later, he secured his certificate of freedom proving his free status in Indiana.[12]

Other people of color soon followed and bought land that developed into the Lick Creek settlement in the hills south of Chambersburg. Benjamin Roberts, David Dugged, and Peter Lindley, some with their wives, were recent migrants from North Carolina. Each purchased forty acres of patented land from the United States of America in 1832. With the exception of Dugged's holdings, these land purchases formed the nucleus of the Lick

Creek settlement. During these early years, Blacks and Whites often lived in the same area and frequently were adjoining landholders.[13]

With each decade, the landholdings and the size of the settlement grew. By 1840, 10 men of color had accumulated a total of 780 acres in the community. The challenging terrain undoubtedly benefited those who may have been secretly moving fugitives through. Sixty-four years after passage of the Northwest Ordinance, however, Indiana voters approved a constitutional provision that stated, "No Negro or mulatto shall come into or settle in the State, after the adoption of this Constitution," further eroding the rights guaranteed by the ordinance. The racial intolerance condoned in article XIII of the provision remained in effect for thirty years.[14]

In the face of such laws, free people of color in Indiana formed a strong family network, maintaining close ties with friends and relatives in other settlements. They visited, shared holiday celebrations, and participated in social and religious activities, including revivals, camp meetings, and homecomings. Intermarriages bound unrelated families and expanded the geographic reach of the small rural enclave. By 1855, the settlement reached its maximum size of more than 1,500 acres.[15]

People of color migrated to Indiana and settled in Black settlements to gain some measure of control over their lives. Banister Chavis's probate records from the same year present an interesting picture of the holdings one Lick Creek farmer was able to amass. Each piece of property was listed with its appraised valuation. The probate included home furnishings such as split-bottom chairs, beds, and cupboard ware. Bed clothes counted among the possessions. The probate showed that Chavis had important implements necessary for a successful farmer.

The list of possessions included a chopping axe, a scythe and cradle, gardening tools, and two plows plus a two-horse wagon. His livestock included: two bay mares, six head of sheep, a spotted sow, one black sow, six fat hogs, five geese, one red cow, one red heifer, and two yearling calves. In addition to a stack of oats, the farmer had a lot of tobacco, shock corn, and one field of corn at the time of his death. Included among his effects was one note to Elias Roberts due twelve months after date for $425. Chavis had prospered in freedom.[16]

## Quakers and Free Blacks at Lick Creek

Quakers came to Indiana fleeing racial persecution and disavowing increasingly restrictive laws in North Carolina bent on constraining free Blacks and their growing legal status. North Carolina's legal stand forced Quakers, particularly from Guilford and Chatham Counties, to resettle in the free states with many migrating to Indiana. North Carolina's political and racial climate had a major impact on Black migration out of the state as well. By the mid-1790s, the North Carolina assembly restricted both manumissions and movement of free Blacks under its control.[17] North Carolina law, with the exception of freedom for "meritorious service," allowed no manumissions but it was unevenly and loosely enforced. After the Revolutionary War, an overall pattern took hold; each step intended to facilitate emancipation was thwarted by a governmental step to counteract the freeing of captives. The $1,000 bond required by North Carolina for emancipation loomed as a financial obstacle of considerable magnitude for Blacks seeking their freedom from slavery. After payment of the bond, North Carolina law required the newly freed former slaves to immediately and permanently remove themselves from the state. By 1818, forty-six migrants had entered Indiana from North Carolina, and Lick Creek became one of the destinations.[18]

According to historian George Cox, Quaker Friends, in addition to the population in general, "were effectively constrained from making general emancipation practical, and they even had problems ridding their own denomination of the taint of slavery."[19] Quakers in general were as conflicted over slavery as other religious groups and tended to accept the views of racial inferiority held by the majority of the White population. Many Quakers, representing the largest religious body in the colony during the late seventeenth and early eighteenth centuries, adopted slavery for their own Carolina plantations. They treated Blacks with paternalism and failed to welcome former slaves as full-fledged members of the Quaker body.

North Carolina Quakers, however, also had a long history of condemnation of slavery. From the Revolutionary period to the Civil War, the sect exerted the strongest antislavery influence in the state. Increasingly though, North Carolina Friends found themselves adhering to unpopular antislavery abolitionist beliefs in the midst of slave territory. As Quakers became uneasy with slaveholding, pondering ways to circumvent the rigid 1741 restrictions against manumission in North Carolina, they decided to establish a trusteeship system. Assignments of captives received from slaveholding Quakers would be held in trust until the enslaved persons could be freed and colonized outside the United States or resettled in one of the free states.[20]

James Guthrie, one of the Black migrants who came to Lick Creek with Quakers, obtained his freedom under the trusteeship system. North Carolina Quaker Nathaniel Newlin had purchased Guthrie's freedom in 1842, as part of a Quaker emancipation scheme. Newlin was intent on freeing Guthrie, but the laws of North Carolina prevented him from doing so. Looking for an alternative solution, Newlin then deeded Guthrie to his brother, Thomas, with the stipulation that Guthrie be granted his freedom. Thomas Newlin in turn moved Guthrie to Paoli in Orange County and entered a Certificate of Freedom for him. Five years later, Guthrie, who was described in "the Register" as a six-foot "pureblooded African," had purchased forty acres of patented land from the United States of America.[21]

Friends, as well as other religious and benevolent organizations including Presbyterians, in North Carolina, tried various means of dealing with the problems of slavery. Migrations of Blacks to the American Midwest as well as to Liberia were conceived as solutions. Quakers and Presbyterians, therefore, supported and worked in close cooperation with the American Colonization Society (ACS) after concluding that free Blacks were a problem and that colonization in Africa was a viable solution.[22] Members of the ACS attempted to make colonization a condition of freedom. Friend Levi Coffin thought it "an odious plan of expatriation concocted by slaveholders . . . to get rid of free Negroes whom they regard as a dangerous element among slaves."[23]

Between 1825 and 1831, the North Carolina Quaker yearly meeting looked closely at the work of the ACS. Members such as Coffin looked upon it as little more than an adjunct of the Slave Power. Nevertheless, the Society of Friends worked in harmony with the ACS, sending hundreds of newly freed Blacks to Liberia and Haiti. Friends acted as a sort of agent for the society and contributed more than $2,000 to its funds.[24] These colonization schemes resulted, in part, from reluctance on the part of various Quakers to live among freed Blacks, with prejudice in Indiana among Quakers equaling prejudice in North Carolina among Whites in general. By 1836, however, the Indiana Yearly Meeting of Orthodox Friends warned its members against joining any association that advocated colonization as "the unrighteous work of expatriation."[25] The Indiana yearly meeting at Richmond simultaneously took a stand against colonization, discouraging its members from going outside the Society of Friends in any antislavery work.

Once that realization took hold, Quakers devoted themselves to pressuring the government to end slavery and used their piety in service of the Underground Railroad. Because of their antislavery work, Quakers have enjoyed an uncritical place in American history and in the history of the Underground Railroad as the penultimate liberators of enslaved African Americans. Indeed, the sect was at the forefront of the antislavery cause and was "the mainstay of the antislavery movement" in their challenge to slavery.[26] At best, the all-important work of free Blacks was viewed as little more than incidental.[27]

## Origins of the AME Church

One consistent site of refuge for free Blacks as well as escapees was the independent Black church. In Lick Creek and throughout much of Indiana, the activism and organizational efforts of the AME denomination were at the center of the rural enclaves. These tiny congregations made up the larger AME conference and kept remote outposts connected to the liberation theology of the denomination.

In 1836, AME elder William Paul Quinn built churches southwest of Lick Creek along the Ohio River across from Louisville in New Albany, Floyd County, Indiana. Quinn came to Indiana in conjunction with his work in establishing Quinn Chapel in Louisville, indicating the denomination's penetration into slave states. During the 1830s and early 1840s, Elder Quinn led several hundred midwestern free people of color into the AME denomination. He participated when Indiana formed the sixth AME conference at Blue River in northern Rush County. North Carolina–born Black abolitionist Willis Revels was among the pioneering participants and founders of the conference. Bishop Morris Brown assigned Quinn oversight of all the circuits of the conference. After decades of traveling, Quinn finally moved to Richmond, Indiana, a center of Underground Railroad activity, which remained his primary residence until his death in 1873.[28]

The church maintained an essential position in the Lick Creek community and was the focal point of the settlement. The congregations sustained the church for the twenty-five years between 1843 and 1869. Land transactions bound Bishop Quinn directly to the settlement. By 1863, Quinn sold the one-acre church lot along the north side of the section to Eli Roberts. The new AME church possibly replaced the nearby colored Methodist Union Meeting House. Built in 1837, the new church stood on land deeded by Revolutionary War veteran Ishmael Roberts and his wife, Lucretia, to Lick Creek residents David Dugged and Martin Scott.[29]

## William Paul Quinn in Indiana

Elder Quinn maintained strong ties to Quakerism and an easy comfort among the Quakers in the Lick Creek vicinity. He became acquainted with the sect through a Quaker English woman and had been befriended and instructed by one of the most controversial Quakers of his time, Elias Hicks. Hicks led the Separation of 1827–28 that resulted in formation of the Hicksite Friends. As a staunch and uncompromising abolitionist, Hicks stood at the forefront of a campaign against the use of slave-made produce.[30]

Quinn, a dynamic circuit-riding itinerant preacher spent much of his time traveling from church to church in the wilderness, converting thousands to the AME faith. The denomination relied heavily on itinerant ministers to penetrate the far reaches of the frontier. Quinn left a legacy of radical activism. He was present at the organization of the AME Church in Philadelphia in 1816, a seminal moment in American history, and he witnessed the bold radical consciousness that launched the independent Black church. He defied slavery and organized churches in St. Louis, Missouri, as well as Louisville, Kentucky, and ordained ministers in New Orleans a decade before the Civil War.[31]

The AME Church facilitated deep connections. Circuit riders such as Quinn established churches and returned on occasion to preach while relying on lay preachers and local ministers to reinforce the efforts of the itinerant ministers. As part of his duties in presiding over the Indiana circuit, the far-reaching pastor founded Allen Chapel AME in Terre Haute, Indiana, in 1837. Here again, Quinn left his imprint on the congregation of former slaves who originally came with Quakers to Vigo County. Congregants gathered in a plain white wooden house that served as a church and as an Underground Railroad station.

Quinn owed much of his effectiveness to the intertwined relationships he formed with families as he traveled across the nation. The charismatic minister befriended the Woodson family in Ohio and the Revels brothers, Willis and his younger brother, Hiram, in Indiana.[32] Following a familiar pattern, the families were active across a range of Black institutions. For example, Quinn's friend Hiram Revels initiated a private subscription school for Black children in the basement of the Allen Chapel in Terre Haute, one of the Underground Railroad churches in Indiana. The Chapel, the oldest church in western Indiana, also hosted the first Indiana AME convention. When St. Andrews AME in Sacramento, California (originally Bethel AME), filed a petition to be admitted to the Indiana Conference of the AME Church in 1850, it was Willis Revels who sent a letter of welcome to the new congregation. Similar to the activism of Allen Chapel, the church hosted three of California's Colored Citizens' Conventions. Such was the reach of Quinn's vast network.[33]

The influential minister traveled to New Albany, Indiana, as a circuit preacher in conjunction with establishing Quinn Chapel in Louisville. Known as the "abolitionist church," Quinn Chapel AME "was a lynchpin of organized AME activity along the Ohio River border"[34] (see map 5). Bishop Quinn connected the small churches to his expansive world; the Kentucky church connected other small AME congregations in southern Indiana and Ohio. Willis Revels, who eventually became a physician, served as an AME preacher at the Lick Creek settlement church and went on to pastor Quinn Chapel in Louisville. Quinn Chapel linked the north-central Kentucky Underground Railroad network. Revels also served as the longtime pastor of Bethel AME in Indianapolis, one of Indiana's most notable Underground Railroad stations. Following in the footsteps of his mentor, Quinn, Revels ministered to three Underground Railroad churches. Willis Revels maintained a close lifelong relationship with the "pioneer of the West."[35]

Bishop Morris Brown ordained Elder Quinn as the fourth bishop of the AME Church in May 1844. After Brown's death in 1849, Quinn was elevated to senior bishop and served the church in that capacity for the rest of his long life. By the time of his death in 1873, Quinn's far-reaching influence stretched across the United States and into Canada, from New Jersey through Wisconsin, to Sacramento, California, penetrating from Louisville to New Orleans, the very heart of the South. Quinn's associations with the larger world brought the little, out-of-the-way churches into what is emerging as the greater AME, Black church Underground Railroad network and into Quinn's extensive political world. The "militant soldier of the cross" served the church until his death in Richmond at eighty-five years of age. Willis Revels, a disciple to the end, participated in the memorial service for his old friend. These African community leaders had deep connections with one another, tied together through family relations and intermarriage, church organizations, and the fraternal structure of the Prince Hall Masons and the secret work of the Underground Railroad.[36]

## The Underground Railroad

Escape routes in the Lick Creek area originated near Brandenburg, Kentucky, before moving on to the natural protection of the hills and hollows around Corydon, diverging on to New Albany and Paoli Pike. The Ohio River separated the southern boundary of Indiana from the slave state of Kentucky. Those fleeing slavery often made their way to the border and crossed from Kentucky into Indiana en route to Michigan or Canada. Others, however, made Indiana their permanent home. In the settlements on the Indiana side of the Ohio River, Blacks actively helped runaways cross the river and offered them shelter in their homes or communities before sending them farther north. Free people of color in Indiana often exchanged signals with their counterparts on the Kentucky side, using lighted hilltop bonfires. As the way cleared, runaways were ferried across the river in skiffs.[37] The Kentucky border was a mere twenty miles from Lick Creek; runaways escaping from Kentucky to Indiana were in the vicinity. According to early histories, Chambersburg, one half mile north of Lick Creek, operated as a station on the Underground Railroad. Apparently, it was a first stop north of the Ohio River in Indiana.[38]

The Quakers in the region were instrumental in moving escapees through the area. Relatives point to the Eli Lindley House north of Chambersburg as a station.[39] Eli and Elizabeth Lindley's descendant, Friend Howard Hall, lived near Lick Creek before Indiana became a state. Hall was born in an old log house and explained that the fireplace hearth had a trap door that opened into an 8 ft. x 6 ft. pit. During daylight hours, a rug covered the trap door where freedom seekers were hidden out of sight.[40] Isolated occupants continually offered aid and assistance to runaways seeking freedom.

Underground Railroad scholar J. Blaine Hudson, in his analysis of the Underground Railroad in Kentucky, one of the states from which escapees left on their way to Indiana, observed the difference between African American and White perceptions of assisting runaways. The majority of African Americans who rendered or received aid considered their actions unrelated to an organized Underground Railroad. "Most African Americans in the Kentucky borderland viewed assisting runaway slaves as an extension of their community values, but viewed the Underground Railroad as an organization 'staffed' by Whites or by other African Americans who lived elsewhere," which frequently meant to the north. For runaways who were largely in contact with other African Americans, the Underground Railroad "was peripheral, rather than indispensable, to the success or failure of their escapes."[41]

Josiah Henson, the purported model for Harriet Beecher Stowe's *Uncle Tom's Cabin*, was in actuality an escapee from slavery whose first footsteps in freedom were taken in southern Indiana. With the exception of the help he received after inducing "a fellow-slave to set us across the [Ohio] River," he, his wife, and their four children hastened through that portion of the state. Henson observed, "We had no friends to look to for assistance, for the population in that section of the country was then bitterly hostile to the fugitive. If discovered, we should be seized and lodged in jail." With little time to reflect on their new liberty, the family made its way to Cincinnati, where Henson searched for his friends. "They welcomed me warmly, and just after dusk my wife and children were brought in, and we found ourselves hospitably cheered and refreshed" before heading on to Buffalo and eventually Canada.[42]

After he had established himself in Canada, Henson ventured back into Kentucky, Ohio, and Indiana, rescuing family members of friends in his new home. Leaving Canada and traveling approximately four hundred miles alone and on foot, Henson made his way to the Kentucky border along the Ohio to rescue the parents, sisters, brothers, nephews, and nieces of James

Lightfoot, but the family, for a variety of reasons, was unable to return to Canada with Henson. Similar to Harriet Tubman, the undaunted Henson did not waste his liberty mission. Traveling deeper into Kentucky, he learned of about thirty people in Bourbon County who were willing to risk escape. With this group, he traveled through Cincinnati to Richmond, Indiana, where they found assistance before moving on to Toledo and taking passage to Canada. Henson also returned as promised to accomplish the successful rescue of Lightfoot's brothers, taking them through Cincinnati and Indiana where, after a harrowing near miss with slave catchers, a Quaker farmer helped them before they set sail for Canada. Henson estimated he had been "instrumental in delivering one hundred and eighteen human beings" out of bondage.[43]

Indiana's most notable Quaker and Underground Railroad worker, Levi Coffin, observed that other Blacks usually helped escapees from slavery. Coffin asserted that runaways generally stopped in a neighborhood of free Blacks near Newport, Indiana, now known as Fountain City, at the center of the state. This settlement was composed largely of Black descendants of those manumitted by North Carolina Quakers years before. Paul Quinn, who had been accustomed to living among Quakers, also had ties to the area and owned a 17-acre horse farm outside Newport. Coffin had lasting ties to the North Carolina community in Indiana. He was a North Carolina native who had come to Indiana from Guilford County in 1826. After Coffin learned of the recaptured escapees, he began using his house as a place of refuge.[44] Levi Coffin, "reputed President of the Underground Railroad," knew of the Black settlements in the southern regions of the state near Paoli in Orange County and Salem in Washington County, Indiana, where he spent time visiting relatives.[45]

Quinn's close association with Quakers held important implications in Indiana. His affinity with Quakers continued throughout his long life and extended to the area around Richmond, Indiana, where he eventually settled. The preacher's interest stemmed from the friendly nature of the Black-White relations there and from the city's strategic location in Indiana, situated along an Underground Railroad route surrounded by churches he helped establish in Randolph County.

## The Civil War

Antislavery efforts of free Blacks, Quakers, and citizens of conscience working on the Underground Railroad on behalf of escaped slaves helped fuel the strife that pushed the country toward sectional conflict. Participation in the Civil War perpetuated African American quests for liberation. Nearly

1,400 Blacks representing 73 Indiana counties served in the U.S. Colored Troops (USCT); most were volunteers. The majority formed a battalion of Indiana's Black troops, the 28th Regiment.

Consequences stemming from the strategic proximity of the Kentucky border to Indiana continued during the Civil War. Enslaved Black men from Kentucky crossed the Ohio River to join the 28th USCT. After eight runaways fled from Owensboro, Kentucky, one was captured at Vincennes while the other seven successfully escaped to Indianapolis, where they enlisted in the Black regiment. Their enslavers also ventured to Indianapolis "for the patriotic purpose of getting the bounty money allowed by the act of Congress to loyal masters."[46]

More than half of those recruited for the 28th USCT hailed from Ellicott Mills, Maryland, near the location of John Brown's farmhouse headquarters. The 28th, in addition to the 109th and 127th Colored Infantry, included among them men who were friends of John Brown and his fellow conspirator, Osborne P. Anderson. AME minister Willis Revels, former pastor at Louisville and first cousin to Leary Lewis, another fighter in John Brown's army, recruited for Indiana's 28th USCT. Revels acted as a frequent correspondent to the *Christian Recorder*, the AME newspaper that reported on the progress of the Indiana 28th. Mary Ann Shadd also traveled from Canada to the United States recruiting for Indiana, among other states. Empowered by a certificate of authorization to act as Martin Delany's agent in recruiting for the 28th, Shadd Cary exemplified dozens of American women who defied gender conventions by engaging in wartime efforts.[47]

Simon Locust, the sole veteran listed in the Orange County records, was drafted in September 1864, mustered in at Jeffersonville, Indiana, and served one year in Company E of the 13th Infantry Regiment of the USCT.[48] Two other residents of Lick Creek also fought in the war. Civil War veteran, Martin Scott, listed in the 1860 Owen County Census as a Negro and described in the literature as mulatto, enlisted and fought with local White troops in Company I, 19th Indiana Infantry, in 1864. Wounded at the Battle of the Wilderness, Pvt. Scott was captured and held at Andersonville until he mustered out on May 24, 1865, and then was discharged from the 20th Indiana Infantry. Scott died in 1918. His obituary described him as "no darker skinned than the majority of the weather tanned Yankees." The article pointed out just how daring Scott had been, "Had it been known by the confederates that he was a Negro, they would have shot him forthwith."[49] James A. Seddon, Confederate secretary of war, ordered captured Black Union soldiers put to death on the spot and without trial. Considering that Confederate troops rarely held Blacks captive in southern prison camps,

Scott took a calculated and potentially deadly risk. Captors frequently shot Blacks, putting them to death upon surrender or capture on the battlefields, or sold them into slavery.[50]

Solomon and Margaret Newby present a different story of the Civil War. The freeborn North Carolina natives migrated from Orange County in that state to Orange County, Indiana. Subsequently, they lived in Lick Creek from 1840 to 1862. In 1862, the family migrated to North Buxton, Canada West. Their third child and eldest son, James Harling Newby, responded to the call of the Civil War raging in the land of his birth. Twenty-year-old James got himself to Philadelphia and enlisted in Company I, Third Regiment Infantry, USCT, in July 1863. In the British Methodist Episcopal Church Cemetery in North Buxton, Ontario, Canada, stands a gravestone with the following inscription: "Jas Nuby, Co I, 3 U.S.C. Inf—James Harling Nuby, 1842–1928—NATIVE OF INDIANA, U.S.A."[51]

* * *

Underground Railroad narratives give voice to multiple political, spiritual, economic, and ideological functions served by Black settlements and portray their relationships to Quakers in a more balanced light. Coy Robbins, however, argued against the limiting effects of two primary themes in Indiana Black history: slavery and the Underground Railroad. Constricting the historical narrative leaves the impression that the only Blacks to enter Indiana before the Civil War were either enslaved or runaways. As a result, Indiana institutions tended to restrict their collections around these topics. For Robbins, constant focus on slavery implied that enslaved persons and indentured servants were the only people of African descent to participate in early Indiana history. Themes narrowly drawn around slavery disregarded Blacks who arrived of their own volition. The concept that free people of color migrated into Indiana before the Civil War was wholly incomprehensible to proponents of slavery studies.

For Robbins, the Underground Railroad and Hoosier Black history were synonymous, indicating a surreptitious and fleeting Black presence of runaways who slipped into the state and passed through Indiana via a Quaker-driven Underground Railroad. His studies led him to conclude that the Underground Railroad in Indiana consisted largely of Hoosier myths filled with lengthy accounts describing stalwart White males, unusual hiding places, clever signals, displays of compassion toward the wretched, and the kindly sharing of warm food and clothing as Blacks, assisted by sympathetic Whites, moved toward their ultimate goal—Canada. The human passengers rarely emerged; when they did, they were "mystical beings who traveled only at night and often wore disguises waiting patiently for the kindly conductor to transport them to the next safe haven."[52]

This chapter presents an alternative view of African Americans working toward liberation. At the same time, a more realistic view of Quakers and their ambivalent sentiments toward Black equality emerges. Escapees such as Josiah Henson and so many others negotiated either all or the most difficult or dangerous portions of the trip alone or with the help of other Blacks. As Mattie Jackson observed in her narrative, "My parents had never learned the rescuing scheme of the underground railroad which had borne so many thousands to the standard of freedom and victories. They knew no other resource than to depend upon their own chance in running away and secreting themselves. If caught they were in a worse condition than before."[53]

CHAPTER 4

# Poke Patch, Ohio

## A Different Route

Ohio's sustained involvement in the Underground Railroad made the state a viable destination for anyone seeking freedom in the Northwest. At Poke Patch in western Gallia County the Underground Railroad story and African American participation were documented by Underground Railroad historian Wilbur Siebert (see map 1). The significant role of Black Baptists as well as the Methodists distinguishes this settlement from the Illinois and Indiana enclaves. Routes running toward Ohio's iron furnaces in Lawrence and Gallia Counties, leading into and out of Poke Patch, etch lines of resistance in the landscape (see map 4). Greenup County in Kentucky and Cabell County in Virginia had to contend with their enslaved workers escaping to Ironton at the southernmost bend of the Ohio River, Burlington at the midpoint of the broad bend, and Proctorville ten miles to the east—places that connected in one way or another to Poke Patch. Routes connecting iron furnaces throughout the growing county were major pathways to freedom. At Poke Patch, twenty miles from the Ohio River, the liberty line branches shed light on the Black communities that were silently operating in the background.

### Ohio: A Gateway

Of the three earliest states formed out of the Old Northwest, Ohio enjoys the most liberal image as a state with multiple highly developed routes along the Underground Railroad. The first of the northwestern states to forbid slavery, Ohio entered the Union in 1803. Yet, as with Illinois and Indiana, the state instituted Black Codes and intermittently enforced restrictive measures against Black residents.

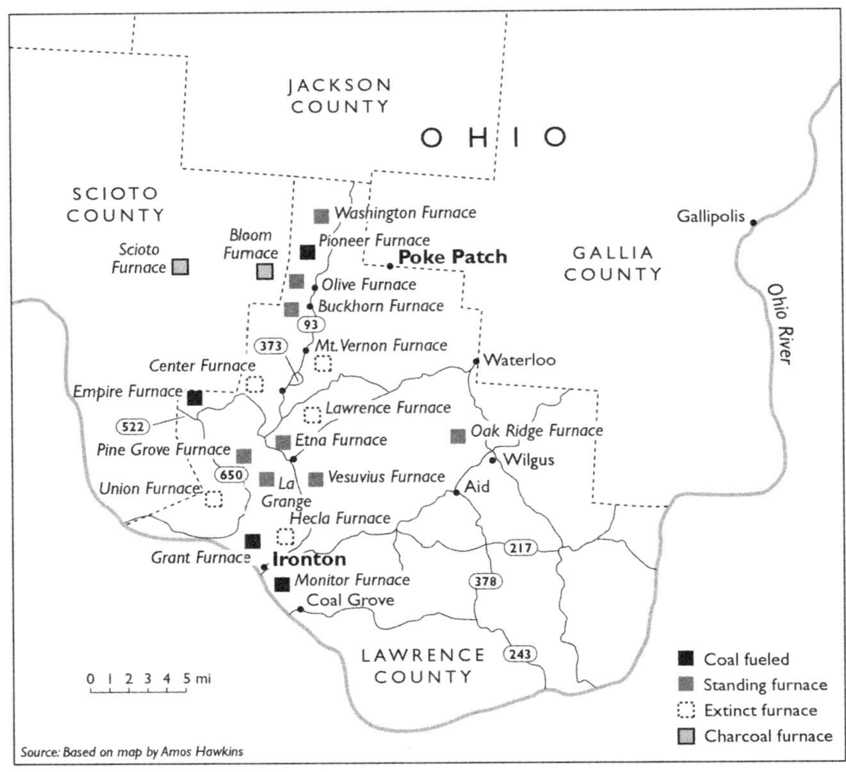


*Map 4*. Iron furnaces map of Lawrence County, Ohio.

Blacks were making their way across the Western Reserve by 1815. At the same time, runaways either found refuge in the area or traveled across the state escaping to Canada through various ports along Lake Erie. By 1817, Kentucky slaveholders complained of their inability to reclaim escapees once they entered Ohio and neighboring free states. What Kentuckians were confronting was an evolving system for moving escapees through the landscape. Over the years, Kentuckians grew furious that Ohio did little to stem the tide of liberty.

As 1820 approached, a basic structure was in place along the routes that developed into the Underground Railroad. The Lawrence County rail lines were in operation by the mid-1830s, if not earlier. These lines eventually caused a shift from the idea of an underground road movement for escapees to the Underground Railroad based on the use of steam railroads that gained in popularity during the 1830s.[1]

Both Baptist and AME denominations established deep roots in the state by 1832. That year Ohio became an Episcopal seat of the AME Church. Four years later the state was the site of the nation's first independent Black regional Baptist conference, the Providence Baptist Association. Members of both denominations assumed a staunch abolitionist stand and many actively worked in the Underground Railroad.[2] By 1860, one church of each faith could be found wherever Blacks lived in Ohio, whether in tiny communities or large cities.[3]

## Poke Patch and the Underground Railroad

Operating a mere twenty miles from the Ohio River, Poke Patch ranked among the most active Underground Railroad sites in southern Ohio. Situated on the western edge of Gallia County, the predominantly African American settlement included many former slaves who worked either as farmers or in the area's booming iron industry. Between 1830 and 1900, the Hanging Rock Iron region produced the majority of iron in the United States (see map 4). Dangerous working conditions left that industry open to Blacks.

During the early existence of Poke Patch, the sole purpose of the tiny community may have been to harbor escapees as they moved northward along the Underground Railroad. Greater than two hundred freedom seekers made their way to the settlement. The residents were ready with food and lodging. Three routes converged at Poke Patch: the Ironton, Burlington, and Rio Grande lines.

Freed African Americans, Whites, mulattoes, and Native Americans settled in the area in the 1820s. Beyond their original purposes in moving there, each of these groups soon became involved in assisted escapes. One founder, Benjamin Holly, was a known underground agent. John J. Stewart and his wife, in conjunction with his four brothers, were also early settlers active in promoting Underground Railroad traffic. Stewart had been born of mixed parentage into a free family from Virginia. Joining the Stewart family in the growing settlement were Peter Coker, his wife, and their five sons.[4]

Black Baptists formed the active religious group in the community. Worshipers constructed the original log church on John Thomas McKeels's farm. After migrating from Virginia to Gallia County, McKeels purchased land and married Amanda Davidson, a relative of Booker T. Washington's wife. His marriage further tied the little settlement to the larger African American social network and kept the plight of rural communities on the minds of the country's Black activists and leaders.

## Hanging Rock Iron Region

Branches of the Underground Railroad passed through stations along the southern borders of the Ohio River before turning farther northward. A minimum of twenty active sites transected the area. Ironton and Burlington functioned as two major crossing points in Lawrence County, southernmost of the Ohio counties. Burlington sat at the extreme southern tip with Ironton to the north and slightly west. The northward route leading to Poke Patch passed through the Hanging Rock Iron Region, a thirty-mile iron ore belt that included Jackson, Vinton, Lawrence, and Scioto Counties and a portion of Kentucky. From Hanging Rock and Ironton, an Underground Railroad route passed through the Mt. Vernon and Olive Furnaces and a western branch passed through Franklin Furnace in Scioto County.[5] One Black conductor, John Mathews, lived at the Olive Furnace and conducted a number of freedom-seeking escapees through the area and on to Poke Patch, Berlin Crossroads, or other routes north.

Iron furnaces played a significant role in the southern regions of Ohio. Wealthy White industrialist and furnace operator John Campbell and others used profits from the prosperous iron furnace industry in the Hanging Rock Iron region to subsidize the Underground Railroad in that area, frequently supplying horses, saddles, and wagons.

Although born in Ripley, Ohio, Campbell settled in the region in 1834. The noted ironmaster and abolitionist was a follower of John Rankin, one of Ohio's most famous Underground Railroad operatives. Such were the sentiments of the founder who christened Ironton in 1840, naming the streets after the furnaces in the region. In 1846, he and his partners purchased 3,600 acres of wilderness 20 miles up the Iron Trail from the County Courthouse. His holdings grew to an interest in fourteen furnaces in the Hanging Rock iron region before the Civil War (see map 4).[6]

At times, ironmasters stood out among abolitionists who exploited their company towns, ironworks, and access to transportation routes to move runaways through the landscape, often from one furnace to another. Campbell and others were responsible for building the Lawrence Furnace and the Mt. Vernon Furnace and shared responsibility with John Peters in the construction of the Olive Furnace. In addition to working at the furnaces, Peters aided runaways who crossed the Ohio River in skiffs. Two African American males lived at the Campbell house, which was advantageously situated on the Ohio River in Ironton. The men acted as Underground Railroad conductors, using the furnaces as a convenient means of moving runaways through the region. The furnaces functioned as major Underground Railroad stops. In *Mysteries of Ohio's Underground Railroad,* Wilbur Siebert maps the route that began in Ironton and ran eastward through Mt. Vernon and Olive Furnaces and connected to Poke Patch as well as a route from Ironton that connected with Franklin Furnace.[7]

Members of the "Order of Twelve," a secret African American organization, conspired with Campbell, chief conductor James Ditcher, and Underground operative Gabriel Johnson to put Ironton at the center of the struggle on the edge of the Ohio River. Johnson's memories of his Virginia birthplace allowed him to put to good use his extensive knowledge of the hardships escapees faced in the South. The Underground Railroad station in Ironton exploited the connections he established on the southern side of the river. Gabriel Johnson handled the organizational and less dangerous operations.[8] At times, though, he too hid runaways in a coal bank at the back of his house.[9] Johnson was at the river's edge to retrieve Asbury Parker from the skiff he used to cross the river from Virginia. That night, Gabe turned Parker over to two men and sent him on his way to freedom through Olive Furnace and then on to Poke Patch. Parker, disguised in a black broadcloth suit, assumed the entitled manner of a freedman and enjoyed the privilege rarely available to those escaping slavery; he traveled by daylight before boarding a train for Columbus.[10]

Gabe Johnson also teamed up with Madison Black in service of freedom seekers. John Campbell maintained in his barn a large covered wagon drawn by four horses that Johnson and Madison Black frequently used to move as many as fourteen or fifteen escapees up to Buckhorn Furnace in Lawrence County or Monroe Furnace in Jackson County.[11]

James Ditcher took immediate charge as the more fearless, zealous worker on the frontlines of freedom. In a five-year period Ditcher piloted as many as three hundred escapees from the Ohio River. Guiding them to inland agents, he delivered eighty or more to Poke Patch.[12] Ditcher avoided detection by shifting from one route to another.

Ditcher and Johnson maneuvered more than sixty-five miles along the river between Portsmouth and Proctorville, originally known as Quaker Bottom. After escapees crossed the Ohio River from Cabell County, Virginia, Ditcher directed them to Poke Patch from Proctorville approximately nine miles east of Burlington. He often began by following the railroad tracks before diverging through the woods to the Poke Patch settlement. Whenever necessary, he followed the creeks that led into other settlements such as Macedonia.[13]

Ditcher once found himself in dire straits when he received a woman and her baby. The pair had been rowed across the river in a skiff by free Blacks from Virginia. Travel, under the circumstances, could not be as swift as desired and slave catchers bore down on them as they landed. Acting quickly, Ditcher rushed to John Campbell's stable, commandeered a horse, and grabbed another from a nearby minister. Riding hard, they managed to reach the Olive Furnace where another free Black man sheltered them. While whiskey waylaid the slave catchers, Ditcher managed to get the mother and child to safety in Poke Patch. From the settlement the pair was able to move farther north. On Ditcher's way back from the rescue, still riding Campbell's horse and leading the minister's horse with a sidesaddle on it, he had to contend with his now sober and questioning pursuers. He presented an implausible, but unflinchingly delivered story. His tall, thin frame and copper-toned skin combined with his quick thinking earned him the nickname "Red Fox of the Underground."[14]

The escape journey may have been less hazardous because Campbell and the iron furnace operations owned much of the land along the escape route. Rescues could fall apart in the blink of an eye, however, and the Fugitive Slave Law made the work all the more hazardous. In 1860, James Ditcher conducted three escapees, a mother and her two children, to Stewart's home in Poke Patch. The following day, Stewart and Ditcher moved the trio to the nearest railroad junction. Despite the cliché about the Underground Railroad—it was neither underground nor a railroad—use of the railroads abounded. After midcentury, Ohio's railroads were used to quickly deliver escapees to the safety of waiting friends in Cleveland or Detroit. On this day, however, the slaveholder was onboard waiting in anticipation. Disregarding the mother who had become old and useless to him, the slaveholder condemned her two children back to slavery on his Kentucky plantation and Ditcher had to disappear to avoid prosecution.[15]

Keith Griffler indicates this is the only instance where Ditcher lost anyone under his care during his two decades of Underground Railroad work. Gabriel Johnson recorded a different episode, however. John Ditcher and James C. Stewart, another member of the pivotal Poke Patch family, moved the last of a group of runaways from John J. Stewart's Poke Patch cabin to the Washington Switch of the Hocking Valley Railroad. James Stewart worked the Galleon Furnace to the northeast. He was an active agent of the Underground Railroad during the time John Campbell appointed him ironmaster. Stewart and Ditcher took a brother and sister, Tom and Julia, under their charge. In this case, slave catchers seized the pair and returned them to slavery.[16] Not every escape was successful; not every story ended with freedom.

After leaving Ironton, escapees moved up from the Mt. Vernon Furnace to the Olive Furnace along the route leading to Poke Patch in Gallia County or moved on to the Buckhorn Furnace, nine miles northeast of the Olive Furnace.[17] At the Buckhorn Furnace, Campbell's superintendent sent the runaways twenty miles northwest to the town of Jackson in Jackson County. Once the freedom seekers left Gallia County, Johnson and Madison Black might drive John Campbell's wagon to deliver them to the Monroe Furnace. The map of the town of Ironton makes a clever guide through the Hanging Rock Iron Region; each street name corresponds in sequence to the furnaces in Lawrence and Jackson Counties.[18]

John Campbell's funding of Underground Railroad activities conformed to a familiar pattern of wealthy individuals dedicating funds to ensure safe passage of runaways. Each gave according to his means and access to vital resources. Prosperous Black abolitionists such as James Forten and Robert Purvis in Pennsylvania contributed monies to aid escaped slaves.[19] The White antislavery worker Thomas Garret in Delaware used his money to purchase shoes; in upstate New York, Gerrit Smith contributed land for the Timbuctoo settlement in North Elba. The Tappan brothers invested enormous sums in the cause of liberty. Train conductors allowed safe passage as did ferrymen. Runaway advertisements cautioning ferrymen not to give aid to the fugitive was a stock phrase that came at the end of a high percentage of runaway notices. The sentiments of the boatmen were straightforward: if you could pay, you could travel. One of the Underground Railroad patterns that heightened effectiveness stemmed from men such as Campbell who applied their resources to circumventing the law.

## The Black Baptist Church

According to Wilbur Siebert, Blacks, Quakers, Covenanters, Wesleyan Methodists, and other abolitionists operated Underground Railroad routes in the region.[20] Rather than identifying African Americans involved in the Underground Railroad by race alone, different religious affiliations clarify the operations. Small Black settlements along the route into and out of Poke Patch contained Black Baptist churches active in the rescue work.

The Union Baptist Church served the religious needs of the area. Worshipers from Black Fork, an African American company town founded by the Washington Iron Furnace Company, and the adjacent Poke Patch community, attended services. Organized in 1819, the church predated the formation of the Providence Anti-Slavery Missionary Baptist Association, formed in 1821. The church and the people of Poke Patch actively engaged in antislavery activities from that early date.[21] For the convenience of each community, congregants had a new church built between Black Fork and Poke Patch.[22]

Both enclaves were heavily involved in the Underground Railroad. A route ran north to Poke Patch from two adjacent Black settlements in Burlington and Macedonia, roughly thirty miles to the south along the Ohio River border. These communities were not "towns" per se, but rather a loosely knit system of farmsteads spread over the rural landscape usually within a five-mile radius.[23] The congregation of Macedonia Missionary Baptist Church in Burlington first assembled in one another's homes around 1799. Early records distinguish this place of worship as the first African American church established west of Pennsylvania, or in the original states of the Northwest Territory. Early in the first decade of the nineteenth century, the congregation swelled after forty-six newly freed men, women, and children arrived from Virginia and built a house of prayer. For twenty years, Pastor Willis Stewart preached to the congregations at both Burlington and Macedonia. He lived his convictions and led many of the self-liberated to freedom through the dense woods to Poke Patch.[24]

The original church, replaced in 1849, planted the "Mother Church" for the post–Civil War churches to follow. Chillicothe, a very active Underground Railroad station in Scioto County, could be found farther north along one of two routes out of Poke Patch. The seeds of Methodism were planted in Chillicothe 1821 by the ubiquitous William Paul Quinn and Peter James. Reflecting the back-and-forth cycle between AME and Ohio Baptists, the First Anti-Slavery Baptist Church of God in Christ was founded there in 1824. Quinn maintained affiliations with Baptist ministers and their churches.

Although the Baptist Church predominated at Poke Patch, the interaction between church and community parallels the AME Church-community relationship present at Rocky Fork and Lick Creek. Spiritual leadership and families maintained ties with relatives and friends in other southern Ohio communities centered on the church. The 1847 Baptist convention in Brown County and the Baptist Association of Churches in 1848 provided opportunities for delegates from Cincinnati, Columbus, Xenia, and Chillicothe to exchange political and social ideas, in addition to attending to matters of spiritual concern. The returning delegates would have spread not only church news, but also news of other African American communities, as well as Underground Road activities.[25]

Escapees fleeing slavery in Virginia crossed the Ohio River at Gallipolis along the Kanawha River at the southeastern portion of the state. The AME Church was there to offer refuge and solace. Members of the Paint Creek Baptist Church, one of the churches in the Providence Anti-Slavery Missionary Baptist Association, also carried out the work of the Underground Railroad.

## Berlin Crossroads

A system of converging and diverging routes moved on through Porter and Rio Grande, and then diverged either to Poke Patch or to Thurman, all of which are in Gallia County. Another Black man, Noah Brooks, collected escapees forwarded from Poke Patch to Berlin Crossroads. From Thurman, the route also converged at Berlin Crossroads, a small African American farming community fifteen miles to the north in Jackson County.

Black abolitionist, John Mercer Langston, who would go on to an illustrious career as dean of Howard Law School and service as a Virginia congressman, was merely four years old when his extended family, including his sixteen-year-old brother, Charles Henry Langston (Langston Hughes's grandfather), traveled through Berlin Crossroads migrating from Virginia to Chillicothe, Ohio, in 1834. Langston and Charles along with their mother and the remainder of the family had been freed by the terms of their father's will. According to Virginia law, the family registered with the county clerk, secured copies of their free papers, and was forced to leave the state. When they arrived at Berlin Crossroads in Ross County, Ohio, three of the seven travelers had reached their journey's end, deciding to stay at the little settlement where land was cheap and affordable. This was the place to exercise their self-sufficiency now that freedom was theirs.

Jemima and Thomas Woodson, founders of Berlin Crossroads and parents of noted Black abolitionist Lewis Woodson, had lived for a time in Chillicothe, and the two black settlements maintained Underground Railroad connections in addition to family and religious ties. Thomas and Jemima had three children in addition to Lewis, two sons and a daughter, Sarah Jane Woodson, who went on to prominence as the first female instructor at Wilberforce University.

In a quest for equality, the Woodsons purchased the rural county land for the community of Berlin Crossroads in 1829 or 1830. The older generation of the approximately thirty families that eventually settled there had been enslaved in Virginia before escaping to Ohio. The Woodson family moved on to Berlin Crossroads to establish the settlement where they actively engaged in the work of the Underground Railroad and opened their home to escapees.

Prior to establishing the settlement, the Woodsons, after purchasing their freedom in Virginia, first settled in Chillicothe, where they were among the congregants who left the White Methodist Church and formed a new African American congregation that met in the home of Rev. Peter James. The church ranks as the first of forty-four churches formed by William Paul Quinn. The Woodson family would have crossed paths with Quinn as they organized the fledgling house of worship. Lewis Woodson's name was entered among those of his parents and eleven other couples at the founding of the Methodist Episcopal Church. Eventually, the congregants changed denominations and Bethel AME became known as the Quinn Chapel African Methodist Episcopal Church in Chillicothe.[26]

The Woodson family remained faithfully devoted to the denomination and Lewis sustained a lifelong friendship with Quinn. As they matured, the three Woodson sons, Lewis, Thomas Jr., and John, entered the ministry and worked actively on behalf of the enslaved. Educator and reverend, Lewis Woodson fulfilled the duties of secretary for two national AME conferences in Ohio and would go on to become prominent in the Black convention movement.

Lewis Woodson and his brothers had been earnestly involved in the Underground Railroad and continued the family work of rescuing captives from slavery. Lewis is credited with retrieving an enslaved man from Kentucky who had been stolen from Chillicothe by patrollers. Byron Woodson says of his ancestor, "He had a fire in his belly for the elevation of his people." Lewis Woodson's work on behalf of the oppressed may well have been driven by the death of his two brothers, who lost their lives in Ohio in the cause of freeing their brethren from slavery.[27]

The Woodsons, including their sons Thomas and John, received runaways from Poke Patch. The brothers avoided detection by driving their horses to Chillicothe and Washington Court House under the pretense of taking them to market. Escaped slaves were hidden in the hay wagons or disguised as drovers and taken to safety in Ross and Fayette Counties.

The stories of the Woodson brothers help dispel the thrilling and romantic myth of the Underground Railroad. According to family history, on a grim day in September 1846, Thomas Woodson Jr.'s beaten body was found on the side of the road. He had given his life rather than betray the escaped captives he had aided. Six years later, his younger brother, John, received a brutal beating at the hands of Kentucky slaveholders. He endured a year of suffering before he died as a result of his wounds. Following the example set by his brother, Thomas, John had refused to give any information about the escapees he had aided. The family did not crumble under the intimidation, electing to continue their work on the Underground Railroad for as long as slavery existed. The Woodson brothers and the Langston brothers knew firsthand and could speak with authority about the life and challenges inside small, rural free black settlements and the aid they provided to anyone seeking a way out of slavery. The strength and tragedy of his family history shaped Black abolitionist Lewis Woodson throughout his work as an AME minister and nineteenth-century Black activist.[28]

Rev. William Mitchell, author of one of the first books describing the Underground Railroad, was initiated into the business of rescuing escapees in Ross County in 1843. From Jackson County, runaways crossed into Ross County and traveled through Richmond Dale, a Quaker settlement, before heading northeast of Chillicothe through Springfield Township. Runaways continued their journey to stations east of Columbus and then to points farther north.[29]

After Rev. Mitchell relocated eighty miles north to Washington Court House, his home became a permanent stop on the Underground Railroad. His eyewitness accounts of his work on Underground Railroad routes through Ohio infused his work with the voice of authority and authenticity.[30]

Not only were community relationships revealing, but relationships to other abolitionists also held important clues to their activism. Ohio's John Rankin is remembered as one of the state's most important Underground Railroad operatives. The Presbyterian minister's now famous home high atop Liberty Hill in Ripley in Brown County was two counties west of Gallia County. The minister's home may be the clearest example of how the landscape both facilitated escape and thwarted would-be captors.[31] Rankin's association with wealthy furnace owner John Campbell provides a glimpse into the entangled relationships that shaped the antislavery world.

Campbell had been born near Ripley and worked there as a young man until 1831 and returned frequently before he moved to Hanging Rock in 1846 and then into the home he built in Ironton in 1850. John Rankin came to Ripley in 1822 and built his home on Liberty Hill in 1828. Campbell and Rankin were together in the small town of Ripley for a number of years and subsequently became close associates. Rankin had visited Ironton frequently before he moved there permanently after the Civil War; he died in Ironton in 1886. The religious denomination of each participant provides important clues for Underground Railroad research. There is a high probability that

Campbell, like Rankin, was a Presbyterian. Their religious affiliation may have provided a bond that matched their political and moral convictions.[32]

Poke Patch convincingly supports the argument for deliberate strategic placement of an Underground Railroad station in the landscape. The sole purpose of the site appears to have been as a critical junction near river and state borders on the edge of the route through the iron furnace region (see map 4). The demise of the town at the end of the Civil War gives the argument further credence.

Although Bishop Quinn and the AME Church were essential to the success of the Underground Railroad in Illinois and Indiana, Black Baptists from the communities surrounding Poke Patch largely supported the local Underground Railroad efforts. The independent Black church, as the institutional, family, and religious center of life in the small communities, centralized the struggle for freedom. The church offered lifelines to the larger Black world beyond the hills, thickets, woods, and caves of the sequestered rural life of Black settlements. Whether Baptist, AME, or AME Zion, religious-minded men and women displayed an unceasing concern for their brothers and sisters held in bondage.

* * *

Four outstanding historical circumstances set Poke Patch apart from Miller Grove, Rocky Fork, and Lick Creek, providing a counterbalance to the oral and narrative accounts of Rocky Fork and the strictly archaeological sites for which there are no retained oral histories and little documentation. Siebert and other major historians extensively documented the relationship between the Underground Railroad and the free Black community at Poke Patch. He documented routes connecting the iron furnaces but did not discuss iron furnaces as sites of refuge. Identifying iron furnaces as critical to the success of Underground Railroad operations sets this region apart and adds another pathway to the geography of resistance. Although the stories from Poke Patch are unique among the sites presented here, parallel accounts can be found in other iron-producing parts of the country. As upcoming chapters discuss, iron ore-containing regions in Pennsylvania and Maryland, for example, have similar stories to tell.

Poke Patch retains crucial similarities to the Rocky Fork, Miller Grove, and Lick Creek. Larger, better-known centers of abolition such as Ironton overshadowed Poke Patch. More importantly, free Blacks were actively working throughout Ohio for the sake of freedom culminating in their efforts in the Civil War. War veterans buried in the cemeteries point toward a continuous dedication to the cause of freedom. To that end, several soldiers from the U.S. Colored Troops are buried in the cemetery at Union Baptist Church.

The four primary sites in this study evolved under distinct circumstances; however, one important conclusion unites them. The interactions among those fleeing slavery and the Black communities that helped them move along escape routes sharpen when we peer through the lens of the geography of resistance. Although each differs in level and type of documentation, the African American experiences mined from distinct sources confirm the broader findings laid out in part II. The oral record yielded information equal to, if not more compelling than, the written sources. Taken together, the four sites add to a rich and varied understanding of African American rural experiences on the Underground Railroad. Part II explores significant aspects of the geography of resistance that distinguished each settlement.

# PART II
# Geographies of Resistance

Part I tilled the soil so that part II could bear the fruit. In moving away from the individual sites, chapter 5 takes a collective look at how people escaping slavery exploited landforms and landscape features in the service of freedom. This section extends escape routes beyond the iconic homes of abolitionists to include iron furnaces and natural features such as caves, as well as Black communities and churches, which make up the pathways to freedom and the geography of resistance. Using the land as a type of document that encourages new search parameters, this chapter should prove indispensible for anyone laying out or redefining Underground Railroad routes, or trying to recover lost historic Black landscapes.

Chapter 6 continues to reveal the impact of geography on the processes of community formation and the causes of migration that led Blacks to live where they did and flee when they had to. The chapter takes a fresh look at migration by reexamining how people of color used, as well as moved through, their immediate environment. Escape from slavery, in conjunction with both forced and voluntary migration, is the backbone of the Underground Railroad movement.

CHAPTER 5

# The Geography of Resistance

Harriet Tubman thought of freedom as a distinctive destination with dimension, boundaries, and above all safety. When she crossed that "magic line" dividing "the land of bondage from the land of freedom," she lamented that no one was there to welcome her.[1] At the moment of liberation, Tubman expressed her desolation compounded only by her isolation. On the other hand, Josiah Henson, after escaping slavery in Kentucky with his wife and children, had quite a jubilant reaction. "When I got on to the Canada side, on the morning of the 28th of October, 1830, my first impulse was to throw myself on the ground, and giving way to the riotous exhaultation of my feelings, to execute sundry antics which excited the astonishment of those who were looking on . . . It is not much to be wondered at, that my certainty of being free was not quite a sober one at the first moment."[2]

Second only to judicial and constitutional mandates, the landscape was a formidable weapon of oppression against Blacks as well as a site of liberation. This chapter lays out the geography of resistance and the concept of freedom as a place, exploring the connections between freedom and the landscape, and between Black communities and the Underground Railroad. The landscape is an intimate yet underexplored component of the Black experience, where danger lurked and freedom beaconed. Although the land was a site of disorientation, hardship, frostbite, and starvation, it also held crucial pathways out of slavery. Generations of escapees on the Underground Railroad turned to the sheltering anonymity of the land to conceal their journey.

Rapport with the land lent Harriet Tubman's Underground Railroad efforts legendary effectiveness. "Traveling by night, hiding by day, scaling the mountains, fording the rivers, treading the forests, lying concealed as pursuers passed," turning south though journeying north, Tubman mined the landscape, extracting freedom from it as had so many escapees before and after her.[3]

Those who managed successful escapes and those who aided them needed to overcome physical and psychological boundaries. Broadly defined in cultural landscape terms, the Underground Railroad encompassed not only houses but each route forged by the enslaved, each track to freedom enmeshed in what the National Park Service identifies as a "vast network of paths and roads, through swamps and over mountains, along and across rivers and even by sea."[4] Tree hollows, caves, precipices, and sinkholes, high ground and lookout points, forests, thickets, and southern swamps formed natural barriers that protected freedom seekers from their would-be captors. The use of inaccessible land, such as the Great Dismal Swamp, was a hallmark of escape, ensuring success and making the creation of new communities possible.

Not only were river crossings, land routes, iron forges and foundries, waterways, and natural and man-made hiding places crucial to success of the movement, knowledge of the heavens also spelled the difference between success and failure. Geese flying north, moss growing thicker on the north side of trees, and the rising and setting sun brought the heavens into the realm of the geography of resistance; a cloudy night could spell as much disaster as a coursing river.

The egalitarian heavens shared the North Star—"the bright cynosure"—with all who knew its secrets. Blacksmith J. W. C. Pennington reveals the dilemma of using such a nebulous navigator: "my only guide was the *north star*, by this I knew my general course northward, but at what point I should strike Pennsylvania, or when and where I should find a friend I knew not."[5] The enduring symbol of the North Star signifies the dual role of the heavens within the Underground Railroad, one earthly, the other spiritual. A star had guided the wise men to the newborn Christ; heaven held inspiration, the prospect of hope and relief from suffering the horrors of slavery.

Language associated with the Underground Railroad reflected the religious and spiritual character of the movement. Harriet Tubman triumphed as "the Moses of her people"; the flight out of bondage and Black migration mirrored the exodus from the land of Egypt; the Ohio River transformed into the River Jordan; Canada represented both heaven and the Promised Land; escapees were bound for glory.[6] Josiah Henson declared Canada "that haven of promise." He also recognized salvation in the celestial sphere, declaring, "I knew the North Star—blessed be God for setting it in the heavens! Like the Star of Bethlehem, it announced where my salvation lay. Could I follow it through forest, and stream, and field, it would guide my feet in the way of hope. I thought of it as my God-given guide to the land of promise far away beneath its light. I knew it had led thousands of my poor, hunted brethren to freedom and blessedness."[7] Ironically, the heavens and the use of astronomy that had guided slave ships to American shores also guided the captives to freedom. The metaphor of heaven as God's salvation, Canada as heaven, and the North Star as guide in the heavens remained powerful throughout the Underground Railroad years.

Despite the romantic notion and symbolic importance of the celestial navigator, however, at times escapees plainly relied on technology. Freedom seekers around Pittsburgh were sometimes armed with a compass to help them navigate their way out of slavery. Seventeen-year-old James Adams escaped from Virginia with his cousin, a woman, and four children in 1824. Betrayal had diminished their numbers by the time they found help in Ohio. To raise the likelihood of success, they were taught to use a pocket compass, which the escapees "had never seen before." They accepted the instrument that their helper marked with his knife so they would "steer a little west of north."[8]

Escapees were smuggled in steamboats, carriages, stage coaches, railroad cars, false-bottom wagons, and skiffs. They walked and they rode. The Underground Railroad now suffers under the weight of a long-held cliché; it was "neither underground nor a railroad."[9] Yet this inaccurate generalization obscures the complexity of the movement, which was, at times, both physically and metaphorically underground. Although most descriptions of subterranean passageways are relegated to legend, conductors included underground hiding places in their bag of tricks to avoid detection. Levi Coffin leaned toward the effectiveness of dark cellars. Philadelphia's Robert Purvis, president of the organized society of the Underground Railroad formed in 1838, had a carpenter construct a hiding place underneath a room in his Philadelphia home that only could be accessed by a trap door in the floor. This place, Purvis observed, "we deemed perfectly secure, should any search be made by the authorized officials."[10]

True to its name, conductors frequently employed the railroad to transport its "passengers." Harriet Tubman and her passengers rode the "iron horse," referring to the railroad across the Suspension Bridge between Niagara Falls and Canada. Conductors in Poke Patch, Ohio, resorted to booking train passage for their charges. Wealthy Black businessmen and lumber merchants William Whipper and Stephen Smith owned a fleet of railroad cars and canal boats that they used to ship escapees in Pennsylvania across the state on the main line of the Allegheny Portage Railroad.[11] After 1854, the Illinois Central Railroad employees used their jobs to lend an air of normalcy to escape schemes. George Burroughs joined the Underground Railroad efforts in 1857, using his work as a sleeping-car porter to make the Illinois Central Railroad do the work of aiding escapees.[12]

## Landscape of Freedom

Escapees used the shroud of darkness to heighten their chances of successful escapes. Predictable patterns in the night sky paralleled dependable features on the ground. Captives escaping slavery had to contend with losing their way and their nerve, the challenges of the terrain and bad weather, in addition to betrayal, physical suffering, and slave catchers. Once success was within their grasp, much uncertainty lay ahead.

If escapees were fortunate enough to reach a free Black settlement, they would have encountered a combination of family relationships and landscape features that supported escape. Interconnected families formed the backbone of the support structure. Church and community cemeteries gave evidence of the long-lasting nature of the family connections to homeplace. Within these communities, escapees would have understood that homes were scattered and community boundaries undefined. An abundance of natural resources supported the community, giving residents the ability to offer food and shelter to wayfarers. Often, Black communities were settled on inferior or undesirable land, sometimes near iron forges and foundries that punctuated Underground Railroad escape routes. The communities could be found in close proximity to larger, better documented abolitionist centers with confirmed Underground Railroad activity nearby.

Regional terrain, particularly in the rural southernmost regions of Illinois, Indiana, and Ohio, dictated the realities of escape. Freedom seekers moved through a maze of zigzag routes, pathways, and waterways dotted by homes, communities, and safe harbors. In *Runaway Slaves: Rebels on the Plantation*, historians John Hope Franklin and Loren Schweninger found that a large percentage of the free Black population living in cities or separated from Whites in farming areas had the ability to take in fugitives without causing too much suspicion or drawing undue attention. In reality, escapees had to travel through the South and a certain distance into the North before encountering safe havens and collaborators, a distance including extreme southern regions of the free states of Illinois, Indiana, Ohio, and parts of Pennsylvania.[13]

Somewhere in the south-central portion of the northern border states, escapees taking the Canadian route crossed the permeable political and ideological boundary from south to north. That boundary rarely followed state borders. In Illinois, no greater philosophical distance existed concerning race and slavery than between the southern portion of the state and the regions farther north. Beyond that point, discrete Underground Railroad lines branched within the state, providing multiple avenues of escape (see map 1).

The decidedly southern leanings of Southern Illinois prompted one scholar to observe that the National Road, spanning east to west through central Indiana and the southern third of Illinois, provided a truer boundary between North and South than the Ohio River.[14] Slave states to the south and west significantly shaped how escape from slavery operated in Southern Illinois. Southern sections of northern border states combined with northern sections of the southern border states to form a broad band at the nation's midsection. The southern portion of Illinois, Indiana, and Ohio was dangerous territory. Kevin Phillips imagines it as the Lower North, Upper South borderland.[15]

The same can be said of southwestern Pennsylvania where the state jutted into Virginia and shared the length of its southern border with Maryland. Abolitionist sentiment did not take hold in the southwestern Pennsylvania region until 1850, after passage of the Fugitive Slave Law.[16] With passage of the more stringent law came more formal, organized, institutional efforts to assist escapees; moving them through the landscape became more efficient, enabling greater numbers to escape bondage.

Most escapees remained in a small local radius near family in the South. Franklin and Schweninger give example after example of those seeking freedom who faced betrayal or capture before their dreams materialized. For the persevering few who successfully negotiated their way out of slavery and reached the free states, local Black communities became critical destinations, particularly as escapees navigated the treacherous, racially caustic southern portions of Illinois, Indiana, and Ohio.[17]

The valleys of three parallel ranges, the Cumberland, Allegheny, and Blue Ridge Mountains, carved natural pathways leading north. Their great forested interiors blanketed the paths out of slavery. Plenty of limestone caves could be found along the way and were used by escapees and white conductors alike. At Miller Grove, landscape features such as Sand Cave offered both shelter and safety. At times, caves replaced hollowed trees, forests, or mountains. Escape narratives mention barns, haystacks, and corn cribs. Drain pipes, barrels, and trunks were less common hiding places. Old furniture, coffins, and abandoned coal pits provided natural camouflage and temporary seclusion.

### *Caves*

In the first moments of his escape, after walking across a barnyard in western Maryland, J. W. C. Pennington made his way some distance from the main house to a small cave. There, in preparation for his escape, he had hidden a spare bundle of clothing. Recognizing one of the critical components of a successful escape, Pennington returned to the cave to retrieve the hidden clothing that would allow him to divest himself of one of the most conspicuous badges of slavery: coarse, tattered clothing.[18] Historian Laurence Glasco mentions food, clothing, and disguises brought at night to fugitives hiding in the caves around Pittsburgh.[19]

The caves of Maryland, Pennsylvania, and western Virginia, in addition to western North Carolina, Tennessee, Kentucky, and Ohio, offered daytime sanctuary when homes were unavailable. Sand Cave provided refuge near Miller Grove in Illinois. The Underground Railroad routes near Alton began with the caves in the surrounding bluffs.

Between October and March 1856, twenty-two-year-old Winey Petty and her young daughter concealed their escape from Norfolk, Virginia, by hiding in a cave under a house occupied by an enslaved family. The mother and daughter suffered greatly from exposure during the cold, damp, freezing winter months. The mother knew she was scheduled to be sold on the auction block. Having gone through that dreadful experience three times, Winey chose not to endure a fourth and escaped.[20]

In addition to escapees, White as well as Black abolitionists and conductors resorted to using these yawning spaces. In a letter to the great abolitionist Frederick Douglass, Martin Delany supplied a few details during his visit to the hilltop home of Ohio Presbyterian minister John Rankin. Delany revealed one clue to this White abolitionist's great success as an unconcealed Underground Railroad operative. After freedom seekers made their way to his home, Rankin had been known to shelter up to forty escapees at one time, "'packed away' in the underground depot. This depot, as a matter of course, is not in the house of Dr. Rankin, but situated in a cavern about two miles south, of the whereabouts of which none but abolitionists are aware."[21] By this method, Rankin thwarted slave catchers when they forced their way into the home to find only the women and children.

After Jermain Loguen's sister and mother had been sold to a brutal master, he caucused in a mountain cave in Tennessee to plot his strategy. His first night's sleep while planning his escape was spent in this cavernous abode. In preparation for his escape, Loguen laid aside his clothes and a new quilted saddle appropriated in reprisal for the theft of his labors. Armed with a pistol, he set forth on his journey to freedom on Christmas Eve, eventually arriving in Indiana.[22]

Caves were important shelters whether escapees were successful on their first attempt or fled multiple times. In Isaac Williams's narrative, *Sunshine and Shadow of Slave Life. Reminiscences as told by Isaac D. Williams to "Tege,"* Williams not only resorted to caves during his attempts but also dug a cave into the side of a cliff. He was captured and jailed after that attempt and overheard his captors remarking that they had never seen "so complete a place to hide in."[23]

### *Waterways*

In North America, rivers and lakes formed natural boundaries between freedom and slavery. For much of its length, the Ohio River divided the nation between north and south. Once escapees made the psychological journey toward the desire for freedom, the great American waterways had to be conquered. The Great Lakes to the north and the Ohio and Mississippi Rivers to the south and west coursed through the geography of resistance. The Illinois, Wabash, and Detroit Rivers led northward. Add to this list the Delaware and Susquehanna Rivers and the majestic Chesapeake Bay farther east as well as innumerable brooks and streams, all of which simultaneously offered speedy alternatives to escape by land and presented seemingly insurmountable obstacles. In the South, bold free Black sailors, "angels of liberty" as historian Jeffrey Bolster referred to them, stowed escapees aboard ships.[24] Harriet Tubman's effectiveness came in part because she had grown up working around the Chesapeake Bay, navigating the rivers, streams, and marshes on Maryland's Eastern Shore.

Narratives are full of anxious, harrowing moments spent at the water's edge in search of a way across. In the counties along the Ohio River, authorities were on the lookout for freedom seekers. One old plantation woman asked an enslaved nineteen-year-old Arnold Gragston to help a young woman get across the Ohio River from Kentucky to Ripley, Ohio. The old woman gave him specific instructions about when to go and where to leave his passenger. He agreed and rowed into the depths of darkness of a moonless night; Gragston described it as "the 'black nights' of the moon." The trembling Gragston struggled against the current as he looked for the tall light to guide him as he had been instructed. After delivering his charge safely to Ripley on the other side and overcoming his initial fears, Gragston evolved into a regular conductor, braving the trip and evading lookouts, rowing "two and three people" across, sometimes a "whole boatload, three or four times a month."[25]

On a shadowy night, Josiah Henson's escape with his wife and children also ended in a brief but life-altering encounter with a lone, unidentified Black man who silently rowed them across the river. As Henson reported, "We got into the little skiff in which I had induced a fellow-slave to take us across the river. It was an agitating and solemn moment. The good fellow who was rowing us over, said this affair might end in his death; 'but,' said he, 'you will not be brought back alive, will you?' 'Not if I can help it,' I answered. 'And if you are overpowered and return,' he asked, 'will you conceal my part of the business?'" Before the family landed on the shores of Indiana, Henson reassured his anonymous helper that he had nothing to fear. The rower replied, "Then I am easy . . . and wish you success."[26]

Ice floes, skiffs, low points, draughts and flooding, boats and ferries occupied the minds of self-liberators who faced the challenge of crossing a major waterway. After abandoning his Tennessee cave, Jermain Loguen and his companion led their horses across the frozen Ohio River and into Indiana during the Christmas season. Although the Ohio River was heavily patrolled and skiffs were pulled up, padlocked to trees, and the oars removed, free people of color who owned skiffs and canoes hid them in the secret bends and coves of the river to aid escapees.

Harriet Jacobs, one of the most famous Underground Railroad passengers, revealed how the Edenton, North Carolina, African American community, including Black seamen, arranged for her escape on a schooner bound for Philadelphia. So entwined were waterways with the Underground Railroad and the narrative of escape that the last lines of many runaway advertisements invariably forewarned ferrymen, "All Masters of Vessels, or Captains of Privateers and others," that aiding runaways would be "at their peril."[27] Waterways connected rural sites to the footpaths of freedom, to city centers and marketplaces, and to safety.

Knowledge of American rivers is essential for understanding Underground Railroad operations within the geography of resistance. Black communities were often settled near bodies of water—large and small. Many of the major Underground Railroad towns and cities such as Boston, New Bedford, and New York, in addition to Philadelphia and Baltimore, thrived as port towns. Free Blacks ran an active Underground Railroad operation in Middletown, Connecticut, on the shores of the Connecticut River. In New York, Syracuse, Rochester, and Buffalo ranked among the major waterfront outlets and Underground Railroad cities. Pittsburgh sits on the Ohio River at the confluence of the Allegheny and Monongahela Rivers. The slave state of Kentucky is visible from Cincinnati's northern setting on the Ohio River. Cleveland, Sandusky, and Toledo in Ohio rimmed Lake Erie. Similar to Chicago and Detroit, these cities stood as western portals to Canada. In addition to the great rivers, little creeks provided access to rural havens such as Rocky Fork or Lick Creek. Farther east, the small enclaves of Springtown and Timbuctoo in New Jersey were similarly situated.

### *Iron furnaces*

Iron furnaces and forges operated along the hidden Black pathways to freedom before the Underground Railroad got underway. Iron furnaces as sites of refuge add an intriguing aspect to the flight to freedom. Blacks have had a long relationship with blacksmithing and ironworking and during the early period, many enslaved Africans hailed from countries that worked with metal, particularly iron. In the early period of ironmaking in the United States, American ironmasters may have deliberately turned to Africans from iron-working cultures with specific knowledge and ironmaking skills. These expert workers may well have formed the "backbone" of the American iron industry.

In his narrative, Pennington spoke of himself and his profession with pride. Blacksmiths, enslaved and free, commanded respect; they were an imposing group. The position of ironmaster implied power, expertise, and capacity. Ironmasters and ironworking held considerable significance in the lives of Blacks, particularly in relation to the Underground Railroad.

Furnaces and forges, scattered across much of the United States, were particularly numerous in Maryland and Pennsylvania, as well as farther west in Ohio and Michigan and throughout the southern United States. Slavery took on a crucial role in the growth and development of the iron industry. Ironworks gobbled huge numbers of skilled and unskilled laborers.

Slaves escaping prior to 1830 invented ways to flee slavery that predate organized efforts. Across several states, enslaved ironworkers indispensible throughout the industry fled from the harsh labor environment. Long before the advent of the Underground Railroad, colonial-era newspapers indicate the size of the problem of workers fleeing from foundries. In Maryland, enslaved workers were escaping from the Baltimore Iron Company, from the Marlboro and the Patuxent Iron Works, and from Ridgely, Northampton, Kingsbury, Catoctin, and Antietam Furnaces before the Revolutionary War. When African-born Tom fled Maryland's Elk Ridge Furnace in 1762, the four other escapees with him "spoke very little English."[28]

Enslaved ironworkers were among the occupational group able to achieve successful escapes during this era. In fact, more escapes occurred from iron foundries than from any other nonagricultural industry. Similarly, historian Gerald Mullins reports that of all the small-scale extractive and craft industries, escapes by ironworkers ranked the highest. Among the more specialized ironworkers, highly skilled blacksmiths were always in demand. Often permitted to hire their time, ironworkers experienced greater independence and familiarity with their surroundings, making escape more accessible. J. W. C. Pennington had been quite proud of the quality of his work while he had been held in slavery. His narrative, *The Fugitive Blacksmith or Events in the History of James W. C. Pennington*, describing his life in slavery and his successful escape from Maryland, brought the subject to the fore.[29]

Escape routes in Pennsylvania paralleled the operations around Poke Patch. Ironworkers knew that iron forges generally lay along a route that followed a vein of ore through a region. Those who escaped from the South, particularly Maryland, made their way north to a place like Berks County, Pennsylvania, where numerous forges dotted the landscape. A series of forges—Pine Forge, Hopewell Furnace, and Joanna Furnace—ran along the Underground Railroad route between Morgantown and Hamburg.[30]

Beginning in 1835, remote areas around Hopewell played an important role in the Underground Railroad. Escapees from the South crossed the Pennsylvania border, traveling to Berks County over hilly obstructions to the home of Elizabeth Scarlet and her son, Joseph, the Quaker owners of Scarlet's Mill. Here African Americans who had escaped bondage in the South formed a community in the valley of Six Penny Creek, close to Hopewell, Joanna Furnace, and the forges in Birdsboro. Joanna Furnace owner Levi "Bull" Smith aided runaway slaves by sending them to the most remote areas of the woods surrounding the furnace, staying with them until danger passed.[31] African Americans passing through Hopewell Furnace were employed for short periods. Many former slaves earned their living supporting the iron industry working as woodcutters, colliers, and teamsters. The names of runaway slaves employed in various activities were not reliably entered into the furnace records in order to protect their identities.[32] To avoid pursuers, some fugitives hid out in the woods in huts of charcoal burners working for Joanna Furnace. But mostly they lived quite openly and unmolested.[33]

Industrial historian Joseph Walker observes that the belief that runaways from the South were able to find work in the forges and furnaces in the North is highly probable based on their disappearance from the account records, but it is difficult to prove. Most forges had a combination of workers ranging from free to enslaved. Escaped slaves landed somewhere in the murky space between the two. Free Blacks became artisans and entrepreneurs.

In the Shenandoah River area of Virginia, African Americans worked near the arsenal and musket factory complex at Harpers Ferry. The development of the area's iron industry satisfied the demands of the arsenal that had relied on Africans as a source of the bulk of its labor supply. John Brown came among these powerful ironworkers to recruit men for his planned raid on Harpers Ferry. In making his decision about the best place to strike, Brown relied extensively on the combined knowledge of Blacks from the region and his own deep understanding of Underground Railroad routes. Free Blacks in the area surrounding Harpers Ferry were concentrated in small self-contained communities or towns such as Johnsontown. Quakers and Free Will Baptists bordering the town provided a protective buffer for the Black community. Free Blacks along with Quakers and the local enslaved workers operating the ferries in Harpers Ferry and nearby Shepherdstown were well positioned to help escapees along the Great Black Way.

The area's active Underground Railroad connected to the iron furnaces. White Underground Railroad operative Hiram Wertz laid out the route. "The route was by way of South Mountain from the Potomac River to the Pennsylvania border. The first station was . . . called Shockey's . . . by the way of Wertz's father's barn at Quincy, then on to Africa near Caledonia Furnace, owned by the great champion of the slaves, Thaddeus Stevens. From Africa escapees were piloted through the mountains by way of Pine Grove Furnace, Mt. Holly and Boiling Springs, Pennsylvania and then went safely over the Susquehanna."[34]

At Chambersburg, George Cole, a free Black man, also exploited the Boiling Springs route. According to Cumberland County, Pennsylvania, Circuit Court records, the Black conductor aided a group of thirteen who had escaped from Williamsport, Maryland, in October 1847. As he guided them north through Shippensburg, he followed a route that used iron furnaces as safe havens, stopping at Mills Furnace, Huntsdale, and Salome Forge. His intention to continue on to Ege's Forge at Boiling Springs was thwarted, however, and the group diverted to a nearby barn for shelter.[35]

Recognition of connections between iron furnaces and forges and the Underground Railroad has been sporadic. Freedom seekers both escaped from iron forges in the South and used furnaces and forges in the North as sites of refuge. Moreover, ironmasters participated in the Underground Railroad and, it appears, offered protection to escapees under the guise of giving them work.[36] Farther west, iron furnaces located in places such as Poke Patch formed important escape routes in the southern regions of Ohio. Information is scattered across narratives, mixed together in runaway ads, and buried in court records and account books. Similar to waterways, the routes leading from one forge to the next are a powerful, though understudied branch of the geography of resistance.

### *Houses*

The homes of abolitionists represent the most stable artifacts of the Underground Railroad. Iconic among them are the hilltop home of John Rankin and the nearby riverfront location of Black abolitionist John Parker. Both exemplify how the geography of resistance operated—Rankin as the unconcealed White abolitionist and beacon of hope and freedom high at the end of the freedom stairway, Parker as the silent African American operator at the more dangerous water's edge providing immediate access to that freedom. Both strategically situated at the water's edge offered maximum aid and optimal security through either vantage point or seclusion, two consistent landscape features of the Underground Railroad synonymous with the geography of resistance.

Both homes survive as the signature of the Underground Railroad in the landscape. Rankin lived in a neighborhood frequented by freedom seekers. His reputation as an antislavery activist and the hilltop home—visible for miles—overlooking the Ohio are nothing less than legendary. Homes of abolitionists capture the imagination. In 1848, Black abolitionist Martin Delany visited Rankin's refuge, describing it as "the resting place for the way-worn and weary for years, to the great chagrin of the slaveocrats of his neighborhood, and the slaveholders of Kentucky."[37] Rankin's Ohio River perch and the nearby location of Black abolitionist and ironworker John Parker operating at the river's edge are among the most dramatic. Many times those who escaped by crossing the Ohio River at Ripley, the famed seat of abolitionism in Ohio, were assisted by ironmaster John Parker and hidden at the nearby black settlement of Africa Hill.[38]

Small Black settlements connected to the Underground Railroad such as Africa Hill have largely disappeared from the landscape. Few examples of the homes of Black families who sheltered escapees have survived. W. Paul Quinn's name appears on multiple deeds in the city of Richmond and his home will be an important addition for consideration to the Network to Freedom and the National Register of Historic Places. Elaine Welch emphasizes the pivotal time Quinn spent in Richmond, where his commitment to the Underground Railroad deepened. As a circuit-riding preacher ministering across conferences and throughout the denomination, Quinn practiced one of those meandering professions that allowed him freedom to move about the countryside and remain above suspicion of fueling the Underground Railroad.[39]

## Inferior or Undesirable Land

Most free Blacks, whether through economic constraints or racist policies, often found themselves saddled with the least desirable land. Up in the hills or tucked away on rocky outposts, Blacks had to contend with racism in the landscape and the harsh realities of the land as one more problem to surmount. The historic free Black community on Mt. Joy Street on the north slope of the Beacon Hill section of Boston sits atop one of the highest points in the city. The terrible soil and drainage plagued the church and the surrounding community for years. Free people of color were also settled on inferior land at Concord, Massachusetts, the home of the Transcendentalists. In the early history of Massachusetts, newly emancipated former slaves were permitted to squat at Walden Woods in the most remote and infertile places. The sandy soil did not retain water well, prompting Henry David Thoreau to acknowledge the land for what it was—sterile soil.[40]

The quality of the land was also an issue for settlers at North Elba in upstate New York. In 1845, White abolitionist Gerrit Smith made land grants of forty-acre tracts to poor Black men to start a settlement for free people of color, North Elba or Timbuctoo, in the Adirondacks. A year later, he began giving away 120,000 acres of land that he had inherited from his father. Smith had visions of the Adirondack wilderness offering refuge, put into the hands of Black families from Brooklyn to Buffalo, "without money and without price." Local historians remember the area as "rich in the variety and magnificence" of its scenery and "exhaustless" resources. The land was to be "settled and improved, and the wilderness made to bud and blossom as the rose." The "deep seclusion" and "the wild solitude of the place" awed and impressed. In 1849, John Brown purchased land in North Elba from Smith with the intention of settling his own family there. Brown was also interested in helping settlers establish the Timbuctoo colony.[41]

Although the area had "inexhaustible" lumber resources, the altitude of the town was "greater than any other cultivated lands in the state." The black loam that prevailed for miles gave way to large tracts of poor sandy soil that gave the place the euphonious name of the "Plains of Abraham," or "Abraham's Plains." Discouraged by the discovery that the land, which seemed to hold so much promise, was too rocky for farming or much else, Black settlers moved on.[42] Blame for the demise of the experiment, however, is often laid at the feet of its Black settlers. Gerrit Smith realized and admitted that the land was not at all suitable, neither fit for farming nor capable of producing crops; much of it was undesirable despite the considerable timber. Conventioneers at 1847 Proceedings of the National Convention of Colored People in Troy who listened to Gerrit Smith pledge 140,000 acres of land at the disposal of some 3,000 free Blacks began to have doubts and concerns about the success and viability of the venture. The intractability of the land was one of the primary factors that led to the failure—to the lack of success of the endeavor.[43]

The problem followed Blacks as they migrated to Canada. The land White abolitionist Rev. William King set aside at the Elgin Settlement in Buxton, Canada, was intended to have a positive impact on Blacks in America. Education and religion were the cornerstones of his philosophy. The land set aside for the settlement was "less than ideal." "King either overlooked or ignored warnings about the quality of the land. Government surveyors and others had done their best to alert him to the problem. One licensed surveyor reported that the northern section of the tract, though composed generally of good soil, "was much depreciated for want of roads, and thorough drainage." The southern section likewise suffered from a lack of drainage as well, "but little of this land could be made available unless an expensive and systematic system of drainage [was] resorted to."[44] The settlement survived the poor drainage problems and went on to become one of the most successful and enduring of the Canadian settlements.

Inferior land relative to the surroundings in some cases was the ultimate cause for the community's failure. There are numerous examples across the nation of Blacks being settled on the most unforgiving land—the Gist settlement in Ohio, Rocky Fork and Brooklyn, Illinois, the Beech and Lick Creek settlements in Indiana, Timbuctoo or North Elba in New York, Walden in Massachusetts, and Timbuctoo in New Jersey—and then being held accountable if the community failed.

Free Blacks maintained the wherewithal to purchase affordable land from the meanest wages. Expending enormous sums to purchase their freedom or the freedom of their families and loved ones or meeting the exorbitant financial drains required to post bonds often left people of color in greatly reduced financial circumstances. Whether African Americans were relegated to poor-quality land or they purchased what they could afford are two sides of the same question. Racial policies condemned Blacks to either the least desirable spaces or restricted access to economic opportunities. The ability to buy quality land hung in the balance. At times, people of color were latecomers who chose to settle on less desirable land in more inviting regions rather than on quality land in dangerous areas.

As challenging as farming on rocky, sandy, or infertile soil could be, people of color found alternatives to survival by supplementing their farming with activities such as lumbering. The natural bountifulness of the surrounding land often bolstered them. Fish and game, wild berries, nut trees, eggs, and vegetable gardens along with plentiful fresh water sustained them when the ground would not. What the soil refused to yield in food it often produced in the form of bricks that could be sold. Timbering, charcoal, and baked goods supplied alternative means of support.

Topographic and soil analyses of historic Black settlements would be a most revealing landscape study of how racial oppression, injustice, and economic inequality operated in the landscape and on the ground. The landscape reinforces our understanding that policies of injustice and disadvantage against people of color were rampant throughout society, becoming particularly visible in the geography. Poor-quality land functions as an important marker for locating Black settlements along Underground Railroad routes.

## Dispersed Settlement Patterns

Rural Black settlements were arranged so that families resided on their own individual plots. Families did not live near one another or in a village center.[45] At times, Rocky Fork residents did place their houses toward the edges of their lots, nearer their neighbors. In Timbuctoo in New Jersey, archaeologist Christopher Barton found that families placed their homes closer to one another.

Archaeologists have the ability to reconstruct settlement patterns using a combination of excavation and mapping. With so little existing aboveground evidence, archaeology is crucial for understanding where Black settlements were and how Black communities in the North were laid out.

Churches often sat on the edge or at the corner of the settlements, rather than centrally located in accordance with European "centralized" landscape planning. Since these long forgotten, loosely defined, poorly preserved communities rarely survived, standing churches or cemeteries are the indicators of communities. Looking for church cemeteries combined with archaeology and mapping are the best techniques for recovering community history.

## Close Proximity to Larger, Better Documented Underground Railroad Activity

Whether in Alton, Illinois, or Salem, New Jersey, the history of better known abolitionist havens overshadows small Black communities and their churches. Abolitionist and Underground Railroad activity generally operated within a two- to three-mile radius of small Black enclaves, with identified Underground Railroad routes in the vicinity (see map 5). Routes, safe houses, and lookout points in addition to caves and other landscape features contributed to suspected or confirmed Underground Railroad action. Legal proceedings and runaway slave notices often pinpointed suspected destinations or sites of capture or detention. This pattern repeats itself across multiple regions. A better known abolitionist center was connected to each Black community in this study.

### *Cemeteries*

Where towns or churches no longer exist, tombstones and grave markers remain as the last vestiges of a once vital Black settlement. At times, flowering plants, daffodils or irises, or whatever the region and weather supported, poke through the choking weeds to serve as a grave tribute or to signal that this land was once cultivated. At Miller Grove and Rocky Fork in Illinois, inscriptions on gravestones provide genealogies for interrelated families living on the early Black frontier. Cemeteries mark free Black communities and connect them to the Underground Railroad.

U.S. Colored Troops graves point to the consistent dedication to freedom of the residents. To this day, cemeteries containing the graves of family members interspersed with the graves of Civil War veterans, Colored Troops or Infantrymen, remind the nation that the Civil War came at the end of a long line of strategies for freedom. The war marked the logical conclusion of the Underground Railroad movement. Nothing is more emblematic of the free Black community's commitment to freedom and equality than the Civil War graves and markers that stand as centurions, often the sole reminders in the landscape of the communities that came together to take a stand for the promise of America––freedom, equality, and democratic self-determination.

CHAPTER 6

# Rethinking African American Migration

## Escape as Migration

The caves, mountainous terrain, lookout points, and forests that provided isolated, difficult to penetrate landscapes for the residents of Rocky Fork or Miller Grove, or at Lick Creek or Poke Patch, characterize hallmarks of maroon communities formed by escaped slaves across the Black Atlantic. Escape of tens of thousands of freedom seekers fueled one of the most important migrations out of slavery. Physically fleeing bondage stands out as the captive's first response to oppression. This chapter looks at the relationship between migration, displacement, and the Underground Railroad movement. Migration, both voluntary and forced, courses through the Black experience.

### *Maroon Settlements*

From the earliest moments of the African diaspora, men and women fled slavery to reject their condition. Escape and the formation of settlements in southern swamps or forbidding, rugged terrain ranks as the most frequent response to slavery; fleeing was the solution of first resort. Maroon communities functioned as the diaspora's first free Black settlements. Whether in midwestern hills, the Great Dismal Swamp, the Florida bayou, or the remote regions of Cuba, Brazil, or Jamaica, communities of escaped slaves proclaimed their right to be free. Maroon communities began the progression to free Black settlements and the Underground Railroad.

Relatively large numbers of Black men and women demonstrated a willingness to live outside the nets of White law and order.[1] For Sundiata Keitha Cha-Jua, maroon communities, freedom villages, and "organized Black communities" communicated the earliest expressions of "territorial Black nationalism," the initial vestiges of cohesive solidarity. In conveying "a living message" of the possibilities of freedom for those still held in captivity on plantations, farms, and homes, communities of self-liberated slaves undermined the slaveocracy in the same ways that escape from slavery and the Underground Railroad challenged slaveholders and lawmakers.[2]

Freedom's pioneers using the "first underground railroad" fled South Carolina by foot and moved through the swamps and marshes of coastal Georgia by dugout canoe to find freedom and protection in Spanish Florida.[3] Between 1672 and 1864, no fewer than fifty maroon colonies existed in the American South, foreshadowing the rise of the Underground Railroad.[4] Within the first decade of colonial rule, hastily written laws mandated brutal punishments for recaptured runaways. It took sustained military action to dislodge entrenched, self-liberated, freedom-appropriating maroon communities. Before Florida and Texas entered the Union as slave states in 1845, those lands offered sanctuary at America's foreign edges. In addition to domestic locations such as the Northwest Territory, refugees fled to Canada, primarily, but also to Mexico, the Caribbean, and South America. Africa and England also existed as possible sites of asylum, revealing a constant migration toward freedom beyond the narrow parameters of the Underground Railroad. Stamped with the image of fugitive slaves, these early maroon sites are generally not recognized among the first free Black settlements.

Fugitives appropriated and seized freedom rather than waiting for its bestowal, but it was freedom nevertheless. Lack of agreement on the numbers of escapees in the United States hampers accurate estimations. Some historians have claimed the number hovered near 40,000. Others think it more probable "that somewhere between 40,000 and 100,000 African Americans . . . found freedom." Analysis of the many different figures listed for runaways would constitute a study in itself. Donald Simpson observes that estimations for the total number of Blacks in Upper Canada range from 20,000 to 70,000 but he believes the figure is in the 40,000 range. Canadian historian Robin Winks cites an average of 60,000 refugees in Canada alone. These estimates do not consider the large numbers of escapes and displacements outside the traditional Underground Railroad.[5]

### *Migration and Displacement*

Black community formation and the Underground Railroad shifted between constant migration and displacement that began with the Middle Passage, moved through maroon settlements, took on an international scope during the American Revolution and the War of 1812, and progressed to the Underground Railroad. The last escapees from slavery filled contraband camps of the Civil War. African American migration after the war transformed into a people in search of family and kin, before moving on to the Great Migration of the twentieth century. This last migration has overshadowed all others. In *The Warmth of Other Suns: The Epic Story of America's Great Migration*, Isabel Wilkerson calls the Great Migration the "first mass act of independence by a people who were in bondage in this country for far longer than they have been free."[6]

The numbers of migrants out of slavery did not escalate into the millions and therefore may not be deserving of the word "great." Yet, if length of time carried as much as weight as numbers of people, the actions of runaways who were escaping oppression in response to slavery for more than two hundred years qualifies as heroic if not great. Escape from slavery stands beside the slave trade as the longest, if not the greatest migration of African peoples, two centuries before the Underground Railroad began to take shape and 250 years before the Great Migration of the twentieth century.

Three large pre–Civil War migrations occurred between the Middle Passage and the Great Migration: the mass exodus resulting from the Revolutionary War; the heart-wrenching displacements of the internal, domestic slave trade—forced migrations that moved millions of enslaved captives to the Deep South after the closing of the slave trade in 1808; and the dispersed, often individual, escapes culminating in the Underground Railroad.[7]

The American Revolution set in motion one of the largest migrations unrelated to the slave trade throughout the diaspora. At the end of the Revolutionary period, thousands of Black Americans who had fought for the British escaped with them to Nova Scotia in Canada. Other destinations beyond the colonies fueled a long tradition of international sanctuary from slavery that widened freedom seekers' options.

At the end of the war, the defeated British used *The Book of Negroes* to capture the names of the approximately 5,000 African American men, women, and children who fled America in fulfillment of Lord Dunmore's promise of freedom to Black loyalists who fought for the Crown. Another 3,000 or more sailed out of New York harbor with the Royal Navy. These figures do not reflect the hundreds of unregistered escapees who left New York and other ports onboard private vessels. Benjamin Quarles estimates that upwards of 15,000 Blacks claimed their freedom by evacuating with the British alone. Approximately another 5,000 had departed previously with the French.

After the Revolution, the domestic or internal slave trade continued the great displacement of millions of African captives set in motion by the closing of the international slave trade in 1808. Millions of enslaved men, women, and especially children were bought, sold, and traded to the Lower

South. The new nation changed from a society dependent on economic wealth derived from an enslaved workforce to a society tolerant of slavery in specific geographic locations; freedom became a place rather than a right as the domestic slave trade took root in the newly formed United States of America.[8]

As the frontier beckoned, Horace Greeley urged settlers to "Go West." With the expansion of the country, several factors affected migration. Blacks made their way westward in the nineteenth century to the Old Northwest territory and beyond to California. African Americans moved out of the South toward a dream of more racially tolerant frontier environments in Ohio, Indiana, and Illinois and anywhere else holding the promise of a better life.

## Emigration and Colonization Schemes

Emigration schemes of the pre–Civil War abolitionist era further influenced displacement and migration patterns, ranging from the American Colonization Society endeavors, to Quaker-sponsored mass departures, to Black Nationalist ventures to relocate Blacks in Liberia, Sierra Leone and Haiti.[9] Reactions to colonization and emigration ranged from despair to hope. At various times and for various reasons Blacks and Whites conceived of colonization and emigration as both a problem and a solution to the problems associated with the racist policies at the state and national levels.

The presence of free Blacks, and particularly their success, refuted the "truth" of claims about racialized inferiority espoused by so many of the nation's founders and leaders. A free Black presence in American society challenged the idea that "Black" and "slave" were necessarily synonymous and inferior. Free Blacks concentrated in northern and southern urban areas posed a danger, both real and imagined, to the slaveholders' efforts to maintain a tight grip on slavery.

White emigrationists saw colonization schemes to send Blacks mainly to Liberia as an ideal opportunity to rid the country of free people of color, considered a dangerous threat to the slaveholding republic. Steven Vincent pointed out that "Many North Carolina Friends viewed free people of color with considerable disdain and resentment, in part because of the heavy toll that the struggle against slavery had taken on the Quakers themselves." A number of Friends blamed Blacks, both slave and free, "for at least a portion of their problems and wished they could be entirely rid of their presence."[10]

The ever-increasing numbers of free Blacks in American society left White Americans to imagine multiple problems posed by their presence. Free people of color occupied a contradictory position in a society based on exploited labor from an enslaved population. Vincent explains, "If Blackness was inherent to slavery, then slavery could never be completely abolished unless Black skin itself could be abolished."[11]

Whites viewed free Blacks ambiguously, both as competition and as a burden to society. Fears of free Blacks and their perceived capacity to foment rebellion were heightened in the aftermath of Gabriel Prosser's rebellion near Richmond, Virginia, in 1800, leading Vice President Thomas Jefferson to consider colonization carefully. Jefferson believed that if Blacks were freed, they should reside in a distant colony beyond the limits of the United States on the northern boundary.[12]

As Carter Woodson indicates, there were other schemes to relocate Blacks on "a few thousand acres of land at some distant part of the national domains for the Negroes' accommodation and support." The Kentucky Abolition Society was interested in colonizing free people of color on public lands of the Northwest Territory.[13] Blacks, however, had already appropriated the land that became the Northwest Territory as a place of freedom, by escaping slavery and finding refuge there prior to the Revolutionary War.

Maryland began supporting the idea of colonization in 1816. The American Colonization Society (ACS) was, for a time, a most powerful leader in the emigration movement. Whites saw emigration as a chance to remove free Blacks from within their midst. For a time, abolitionists such as Quaker colonizer Benjamin Lundy and other southern Friends supported the work of the society. Between 1825 and 1831, the North Carolina yearly meeting, from which the Lick Creek Friends community migrated, was particularly interested in colonization. Quakers embraced what were essentially deportation solutions of the ACS, contributing more than $2,000 and fitting a vessel, which sailed carrying 119 emigrants from Beaufort, North Carolina, to Haiti.[14] In 1826, the Greensborough *Patriot*, reporting on the manumission and colonization efforts of the Guilford County Friends in North Carolina, noted, "120 Blacks were going to Haiti, 316 to Liberia, and 100 to the non-slave-holding states of Ohio and Indiana. Eleven had already gone to Africa, forty-seven to Liberia and sixty-four to Ohio."[15] By 1836, however, the Indiana yearly meeting of Orthodox Friends warned its members against joining any association that advocated colonization as "the unrighteous work of expatriation."[16] By 1838, Quakers reached the apex of their antislavery development, moving away from a gradualist mentality toward abolitionism. As it became clear that the ACS plans were little more than deportation schemes, Quaker support waned.

An article from a Richmond, Indiana, paper reported free Blacks arriving at the instigation of the North Carolina Society of Friends, and expressed the hope "that the Negroes will either be retained there [North Carolina] or transported to Hayti or Africa."[17] By 1848, when North Carolina Quakers saw their work as largely complete, 525 Blacks had been sent to free states, 681 to Haiti, and 479 to Liberia for a total of 1,685 people.[18] Colonization tactics resulted, in part, from reluctance on the part of some Quakers to live among freed Blacks with prejudice in Indiana equaling that in North Carolina.

As an outgrowth of the anti-colonization movement in the east, Underground Railroad, abolitionist activities, and antislavery sentiment brought structure and unity to Black abolitionism. Black leaders convened the first national Black convention as a response to colonization attempts. Members stood firm against the ACS, evoking nationalist rhetoric. "However great the debt which these United States may owe to injured Africa . . . we who have been born and nurtured on this soil, we, whose habits, manners, and customs are the same in common with other Americans," would never consent to the emigration schemes of the society.[19]

Alarmed by the enactment of laws against Blacks in several states, particularly Ohio, the first article of the constitution of the earliest Black national convention held in Philadelphia in 1830 recommended the formation and establishment of a Parent Society "for the purpose of purchasing land, and locating a settlement in the Province of Upper Canada." The convention over which Richard Allen presided was interested in affording a place of refuge "to those who may be obliged to leave their homes, as well as to others inclined to emigrate with the view of improving their condition."[20]

For more than thirty years, the concept of self-governance through emigration circulated intermittently within the Black community as a solution to American racial policies. Black Nationalists formed the opposite side of the colonization equation. Early in the nineteenth century, Massachusetts Black Nationalist Paul Cuffee transported several Black families to Liberia. Cuffee was part of the first wave of Black Nationalist "back to Africa" movements viewing African emigration as a commitment to the universal improvement of the African condition.[21]

For decades, legal sanctions resulting from slave revolts also drove African American migration. Gabriel Prosser's Rebellion in 1800 and Nat Turner's 1831 insurrection heightened fears and catalyzed deportation schemes. John Brown's attack on Harpers Ferry also held numerous implications for Black migration. After November 1859, Arkansas, the first state to react, passed legislation ordering free Blacks to leave the state by the start of the New Year or face reenslavement. Some exiled Arkansans went west. In 1860, Minnesota considered similar measures barring Blacks from coming into the state and requiring registration of those already there, but the measure was defeated. Indicating the scope of the problem, the Pennsylvania state legislature also considered several proposals in early 1863 designed to prevent Blacks from settling in the state.[22]

Between 1850 and the eve of the Civil War, emigration movements to Africa, Haiti, Central America, and the West Indies proliferated among African American male leadership.[23] Demonstrating the prevalence and concern for such issues, by 1853 and after much discussion and modification, the First Convention of the Colored Citizens of the State of Illinois regarded "all schemes of colonizing the free colored people of the United States to Africa, or any other foreign land, as most wicked attempts of Southern slaveholders and their Northern abettors to force us from our native homes, and by that means perpetuate slavery in this country . . . We will plant our trees in American soil, and repose in the shade thereof."[24]

Yet Haiti loomed large in the Black imagination. Black Nationalist J. T. Holly promoted Haiti over Canada as an asylum from American slavery. Martin Delany preferred Liberia and Henry Highland Garnet eventually chose to emigrate permanently to Jamaica. England, too, provided a welcoming, financially lucrative mooring, even if only temporarily, for several of America's most famous escapees.[25]

By the end of the Civil War, the push to remove African Americans from their country did not end with the Union victory. With the aid and support of the ACS, President Abraham Lincoln attempted to implement several colonization efforts. Black communities around the country, with White abolitionists and government officials, strongly opposed the administration's plans, which ultimately met with little support and major criticism.[26]

Slaveholders tried to bind manumission to emigration, particularly in their last will and testaments. Death of the slaveholder and subsequent manumissions by last will and testament often meant disruption and movement for the newly freed. During the slaveholders' dying moments, many attempted to absolve themselves of a lifetime of slaveholding by granting freedom to those they had held in bondage. Both free Black communities and the Underground Railroad were shaped by forced migrations that often resulted.

At Miller Grove a postmortem manumission by William Sheppard released Jeremiah Sheppard from the grasp of slavery in 1835. Aspects of Jeremiah's story highlight the community experiences of newly free Blacks. His enslaver followed the ACS attempts to yoke manumission with emigration, primarily to Liberia. "Some emancipators forced their slaves to migrate by giving them a choice between Liberia and bondage." Sheppard's will stipulated that Jerry should serve the slaveholder's estate for "three years and afterwards should be hired out or hire himself until he had acquired money sufficient to transport himself and wife Dinah to Liberia."[27]

Jerry not only obtained the funds to finance the trip to Liberia, he also purchased the freedom of his wife. Jeremiah "procured money sufficient for his removal but owing to changes in the management of the colony of Liberia and difficulty of procuring a passage there" he decided to go to one of the free states. To overcome the difficulty of obtaining his free papers, Sheppard gave bond and security as assurance that he would leave the state of Tennessee where he had been manumitted in twenty days as the law required. After ten years, the literate freedman and his wife migrated to Illinois, where he opted to "spend the remainder of his days preaching the gospel" and spreading the word of God as an AME preacher. Sheppard bought several parcels of land in Miller Grove.[28]

## Agrarian Settlements and Experiments

For Blacks, agriculture and land ownership were paths to freedom and an opportunity to demonstrate self-reliance while refuting racist myths of Black inferiority. After the 1830s, a few Black abolitionists took an Americanist stance and began encouraging resettlement on the American frontier. They claimed that separate communities offered Blacks a "sanctuary from discrimination without abandoning their American birthright."[29] The idea lingered and resurfaced from time to time. Sundiata Keitha Cha-Jua estimated a hundred or so Black towns developed in the United States between the early 1800s and the mid-1900s.[30] A detailed study could uncover more. Several of the settlements remained viable into the third quarter of the twentieth century.

Land ownership also provided the ability to offer much-needed sanctuary. Lewis Woodson, following in his parents' footsteps in Ohio, established a Black settlement in Jackson County, Ohio. He argued for land ownership; becoming "*owners* and *cultivators* of the soil" was the key to empowerment. "The possession of houses and lands, and flocks and herds, inspires the possessor with a nobleness and independence of feeling, unknown to those in any other business." Land ownership offered independence, the "*unmolested* enjoyment of the privileges of social life, the ability to establish churches on land controlled by congregants, a refuge and a home for extended families."[31]

An 1838 article in the *Colored American* sparked a discussion of the virtues of Black agrarianism. Lewis Woodson wondered whether it was wise to begin such settlements within the jurisdiction of the United States, or any of the individual states. Frederick Douglass also found the agrarian movement problematic, citing the difficulty of getting Blacks to undertake scattered settlements across the landscape, as they often preferred to congregate in large towns and cities. The great abolitionist thought slavery inculcated a lack of self-reliance, leaving Blacks unsuited "to go into the western wilderness, and there to lay the foundation of future society."[32] Douglass also saw agrarian experiments as a band-aid, stating that agricultural pursuits were no remedy for the evils of poverty and ignorance in which so many people of color found themselves.[33]

The idea of agrarian settlements persisted. Black state conventions of colored citizens followed the lead of the national meetings. By 1841, the idea of Black farming and community formation was on the agenda of the state-level convention held in Pittsburgh. Members Lewis Woodson and Martin Delany held the opinion that no calling was "more honorable, independent, and virtuous, than farming." To those who could not become successful mechanics, they encouraged, work the land.[34]

Emancipated men and women from Virginia and North Carolina helped establish dozens of flourishing Black farming settlements in Ohio and Indiana between 1808 and the Civil War. Moved by their success, the Black national convention, held in Buffalo in 1843, recommended formation of Black farming settlements in Michigan, Illinois, Iowa, and Wisconsin and, as a result, sizable Black farming settlements took root by 1860. The Committee Upon Agriculture reported its plan for farmers and emigration to the West. "Let twenty families . . . with health, habits of industry, and economy, with intelligence, a sound moral and religious character, with respect for and confidence and interest in each other, who agree, as far as can be, on all great questions of fundamental morality unite together . . . to settle, each adjoining the other, on his own purchased farm, and thus form one neighborhood." The farmers were expected "to unite together in all matters of public interest that are for the good of the whole; such as schools, and churches, roads and bridges." Community members were to "care for each other's welfare" and share alike in "the sorrows and the joys, in the privileges and the privations, and to seek the one, to build up the other as he would himself."[35] For decades prior to the committee's report, African Americans had been migrating west and forming such communities, particularly in Ohio.

The agricultural well-being of the people in the southern section of Illinois stood as a key concern among those gathered at the First Convention of the Colored Citizens of the State of Illinois held in Chicago in 1853.[36] Delegates resolved that people throughout the state "become owners of land, to build houses, and cultivate the soil, as the surest means of making themselves and families independent and respectable." The convention recommended people of color obtain "an interest in the soil," cultivating and improving it whenever it was in their power to do so, believing this to be one of the most powerful means of elevation in the country.[37] After the outbreak of the Civil War, the agricultural plans resurfaced in the hope of yielding an answer to the question of what to do with the freedmen. Black migration, once again, became the solution to the multiple concerns resulting from the aftermath of slavery as well as continuing legal and government-sanctioned racial policies.

## White Philanthropic Abolitionism and Quaker Settlements

Free or newly freed Blacks migrated out of the South with Quaker or Presbyterian abolitionists, former slaveholders, or White philanthropists in the first decades of the nineteenth century. Together, they established numerous midwestern communities. As early as 1773, Thomas Jefferson advocated establishing colonies for free Blacks. Along with George Washington, Jefferson believed Black colonies should be a precondition for emancipation. Between 1819 and the 1860s, White private individuals and organizations formed or aided communal efforts involving 3,500 to 5,000 Blacks. The communities extended from Pennsylvania to the states of the Old Northwest, to Virginia, Tennessee, and South Carolina, to British Columbia and Ontario, Canada.[38] William and Jane Pease overstate the impetus for the formation of organized Black settlements for newly emancipated slaves. They claim that direction came "entirely from White people strongly imbued with the simplest kind of philanthropic zeal."[39] Such a view negates the importance of African American initiatives at places such as New Philadelphia or the Roberts settlement in Indiana.

Although it took Quakers more than a century to reckon with their own slaveholding past, once they realized the implications of their ungodly behavior, the sect was a forceful leader in manumissions and in establishing settlements for freed men and women. Driven more by conscience than experience, experimental communities in Ohio, settlements in Indiana and settlements in Illinois reflect the Quaker commitment to bringing freedom to an enslaved population. Other religious-minded abolitionists such as the New School Presbyterians associated with Miller Grove also purchased land for settlements. At Miller Grove, Lick Creek, and Poke Patch, plans went beyond simple emancipation and resettlement; the communities included both free people of color and their former oppressors, or the former slaveholders lived nearby.

## Freedom through Self-Purchase

The economics of freedom left deep financial scars on the African American family. Self-purchase and buying the freedom of family members throughout the pre–Civil War period substantially depleted the Black community's financial resources. The economic drain of self-purchase added another layer of burden to a heavily strained community. Personal freedom—to own oneself—represented an enormous, expensive, personal and financial asset.

Mother Baltimore, founder of Mother Baltimore's Freedom Village in Brooklyn, Illinois, had been bought and sold numerous times in her life, passing from slaveholder to slaveholder from Kentucky to Louisiana. A Methodist minister, the last in a string of purchasers, permitted her to live under quasi-free circumstances, allowing her to work and retain the earnings. Baltimore took seven years to accumulate the money to purchase herself and obtain her precious freedom papers. Upon obtaining her freedom around 1820, she initially moved to Cincinnati, eventually moving on to Fredericktown, Missouri, where her mother and father were living. Baltimore first harshly berated her slaveholding father for selling her and then managed to purchase her mother's freedom. The two settled in St. Louis, where Baltimore earned a decent living working as a ladies nurse. The resourceful Baltimore also provided the money for her second husband, John Tobias Baltimore, to buy his freedom by mortgaging her home in St. Louis. Shortly thereafter, she lost the home to foreclosure in the late 1830s and then they relocated to Brooklyn.[40]

Depending on location and circumstances, different families faced a host of challenges. Frank McWorter demonstrated his willingness to work within the legal parameters that ruled his life. Unlike Josiah Henson, who escaped slavery by fleeing with his family after a failed attempt to purchase his freedom, Frank chose the legally prudent and equally arduous solution of paying for his family's freedom rather than appropriating it. Frank was forced to constantly evaluate the worth of his family as he purchased his freedom and the freedom of his enslaved wife and children. His unobtrusive act of self-purchase yielded the coveted papers of freedom made necessary by the Black Codes of Illinois.

In 1836, McWorter established the racially integrated farming community of New Philadelphia, Illinois, on the nation's midwestern frontier. After purchasing land to start the new community, McWorter raised money by selling lots to newcomers, both Black and White. Situated twenty miles east of the Mississippi River in the rolling hills of the Pike County countryside, New Philadelphia helped this entrepreneurial free Black man shape the West as part of his journey from slavery in Kentucky to freedom in Illinois. McWorter had endured forty-two years of slavery, first in his South Carolina birthplace and later on the Kentucky frontier.[41]

In addition to income derived from his labors, and commercial farming, McWorter accumulated a portion of the money for the price of freedom of family members from the profits realized from subdividing his land holdings and selling the lots. Land ownership was an important strategy, enabling McWorter to guarantee the coveted legacy of freedom for the majority of his family members. Throughout a forty-year period, Frank weighed each purchase and was shrewd enough to secure his own freedom and the freedom of sixteen family members at a total cost of $14,000.[42] The slave system extracted a heavy toll on the Black family, one that required placing a hierarchical as well as a financial value on loved ones. Choosing who received freedom first was a business as well as an emotional decision. With each purchase, Frank had to face a dilemma—whom to purchase next. Should he free the men, who had greater earning capacity, or free the women before they bore more children, thereby increasing the total expenditure?

Frank secured his wife's freedom first, ensuring the baby she was carrying could be born in freedom and relieving him of the expense of purchasing his child. It was a decision Frank had to face each time he paid another family member's ransom of slavery, or faced an enslaver's refusal to release a loved one. The difficult decision-making process was clearest in McWorter's efforts in freeing his grandchildren. The system of slavery was so self-perpetuating that at the age of sixty-nine, McWorter had set aside enough funds to purchase the freedom of six additional grandchildren. By 1850, two grandchildren and the wife of his son, Squire, were freed. By 1854, he had purchased the freedom of nine of his family members.[43]

The McWorters attained economic stability and amassed money enough to finance freedom for multiple generations. Despite his best efforts, Frank McWorter never secured the freedom of his granddaughter, Charlotte, or her children. After paying more than $14,000 to ransom his family, upon Frank's death at the age of seventy-seven, despite his Herculean efforts, "he had not lived to see the achievement of his dream that his entire family be free from slavery."[44] By 1859, however, the financial legacy he built during his lifetime ensured that his dream became a reality. His son, Solomon, completed the four-generation quest with the purchase of Charlotte, who had given birth to another child, and her children with monies realized from the sale of family-held farmland and New Philadelphia town lots.[45]

Free Frank's investment in land was one among several moneymaking ventures Blacks used to raise funds to free enslaved relatives. After Josiah Henson had been swindled out of the money he had raised through preaching to pay for his freedom, he decided that escape was the only alternative left for him and his family. Runaways such as Henson published autobiographies with the expectation of using the proceeds to purchase the freedom of relatives left behind in bondage. Moses Grandy's narrative was "sold for the benefit of his relations still in slavery."[46] As literary historian Charles Nichols points out, "they wrote to correct impressions rather than to make them."[47]

Neither economic status nor gender predicted who would purchase their freedom. The enslaved chose self-purchase over escape far more frequently than records indicate. Denmark Vesey purchased his freedom. The father of Peter Williams, rector of St. Philip's Church in New York City, purchased his freedom, as did the father of William Still. Still's brother, Peter, purchased his own freedom and then embarked on a fundraising tour to buy his family after the tragic events leading to the failed escape attempt. Elizabeth Freeman, Andrew Bryan, Lunsford Lane, John Parker, and Elizabeth Keckley, among many others, bought their way out of slavery although they remained in the slave states varying lengths of time after procuring their emancipation.[48]

Men no less accomplished than Richard Allen and Absalom Jones shared the same fate as New Philadelphia's Free Frank McWorter, a man who was not taught to read or write. Although McWorter's accomplishments in purchasing sixteen members of his family at a cost of $14,000[49] may be an unsurpassed accomplishment, particularly for one who signed with an "X," numerous men and women amassed financial resources enough to rescue loved ones from slavery. Paying $2,000 each, Richard Allen ransomed his own and his brother's freedom from Stockley Sturgis of Dover, Delaware, in 1785. It took Allen five years, paying on installments, to gather together the money, the bulk of which came from his earnings as a wagon driver during the Revolutionary War.[50] The remainder he earned by sawing cordwood and making bricks. John Malvin used his earnings as a canal-boat operator to secure the freedom of his father-in-law. Noted New York City hairdresser Pierre Toussaint purchased his wife and sister. Walter Freeman, after purchasing his own freedom, secured the liberty of his wife and six children, paying $2,550 to his enslaver, George Badger, secretary of the navy under President William Henry Harrison.[51]

Women who had the financial wherewithal purchased their husbands, mothers, and children as well as themselves.[52] Alethia Tanner bought her four nieces. Sarah Orr, Fanny Jackson's (Coppin) devoted aunt, purchased her freedom during Jackson's early childhood. Enterprising Hester Lane of New York City first secured her own freedom and then went on to pay for the freedom of ten others with the expectation that they would repay their purchase price in installments.[53]

In 1837 alone, of the 18,768 Blacks in Philadelphia, Pennsylvania, 254 had purchased their freedom by paying an average of $278. Cincinnati saw even higher proportions of self-purchasers.[54] Of the 1,129 Blacks in that city during the 1830s, 475 had purchased themselves at an average cost of more than $450, which amounts to a cost of approximately $11,000 in twenty-first-century dollars. In an 1834 letter that revealed the heartache and agony of self-purchase, White abolitionist Theodore Weld wrote to philanthropist Lewis Tappan:

> Of the almost 3,000 Blacks in Cincinnati, more than three-fourths of the adults are emancipated slaves, who worked out their own freedom. Many are now paying for themselves under large securities. Besides these, multitudes are toiling to purchase their friends, who are now in slavery.
>
> I visited this week about 30 families, and found that some members of more than half these families were still in bondage, and the father, mother and children were struggling to lay up money enough to purchase their freedom. I found one man who had just finished paying for his wife and five children. Another man and wife had bought themselves some years ago, have been working night and day to purchase their children; they had just redeemed the last and had paid for themselves and children 1,400 dollars! Another woman had recently paid the last installment of the purchase money for her husband. She had purchased him by taking in washing, and working late at night, after going out and performing as help at hard labor.[55]

Henry Boyd, one of Cincinnati's most distinguished businessmen, accumulated a $420,000 fortune as a bedstead manufacturer, and applied portions of these proceeds to help secure the freedom of others. After first working day and night to purchase his freedom, Boyd went on to secure the liberty of his brother and sister in addition to a number of people unrelated to him.[56]

Few existing statistics enumerate the vast sums spent by the enslaved population and free people of color to purchase their freedom and the freedom of their loved ones. Limited accounting in Philadelphia in 1847 found 275 formerly enslaved residents purchased their freedom at a cost of more than $60,000.[57] The price of buying one's way out of slavery, the costs of an array of bonds enforced by Black Codes, and the financial demands piled on a population historically forced to work for no pay lays bare the tremendous cost of freedom. The level of financial burden for Frank McWorter amounts to a vast sum—approximately $400,000 in twenty-first-century dollars.[58]

Juliet Walker, Frank McWorter's great-great-granddaughter, clearly understood that "Blacks who purchased their freedom learned that the social costs of freedom were not included in the price of manumission."[59] Self-purchasers found themselves in a financial conundrum that required them to participate in the economic exploitation of their own enslavement in order to gain their freedom. Often the threat of reenslavement or kidnapping jeopardized whatever tenuous freedom or security they managed to purchase. Self-purchase and purchase of family members were slavery's extortion.

Buying one's freedom and the freedom of those held most dear was a consistent escape strategy. Slavery's captives worked diligently to acquire the financial means to meet freedom's ransom. Thriftiness, financial acumen, and economic self-control in addition to shrewdness and industriousness were requirements for obtaining the financial means of liberation. Self-purchase achieved legal release from slavery not included in the concept of escape from slavery. At the risk of reenslavement, fines, imprisonment, and violent attack, African Americans used newly acquired freedom to settle in the landscape and begin to effect the freedom of their brethren. Decisions to escape slavery could be driven by a complex, thorny jumble of painful considerations. When self-purchase was not an option or the tremendous sums unavailable, and the desire for freedom burned, then escape and the Underground Railroad became viable alternatives.

## Legal Dictates and Migration

### *Pre–Civil War Black Codes*

The laws of the United States had a tremendous impact on the migration of African Americans. Westward expansion of the country began in earnest with the formation of Ohio, Indiana, Illinois, Michigan, and Wisconsin, the states of the Northwest Ordinance. These states, along with Oregon and Nebraska, implemented Black codes that perpetuated "raced" places in the landscape. The three earliest settled states of the Northwest Territory—Ohio, Indiana, and Illinois—sanctioned legal discriminations against free Blacks until the eve of the Civil War.[60] Most states did the same.

As territories, the three major states resulting from the ordinance, Ohio, Indiana, and Illinois, instituted and enforced rigorous Black Codes requiring a $500 bond ensuring that the individual would not become a county charge. A subsequent act called for a six-month indenture and then removal of anyone unable to pay bond security. States adopted restrictive measures designed to prohibit or at least discourage the migration of free Blacks into the state. Much of the story presented here emerged from descriptions contained in required bonds and indentures mandated by the Black Codes and posted by Blacks migrating into Illinois and Indiana.[61]

To understand the climate that greeted blacks escaping into Ohio one need only look to 1839, when Ohio enacted its own Fugitive Slave Law more extreme than the federal law of 1793. Between 1829 through the late 1840s, White mobs directed four major attacks against Cincinnati's African American residents. Trustees of Cincinnati, alarmed by the increasing influx of Blacks making their way to the fertile bottomlands of the Ohio River, issued a proclamation in 1829 ordering Blacks to comply with a little enforced provision requiring people of color to produce certificates and give bonds. After Blacks resisted enforcement of the code, White rioters burned tenements in Cincinnati's "Little Africa." Older Blacks armed themselves with guns and planned their defense.

The Black Code prompted former Virginia bondsman James C. Brown to form a society to protest these laws and take necessary action to protect the interests of the Black people of Cincinnati. He wrote the lieutenant-governor of Upper Canada seeking asylum and requesting permission to establish a settlement in the province. The riot ultimately displaced 1,200 of Cincinnati's Black residents, forcing them to flee to Michigan, western Pennsylvania, New York, and Canada West where they established the settlement of Wilberforce. [62]

Even the freeborn who had never experienced slavery could not escape the consequences of the Black Codes. As a free person of color, Frances Ellen Watkins Harper, for example, felt unable to return to her native Maryland after the state no longer allowed free Blacks to reside there after passage of an 1853 law.[63] California passed laws discouraging or prohibiting free people of color from settling within the state.[64] As Harper observed, "Indiana shuts her doors upon us. Illinois denies us admission to her prairie homes. Oregon refuses us an abiding place for the soles of our weary feet. And even Minnesota has our exclusion under consideration."[65] Frederick Douglass said of the Black Law of Illinois, "it would seem that the men who enacted that law had not only banished from their minds all sense of justice, but all sense of shame."[66]

### *Fugitive Slave Legislation*

Federal Fugitive Slave Laws were the single most important legislation responsible for pre–Civil War African American migration through escape and the growth of the Underground Railroad. From the drafting of the

U.S. Constitution through the Civil War, repeated laws indicate that the recapture of escaped slaves was uppermost on the minds of statesmen. The ineffectiveness of the Fugitive Slave Clause in the U.S. Constitution led to a second, more comprehensive act in 1793. It was followed by the Missouri Compromise of 1820, which contained its own legislation designed to impose more severe penalties for fleeing. Law after law provides the surest measure of the will to escape.

The Missouri Compromise firmly established freedom as a place. Amid mounting tensions, the state of Missouri had been admitted to the Union as a slave state as part of the Compromise. Coinciding with the gradual abolition of slavery in the northern states, an imaginary line, popularly known as the Mason-Dixon Line, geographically distinguished north from south. With the exception of the boundaries for the proposed state of Missouri, any portions north of the line would be free of slavery.

Following the 1793 Fugitive Slave Act, the 1820 act again stipulated that slaveholders could lawfully reclaim captives escaping into any state or territory of the United States and return them to slavery. The terms applied in free territories and slave states alike. The Compromise helped slavery maintain a vice-like grip on the growing republic, opening a national chasm that engulfed the nation. Most Blacks and abolitionists strongly opposed the Compromise. The majority of Americans embraced it, however, believing that it finally offered a workable solution to the slavery question. Maintaining a balanced number of free states and slave states appeased southern slaveholders. With passage of the Fugitive Slave Act as part of the Missouri Compromise, the Underground Railroad began the long climb toward its peak years, 1850 to 1865.[67]

African Americans had to be aware of the extended reach of state law. Laws enacted in one state affected their freedom and mobility in another. In 1832, the Virginia legislature passed a law offering a $50 reward and 20 cents per mile traveled to anyone apprehending a Virginia escapee in Ohio, Pennsylvania, or Indiana. A person returning escapees from New England or New York received $120 plus traveling expenses. In 1829–30, the threat of slave catchers forced Henry Highland Garnet's family to scatter. His father, George, had fled slavery in Maryland and built a successful shoemaking business in New York City's Five Points area. He managed to escape kidnapping only by climbing out a window and jumping twenty feet from the upper story of their home at 137 Leonard Street into his neighbor's yard. The Garnets lived next door to Black abolitionist Alexander Crummell, who sheltered the father. The elder Garnet barely eluded slave catchers who had tracked him to his doorstep even in that metropolis.[68]

## *The Fugitive Slave Law of 1850*

The Fugitive Slave Act of 1850 added another layer that escalated the forced migration of people of color. Of all the bills that made up the Compromise of 1850, the Fugitive Slave Act was easily the most controversial and the most hated. Black Chicagoans, led by John Jones, rallied at the AME church there and declared their deep resolve to resist every attempt to return any Black person to bondage. "We are determined to defend ourselves at all hazards, even should it be to the shedding of human blood. We who have tasted *freedom* are ready to exclaim in the language of the brave Patrick Henry, 'Give us liberty or give us death.'"[69]

Backed by the power of the U.S. government overseeing the process, the Fugitive Slave Law of 1850 was intended to make it easier to recapture runaways. Increasingly Ohio and other northern states had grown obstinate in returning escapees. The federal government assumed responsibility for enforcement of the statute, and financial incentives propped up the legislation. The act deputized American citizens and forced them to assist in the recovery of fugitive slaves. The act not only made it a criminal offense for any American who failed to help slave catchers, "but to withhold knowledge he might possess of any chance meeting with the fugitive."[70] The act criminalized as fugitives numerous men and women who previously had fled slavery. For those attempting to build lives in the North, the new law was disastrous.

The 1850 law stripped away the last vestiges of due process and was a shocking capitulation of the government to slaveholders. Marshals who were made liable for captives who escaped their custody could legally demand assistance from any citizen. Legal historian Stephen Middleton observed that the law turned federal marshals along with the public into strategically stationed "de facto slave catchers" across the North. Burden of proof hung on captured escapees who were then denied legal power to prove their freedom.

After passage of the law, AME Bishop Daniel Payne personally visited Canada, where well-established escapee Rev. Josiah Henson took him on a tour to determine if "Canada would be a safe asylum for our people."[71] Frederick Douglass said he reached the crisis of his religious life when the Fugitive Slave Bill became a law and the nation became "the enslaver's hunting ground."[72]

The law emboldened and sanctioned kidnappers whose former endeavors now developed into a full-scale enterprise of pursuing free Blacks under the pretense of acting on behalf of aggrieved slaveholders while secretly preparing to sell the captives at auction. At least two AME bishops had narrow escapes from kidnappers and faced the harsh possibility of a lifetime of enslavement. Kidnapping attempts forced both Richard Allen and William Paul Quinn to stare into the mouth of the beast.[73]

Bishop Quinn thought the law more evil than slavery itself. He understood the greed and self-interest of slaveholders but the actions of the federal government "left him choking with rage."[74] With the law came more formal, organized, institutional efforts to assist escapees; moving them through the landscape became more efficient, enabling ever greater numbers of escapes.

At the country's western edge, the Compromise of 1850 allowed California to enter the Union as a free state as one of five compromises. Despite California's inhospitable racial climate and the ambiguities of its law, Blacks viewed the state as another opportunity to escape bondage and migrated there. By 1852, however, proslavery California legislators passed a Fugitive Slave Law allowing White slaveholders to claim escaped slaves within the state. Legislators renewed the law in 1853 and 1854 before allowing it to lapse a year later.

The Fugitive Slave Act revealed the constancy and magnitude with which the enslaved population resorted to flight as an antidote to the poison of slavery. The law exposed the tenacity of the spirit of freedom. Historians understood that the Fugitive Slave Law allowed "some of the most repugnant features of slavery into the heart of Northern cities and towns" and "pushed both Black and White abolitionists into openly avowed and preconcerted" acts of defiance.[75]

Arrests and aggressive enforcement sparked mass exodus among those who had escaped slavery, sometimes years earlier. Like his father before him, Henry Highland Garnet was considered a fugitive. He first left the country, migrating to Great Britain, and then Canada, before ultimately moving to Jamaica in the West Indies. The more famous fugitive slave cases bring to light the destructive effects of the law for the Black community and the moral dilemma it inflicted on people of conscience by imposing a $1,000 fine or six-month prison sentence for aiding escapees.[76]

The Fugitive Slave Act heightened tensions between escapee and would-be captor. Residents surrounding Miller Grove openly sought the cash rewards offered for capturing runaways. The reward incentive made life treacherous at New Philadelphia in Pike County, Illinois, as well. The threat of slave catchers in the county presented an unrelenting danger for the family McWorter had succeeded in freeing. "Whether his family would retain their freedom remained a persistent and fearful question," reported Juliet Walker.[77]

The laws, restrictive slave codes enacted by most states, and the countless fugitive slave advertisements posted by slaveholders seeking their return attest to the magnitude of the problem of escape.[78] After the Fugitive Slave Law's inception, Henry Bibb witnessed the consequences—migration from Indiana into Canada. He reported in 1852, "The Fugitive Slave Law is driving out brains and money." The law resounded "like a drumbeat on the path to the Civil War."[79]

Frances Ellen Watkins Harper, considered by William Still "as one of the ablest advocates of the Underground Rail Road," labeled the Fugitive Slave Law of 1850 "that abomination of the nineteenth-century." Designed to force northern states to recognize southern claims to free labor of enslaved Africans, "it was one of the most unpopular and assailable laws ever passed by a Congress of the United States." After the law passed, Harriet Tubman's sentiments were clear: she could no longer trust Uncle Sam with her people. She began taking them all the way to Canada.[80]

## O Canada!

The first antislavery law facilitating the gradual disappearance of slavery in Canada passed in 1793. No new slaves could be brought into the province. Slaves reaching the province under their own effort as well as all slaves brought in by slaveholders obtained immediate freedom. That same year the newly formed United States enacted the earliest of several Fugitive Slave Laws. Following the Canadian legislation, a small number of American Blacks fled to Canada.[81]

Neighboring and accessible to the United States, Canada stood at the forefront as the most expedient site of refuge. As a group, American and Canadian Black colonies had similar structures and functions. The organized communities established permanent homes, providing platforms for civic responsibility, political cohesion, and, in particular, the education of children.[82]

Once freedom seekers arrived in Canada, Martin Delany advised them to "purchase all the land they possibly can" while the property sold at low rates, in anticipation of the day when "like the lands in the United States generally . . . they may be prevented entirely from settling or purchasing . . . the preference being given to a White applicant."[83] Purchase and ownership of land fulfilled the promise on the masthead of Mary Ann Shadd Carey's Canadian newspaper, *Provincial Freeman*: "Self reliance is the true road to independence."[84] Expatriated Blacks who arrived after the American Revolution made Birchtown and Shelburne in Nova Scotia among their first destinations in Canada after the war. Some among this "first mass group of emancipated African Americans" eventually left Canada and made their way to Sierra Leone, West Africa.[85]

The establishment of the Wilberforce community in Canada grew out of the Cincinnati riots and the Black convention movement.[86] Blacks migrating to Canada established settlements in numerous towns, such as Amherstburg, Toronto, Buxton, and St. Catharines, all of which were Underground Railroad destinations. In addition to these towns, Blacks settled in Dawn, Colchester, and Elgin (Buxton). Dresden, Windsor, and Sandwich received African Americans as did Queens Bush, Wilberforce, and Hamilton. Chatham was a popular destination in addition to the lesser known towns of Riley, Anderton, London, Malden, and Gonfield[87] (see map 1).

When the United States would not concede liberty, justice, and equality, Blacks migrated across the country and around the globe in a relentless search for emancipation, autonomy, and freedom. Whether Florida, the Great Dismal Swamp. or Mexico, no location was thought inappropriate. Fleeing to Africa, Europe, the West Indies, or Central America in addition to Canada forced the international community to bear witness to the racial policies of the United States and its support of slavery. The Underground Railroad offered the immediate, local, incremental solution to the consequences and the aftermath of the African slave trade.

# PART III
# Family, Faith, and Fraternity

The final section fits together the pieces of the Underground Railroad puzzle to form a new understanding of how the Black family, church, and community operated as a powerful yet often unrecognized engine within the movement. Chapter 7 connects family, church, and community. Chapter 8 extends beyond the boundaries of community and church. The chapter focuses on pre–Civil War national political and fraternal organizations that operated through Black community leaders. Many of those at the forefront of leadership in the Black church and community knew through personal experience what it took to escape slavery. Their names repeatedly turn up in Underground Railroad narratives comingled with free Black leaders across the country.

CHAPTER 7

# Family, Church, Community

## Pillars of the Black Underground Railroad Movement

African American communities connected through family relations and intermarriage, church organizations, benevolent societies, and the fraternal structure of the Prince Hall Masons. Despite the fact that the average escapee from slavery was a young single male, maintaining family connections motivated escapes, particularly when imminent sale threatened to break up the family. Black family members understood the costs of freedom and stalwartly offered aid to escapees so they too could taste its fruits. Free Blacks, or self-liberated men and women, succeeded in purchasing freedom for themselves and their loved ones. At times, they also had the wherewithal to purchase land to establish towns and settlements or migrate to areas where other free Blacks had settled.

## The Black Family

African American antislavery families supported the Underground Railroad. Children inherited their parents' activism, brothers and sisters worked together; whole families cooperated in rescue efforts. Activists such as Harriet Tubman and Priscilla Baltimore, Lewis Woodson and John Mercer Langston, and many of the other prominent Black abolitionists had intimate knowledge of free Black communities because they had either lived there or had relatives who continued to settle in Black enclaves across the country.

Daughters as well as sons followed the lead of their families. Mary Ann Shadd Cary, famed editor of *The Provincial Freeman*, was heavily influenced by her father, Abraham D. Shadd, whom she described as a "chief brakeman" on the Delaware Underground Railroad. He opened his home in Wilmington to escapees, and continued his Underground Railroad work later when he moved the family to a farm in West Chester, Pennsylvania.[1]

Harriet Tubman also came under the powerful influence of her father, Ben Ross, and relied on his aid, particularly in engineering the escape of her two brothers from Maryland's Dorchester County on Christmas Day, 1854. Tubman's biographer, Kate Larson pieced together the details of the intricately planned escape missions. Complex networks of Black and White supporters helped Tubman achieve her goals. "Tubman relied heavily upon a long established, intricate, and secretive web of communication and support among African Americans to effect her rescues," observed Larson. "The collective efforts of free and enslaved African Americans operating beyond the scrutiny of whites along the various routes to freedom were crucial to her success . . . it was the African American community from the Eastern Shore of Maryland and the Chesapeake Bay to Delaware, Pennsylvania, New York, New England, and Canada that provided the protection, communication and sustenance she required during the darkest and most dangerous days of fighting for freedom."[2] Flight from slavery, often with close relatives escaping together, underscores the importance of family unity.

Several famous family escapes took place in Maryland. Black abolitionist Henry Highland Garnet had been a mere nine years old when he was literally carried out of slavery. A group of eleven, including his parents, relatives, and sibling, escaped from New Market. After the young Garnet grew exhausted and could no longer keep pace, he was carried on the backs of the more able. Eventually the family made its way to Thomas Garrett in Delaware, who put them on the Underground Railroad. Garnet forgot neither the 1824 escape nor the subsequent family hardships stemming from attempts by slave catchers to recapture his parents and sister in New York City. While at Troy in upstate New York, a way station of the eastern route of the Underground Railroad, Garnet, by then a Presbyterian minister, claimed to have harbored and assisted hundreds of escapees. Garnet, too, worked actively across black institutions, bringing with him the deep personal understanding of the tragedy and pain slavery inflicted on families.

After Anna Murray helped Frederick Bailey (Douglass) accomplish his solitary escape from slavery in Baltimore, Douglass's first act as a free man was to send for his future wife. Black abolitionist David Ruggles arranged for Rev. Pennington, the former blacksmith who was now well-established in New York after his escape, to marry them before sending the newlyweds onward to New Bedford, Massachusetts.

John Weems from Rockville, Maryland, worked tirelessly to free his family in the border state. Weems's partial success brought liberty to his daughters, Ann Maria and Stella, and to his wife. Charles B. Ray, editor of *The Colored American*, is best known for his role in the famous escape of Ann

Maria, one of the more celebrated Underground Railroad cases reported in William Still's work.[3] At fifteen years of age, the comely Weems had a thick head of sandy hair, her most distinguishing feature. A plan was devised. She was snatched from the home of Charles Price in Rockville after his refusal to negotiate a reasonable amount for her sale to her family. Following her escape, the teenager was first hidden in the home of a Black family in Washington, D.C., but that was considered too dangerous and she was moved to the apartment of White abolitionist Joseph Bigelow.

Ann Maria, now transformed into a coach-driving young man, wore a cap covering her hair. On the day of the escape, the young coachman met his passenger at midday on a crowded street. Weems, now dressed as a young lad, jumped into the driver's seat of the coach, took the reins, and drove herself to freedom accompanied by her escort posing as the slaveholder. She arrived at the home of William Still on Thanksgiving eve where he carefully recorded the account of her escape before she was delivered to Ray in New York City. From Ray's home, Weems was moved to the home of AMA philanthropist Lewis Tappan, yet another comrade in the circle, where she spent Thanksgiving eating her turkey and plum pudding feast while hiding in their attic. Weems and her next escort, a Black congregational minister of a colored church in Brooklyn, New York, climbed aboard an express train that crossed the suspension bridge at Niagara Falls headed for Canada. There Weems's extended family, an aunt and uncle who had escaped years earlier with her sister, Stella, was overjoyed at their reunion.[4]

Famed Underground Railroad chronicler William Still frequently boarded escapees at his Philadelphia home before they resumed their flight to Canada and elsewhere. Still, attuned to applying the latest technology to his work, used the telegraph to facilitate cooperation among the distant elements of the Underground Railroad under his control. He worked with Black abolitionist Robert Purvis, also ranked as "president of the Underground Railroad," whose home became a well-known station. With the help of his family, Purvis offered his talent, money, and time along with his ever-ready horses and carriages in the service of escape and freedom.[5]

William Still documented many stories of family escapes on the Underground Railroad. In his writings and in his personal life, Still experienced the price slavery exacted. His mother had been forced to leave two of her sons behind in slavery when she made her escape in 1807, years before Still's birth and decades before organized Underground Railroad efforts. Still begins his book with the story of his lost brother, Peter Still (Gist), and Seth Concklin's rescue of Peter's wife and children from slavery in Alabama. The ill-fated attempt ended in Concklin's arrest and imprisonment near

Vincennes, Indiana, in 1851. Later during the ordeal he was found dead with his head smashed. The unfortunate family was condemned back into slavery in Alabama, victims of the Fugitive Slave Law that made Indiana as unsafe as Alabama. Ultimately, sale of the family was negotiated in 1854 but there was insufficient money to purchase a recently born grandson who had to be left behind in captivity. William Still witnessed the true pain of slavery and the misery the law inflicted on his brother's desperate drive to extricate his family from bondage.[6]

From Pittsburgh—considered the gateway to the West early in the nineteenth century—Hallie Quinn Brown remembered her parents' (Thomas Arthur Brown and Frances Jane Scroggins) work assisting escapees. Pittsburgh ran an active Underground Railroad station in western Pennsylvania.[7] In the early 1800s, Arthursville, also known as the Hill District, was home to a sizable Black middle class, whose churches and other institutions operated a vital terminal along the Underground Railroad.

Below the surface of the Browns' famous hospitality and culture, the family used their spacious home as an Underground Railroad station through the Black community network. One cold winter, Brown's wife was so successful in concealing a mother and five children in the large home that even her family and neighbors did not suspect. The residence served both as a rest for travelers and "a refuge for fugitives."[8]

When traveling to the edge of the frontier, William Paul Quinn, the future bishop, stayed at the Browns' comfortable home on Hazel Street in the Hill District. The former slaves had named their daughter in honor of the pioneer bishop. The Browns hosted many important gatherings for the AME Church in this crucial space inside Pittsburgh's Black community. The gracious hosts set aside a room for visiting bishops, known in the family as the Bishop's Room.[9]

Across the country, Rev. Quinn maintained contact with urban as well as rural families that made important contributions to the Underground Railroad. Over the next fourteen years, Cincinnati resident Hannah Dickson had all nine of her children baptized by Elder Quinn. She had a powerful influence on one among the anointed nine, her son, Moses. In a reflection of Quinn's own radical stand, he blessed the man who grew to become one of the most radical Black abolitionists of his time.[10]

In a long newspaper article, Dickson explained that in choosing to name him Moses, his mother "dedicated her boy to the cause of freedom . . . and predicted that he would, like Moses of old, lead his people from bondage to freedom." His boyhood home had been a gathering place for several prominent antislavery activists.[11] Dickson fulfilled his mother's prophecy. He served several capacities, co-founding Lincoln Institute, the predecessor to Lincoln University, serving as Grand Master of Missouri Prince Hall Masons, and leading the Knights of Liberty in their planned paramilitary work on the Underground Railroad.[12] These early family relationships and associations contributed to Quinn's becoming the "pioneer bishop" of the West.

Farther west, in Illinois, wealthy businessman and Black abolitionist John Jones, alongside his wife, Mary, worked ceaselessly for the Black Underground in Chicago. The former Alton residents' ardent commitment as Underground Railroad workers transformed their family home into "the local headquarters of the underground railroad," sheltering hundreds of escapees in their basement before sending them on to Canada West. John Brown stopped at their home on his way to Canada in the winter of 1858 and 1859 after his sensational "rescue" of eleven captives from Missouri.[13]

The McWorter family of New Philadelphia also helped with escapes from slavery. In the midst of the interracial environment, the founding family was actively participating in the Underground Railroad and risked their hard-earned freedom by aiding runaways. McWorter's great-great-granddaughter, Juliet Walker, explained, "The McWorter family not only gave the fugitives specific instructions on how to get to Canada, but in many instances Free Frank's sons accompanied the fugitives to Canada to insure that they would get there safely."[14] Between 1826 and 1829, Frank's son, Frank Jr., fled to Canada as a fugitive. His father exchanged his saltpeter operations to secure young Frank's freedom. His three brothers must have been quite familiar with the Underground Railroad to Canada because they also traveled the route to Canada to assist escapees.

## Free Black Communities

Operating at the opposite end of highly dramatic fugitive slave cases, rural Black settlements quietly organized in covert collaborative networks under the institutional umbrella of the Black church and the social cloak of the Black family. Nestled in hilly enclaves, sequestered in back alleys, or perched as stand-alone lookouts at precipices, communities of free Blacks offered both shelter and safety within their own concealed Underground Railroad networks. Despite limitations placed on their geographical and social mobility and the steady economic pressures from purchasing freedom or paying fees and bonds, free Blacks banded together to form communities. They adopted one another's children and widows married widowers. Intergenerational households guaranteed care for aging family members and church goers buried their own in the church cemetery. Residents looked after each other's affairs by acting as executors and handling probate proceedings. Cooperation was critical for survival.[15]

The geography of resistance template places freedom seekers at one end of the freedom spectrum, and free Black communities at the other. Over time, the Underground Railroad rose as a central connector between the two. Harold Rose found a consistent relationship between all Black towns and the abolitionist movement, which, in turn, closely supported the Underground Railroad movement. W. E. B. Du Bois confirmed that "Negro settlements in the interior of the free states, as well as along their southern frontier, soon came to form important links in the chain of stations leading from the Southern states to Canada"[16] (see map 1).

Freedom seekers found favorable conditions in the secluded Black settlements near the Ohio River. After escapees crossed the Ohio River around Proctorville, John Ditcher, "the red fox of the Underground," directed them east to Poke Patch. From the edge of the Ohio River in Ripley, blacksmith John Parker could direct escapees to Africa Hill. Escapees who crossed the Ohio at Evansville, Indiana, along the bend of the Ohio were taken along different routes to places where they had friends who moved them farther north.[17] Frederick Douglass was quite mindful of the danger, "for it was not in the interior of the State, but on its borders, that these human hounds [slave catchers] were most vigilant and active. The border lines between slavery and freedom were the dangerous ones for the fugitives." Slaveholders acknowledged the geographic advantages at the border by quickly removing to the Deep South enslaved workers who threatened to disrupt the system.[18]

Where Keith P. Griffler focused on specific Ohio locales, Harold Rose identified every Black town with both the abolitionist movement and organization of the Underground Railroad.[19] Whether urban or rural, Black communities gave sanctuary to escapees. Richard Wright identified every Black settlement in Indiana as a station on the Underground Railroad. Levi Coffin, one of several given the title "president of the Underground Railroad," could speak authoritatively on the subject. He remembered that in Newport, Indiana, fugitives often passed through and "generally stopped among the colored people." These settlements, which have all but disappeared, "did valuable service in the Underground Railroad work." Each one carried on "valiant work in helping the slaves to find Canada." Pamela Peters found the same in her study of Floyd County, Indiana. In describing Underground Railroad operations in Cincinnati, abolitionist James G. Birney reported, "such matters are almost uniformly managed by the colored people. I know nothing of them generally till they are past."[20]

Early Black towns settled in northern and western regions inflamed hostility, fueling fears that large numbers of fugitive slaves would plague the regions.[21] In an 1860 letter, Black abolitionist and moral reformer Frances Ellen Watkins Harper sought to bring her earnest and elevating influence to bear as part of her antislavery work. She hoped that the example set by free Blacks in these farming settlements would reduce the burden of racism for the rest of the race and change the public opinion of the country "not merely by influencing the public *around* them but *among* them."[22]

## The Black Church

Within the Black church, families formed the marrow of the Black community deep in the core of the Underground Railroad. African Americans pulled together to create one of the first Black institutions in the United States. In the words of Martin Delany, the Black church was "the Alpha and Omega of all things."[23] It was the center, the cement, the soul of the African American community. Camp meetings and general and annual church conferences ensured the continued circulation of critical knowledge among small local churches and their rural outposts. As the political and social, as well as spiritual, gathering place, whether in Poke Patch or Chicago, AME Zion or Baptist, the church served as concert hall, school, literary society, recreational center, and meetinghouse. The Black church supported a pragmatic action plan of racial elevation, self-determination, education, and economic autonomy.

Free people of color came together to exchange political ideas and support one another through beneficial aid and mutual assistance. The family remained key. Seven worshipers, often consisting of husbands and wives, were enough for a preacher such as W. Paul Quinn to form a society in advance of a formal congregation. Connections to AME annual conferences or AME Zion general conferences fortified the rural families and communities, folding them into the larger fight against racial injustice.[24]

The Black church and its ministers delivered institutional support and strength at the center of African American community life. Bishop Allen, founder of the African Methodist Episcopal (AME) denomination, began a sacred and secular revolution when he and Absalom Jones led congregants out of Philadelphia's St. George's Methodist Church in 1787 in protest over their treatment. Allen, as the first bishop of the church, lived up to his renown as "the Apostle of Freedom." Throughout his life his tireless advocacy for self-improvement, dignity, and racial equality permeated his life. Churches growing out of this commitment followed the philosophical path he set. The venerable Bishop Daniel Payne reports that Allen was "thoroughly anti-slavery," and that "his house was never shut against the friendless, homeless, penniless fugitives from the 'House of Bondage.'"[25]

Allen founded an American institution dedicated to the cause of liberty. He used his church, and alongside his wife, Sarah, used their Philadelphia home for a higher purpose—sheltering escaped slaves. Walter Proctor, Allen's contemporary and confidant of fifteen years, stated, "The house of Allen was a refuge for the oppressed."[26] Allen and numerous other Black church leaders turned church basements (when they had them) into the secret spaces of the Underground Railroad.[27] Congregants risked their freedom and sometimes their lives harboring escapees.

Known as a friend to the fugitives, Sarah Allen perilously and illegally provided safe haven to runaways and followed the pattern of African American family involvement in the Underground Railroad. Jeopardizing her family and her husband's position, she willingly donated her time, money, and the safety of her family home to facilitate the freedom denied by government and the law.[28] She knew the Black church had to provide a pathway to freedom.

Allen, a strong and forceful leader of the emerging AME Church, encouraged all freedmen to undertake acts of charity and mercy toward those still held in, or attempting to escape, slavery. He had traversed an enormous path, undergoing the transformation from "slave to bishop" and the AME Church reflected his concerns for the fate of anyone attempting to throw off the manacles of slavery. With the death of Allen in 1831, Quinn and other AME ministers upheld their farsighted leader's lifelong principles. From the inception of the Free African Society, precursor to the formal church, racial solidarity, uplift, and abolitionist activity persisted as foremost concerns and spread with the institutionalization of the church.[29]

William Paul Quinn inherited this freedom-minded lineage, which he imprinted on every church he founded, every congregation he shepherded, and every organization he joined. In 1816, this young giant of a man participated in a seminal moment in American history that forever changed his life. Quinn encountered Richard Allen at the founding of the AME Church and witnessed the beginnings of the independent Black church. Although infighting and internal strife accompanied its growth, Bethel Church, in addition to several others, found solidarity of purpose as a station of the Underground Railroad. The church reflected the antislavery, activist component of Allen's self-help philosophy, laid out as an enduring legacy and a formidable blueprint for his ministers.

With the mandate to open the West to the church, Quinn interacted with, visited, and ministered among families of the faithful as he traveled across the country. In 1822, a mere six years after the organization of the AME Church in Philadelphia, the pioneering minister organized Bethel AME in Pittsburgh, one of the first Black churches west of the Allegheny Mountains.

Quinn served as pastor. Lewis Woodson was in Pittsburgh at the time and helped establish the church in the heart of the city shortly after he arrived. Early in 1831, minister Woodson carried the AME standard forward and was already advocating education and self-help. He established the first school for colored children, which was housed in the basement of the church. Serving as the school's first teacher, Woodson took a nineteen-year-old Martin Delany under his tutelage. Woodson began exerting considerable influence on the man who would later be known as the father of Black Nationalism.[30] Beyond the spiritual sustenance of the community, the church supported an Underground Railroad station. Lewis Woodson, an important agent on the Pittsburgh line, pastored Bethel church for many years. Elder Quinn and his friend, Lewis Woodson, imprinted an indelible legacy in Pittsburgh.[31]

The radical stance of the AME Church and its leaders played a hand in insurrection and rebellion. Historian Peter Hinks identified the religious factor as central to organizing any large-scale insurrection. The AME Church and its ministers were implicated in a number of revolts and conspiracies. Several thousand members, class leaders, and religious instructors of the first AME church in Charleston, South Carolina, were involved with the 1822 Denmark Vesey slave conspiracy, planned while Allen was bishop. One of the enslaved Blacks sent to spy on the undertaking reported back that the neighborhood AME church was in the middle of the plot.[32] Hinks pinpoints the Charleston AME church at the center of the Vesey conspiracy.

On city orders, outraged Whites burned the church to the ground. The denomination was particularly vilified for producing and spreading "the sentiment of personal freedom and responsibility in the Negro."[33] Slaveholders did not stop until the church was completely suppressed. Fearing mounting solidarity, Charleston officials hung six of the conspirators and branded the congregation a "hotbed" and jailed suspected Black ministers. Rev. Morris Brown, pastor at the time and advisor to the audacious Vesey, was permanently expelled from the state and quickly fled. Escaping to Philadelphia, Brown rose rapidly, becoming one of the leading lights of the church. Sometime before the Vesey incident, Brown had spent a year in jail for helping enslaved individuals purchase their freedom. As a former slave, Vesey had ensured his own freedom through self-purchase. Upon Allen's death in 1831, Morris Brown rose to presiding bishop; he wisely appointed William Paul Quinn as one of his assistants.[34]

Allen Temple, Cincinnati's oldest black church, was also established during the early growth of the church. The chapel played a pivotal role in the Underground Railroad in Cincinnati, befriending escapees for decades. Blacks first established a Methodist Episcopal congregation in 1823 after refusing to accept the prejudicial treatment heaped upon them by the predominantly

White churches in the city. The congregation joined the AME denomination after it was established in 1824.[35]

Quinn also connected with Reading Bethel in southeastern Pennsylvania. The church typified an isolated small town AME church serving a tiny African American congregation in the first half of the nineteenth century. The Schuykill River courses to the east of the town and the region was once known for its iron foundries and forges, two telltale signs of Underground Railroad communities as defined in the geography of resistance.[36] The ubiquitous Rev. Quinn had been ordained an itinerant deacon a mere two years before he helped worshipers form the Reading African Society, the forerunner to Bethel Church.[37]

William Still discusses the Reading depot or station in his seminal work on African American participation in the movement. Two published escapes pertained to Reading. In the coded language of the Underground Railroad, an agent inquired whether Still had received "those five large and three small packages I sent by way of Reading, consisting of three men and women and children." This shipment represented the first case of the newly formed Fugitive Aid Society. A bit further in the letter, the agent inquired about "signs or symbols you make use of in your dispatches . . . in relation to operations of the Underground Railroad."[38] Several months later a depot operator out of Reading informed Still that the "goods" had been detained. Because of some local excitement, the agents thought it expedient to hold the escapees overnight in Reading.[39] Members of Reading Bethel AME provided food for the escapees as they passed through. The church made the necessary clothing so useful for disguises or transforming from slave to freeman.[40]

In 1840, W. Paul Quinn received the official appointment by the general conference as the general missionary to plant the AME Church in the far West. Although Black abolitionists and journalists Martin Delany, Mary Ann Shadd Cary, and Frederick Douglass criticized the Black clergy for their insolent bearing, accommodating tone, and submissive behavior of their uneducated ministers, nonetheless, Black ministers shouldered the major responsibilities of leadership. Churches and their ministers formed natural alliances in the campaign against slavery.

Free Blacks and the independent African Methodist churches were suspected of implanting rebellious thoughts in the minds of captives. By offering aid to escapees, church buildings served as community centers that the enslaved could use to subvert the system. Captives in Kentucky used the local church as a headquarters for an attempt by twenty-seven persons to arm themselves and escape from bondage.[41] Despite warning to the contrary, Black congregations across the country operated as active stations and their ministers as active agents.[42]

A correspondent for *Frederick Douglass' Paper* described the church as "the site of revolution or reform."[43] The only writings thus far attributed to Bishop Quinn, "The Origin, Horrors and Results of Slavery, Faithfully and Minutely Described," drew verbatim from a four-page section of David Walker's radical-minded *Appeal.*[44] The rise of abolitionism and Black radical thought can be traced to Walker's 1829 pamphlet, which fanned the flames of liberty throughout the North and the South.[45] Quinn's borrowing of Walker's words reflected the profound influence not only of Walker's writings, but also of the AME Church and Bishop Allen, whom Walker liberally cited and generously praised.[46] AME ministers were in print dialogue with Walker, America's most notorious pamphleteer, who in turn dipped deeply into the well of Methodism. He was a practicing Methodist who became a disciple of Richard Allen and may have communicated directly with him in the years preceding the publication of the *Appeal*. Arguably, Walker's pamphlet was among the most inflammatory of all antislavery documents ever published. Not only was Allen quoted within the pages of one of the most commanding documents of Black protest ever written, but Walker also praised him in an effusive testimony and saw to it that the document was widely circulated, particularly in the South.[47]

By the time Morris Brown elevated Rev. Quinn to bishop in 1844, the new prelate could boast of establishing 40 schools teaching 920 students in Illinois and Indiana alone. In his summary report, Quinn noted that within the last ten or fifteen years many of the members who filled the little one-room rural churches first "broke away from the fetters of slavery."[48] Quinn spread the enlightening power of education hand in hand with liberation theology. Moral uplift and education equipped former slaves with the foremost assets.

The reach of the church extended from sanctuary to schoolhouse. After spiritual fulfillment, education was the primary and consistent concern among community members. Sunday schools often met the needs of both. At Miller Grove, where books and slates were among the archaeological finds, Julia Singleton filled the all-important duties of school teacher for the community.

Free Blacks were keenly aware of the strident stance southern slaveholders took against educating Blacks. Frederick Douglass describes the slaveholders' belief that the noble and refining influences of education rendered Blacks unfit to be slaves. "It is almost an unpardonable offence to teach slaves to read," Douglass fumed, best to keep them "shut up in mental darkness."[49] Proslavers viewed African American schools as seditious abolitionist vehicles that undermined slavery's imposed ignorance. Learning empowered people of color to reject the menial status reserved for them. Reading and writing enabled Blacks to forge passes, read runaway notices, and equip themselves with the skills of the literate.

Until 1847, most escapees from Kentucky vanished into the black areas of Cincinnati where two Black churches in the city, Allen Temple AME and Zion Baptist, actively operated Underground Railroad stops. The basement of Zion Church functioned as a regular haven operating in cooperation with the Vigilance Committee.[50] One of the most notable white female Underground Railroad operatives, Laura Haviland, offers an accurate account of how the Underground Railroad often worked. She encountered fourteen newly arrived escapees from Kentucky who were first housed in the basement of Zion Baptist Church immediately after their escape. As they moved on from this first stop on the edge of freedom, the escapees followed the familiar pattern presented in this book and then were taken to a Quaker settlement, a distance of twenty-five miles, and from there were forwarded to Canada.[51] Escapees were often delivered by, and spent their first hours of freedom with, fellow African Americans.

Referencing his own Underground Railroad work, Levi Coffin recounted the story of a man who had arrived in Cincinnati after his escape from slavery. During his initial moments of freedom, the escapee "met with a colored man, who took him to the house of Preacher Green, pastor of Allen Chapel, whom he knew to be a friend to fugitives." In the morning, after this initial contact, AME pastor Green brought the freeman to Coffin's home.[52]

Historians are beginning to appreciate the significant partnership between the Black church and the Underground Railroad. AME minister Jordan Early reports, "Our Church wherever established was called an abolition church, which made the slaveholders suspicious of its proceedings." The term carried a stigma that deterred enslaved members of the community from associating or affiliating with church members. In the Black community of Seneca Village in New York City, for example, the AME Zion church carried the moniker "church militant" in its title.[53] In slaveholding states such as Louisiana, slaveholders found the concept of their captives attending a "Free Negro Church" self-identified as an abolition church intolerable.[54]

Black denominations, AME Zion and the Black Baptists in addition to AME, existed at the heart of these paths to freedom. In southern Ohio, Black Baptists acted as effective conductors who maintained Underground Railroad connections. The Baptist experience in these settlements strongly mirrors AME involvement.[55] The Underground Railroad flourished among AME Zion churches in New York, Connecticut, and New England, where the denomination's influence was strongest. In Boston, Virginia-born hackman Leonard Grimes, an active Underground Railroad agent, ministered to Twelfth Baptist Church, which was widely known as "The Fugitive Slave Church."[56]

Before 1850, Black denominations acted with greater circumspection than either their individual congregations or their White counterparts. The church preferred to limit itself to spiritual matters or, in the case of the AME Church, to equivocate on antislavery issues out of concern for southern congregants still held in bondage.

Competing and multiple considerations confronted and constrained the men of God at the helm of the churches. The public figure operated in a socially, politically, and racially controlling White world. The religious leader was responsible for his flock of both enslaved and free congregants. The political activist operated in the world of Black abolitionism and Black radicalism. Such were the multiple tensions and seemingly opposing ideologies religious leaders had to navigate.

After 1850, however, the Fugitive Slave Act provoked the church to a more public and drastic stance. Black churches moved toward sustained radical self-help activities, demonstrating an increasingly militant opposition to slavery. In their own time, Bishop Allen, Bishop Quinn, and Payne chose not to speak directly concerning the Churches' or their own personal complicity with the Underground Railroad or freedom seeking escapees. Nevertheless, each was intimately acquainted with the plight of his enslaved brethren. With the possible exception of William Paul Quinn, all the early bishops of the church had once been enslaved.[57]

Quinn oversaw not only the westward and southern expansion of the AME but also its internationalization. The bishop presided over the seventh AME conference held at the Queen's Bush, Canada West, in 1846. When Canadian Whites accused church ministers of fostering anti-White prejudice in their congregations, the bishop and fifteen other ministers took up the issue at the Queen's Bush Conference. Arguing that White racism represented the main factor leading to the formation of the church, ministers affirmed their right to control access to their pulpits and the messages delivered. Quinn also presided over the 1853 Canadian conference where delegates drafted a resolution recognizing Canada as safe haven for fugitive slaves. In addition to Canada, the church under the pioneering minister's leadership planted the seeds of Methodism in Jamaica, West Africa, and Haiti.[58]

The outspoken clergyman, remembered as a "militant soldier of the cross" among church historians, formed numerous churches implicated in the Underground Railroad movement, including the churches at Rocky Fork, Brooklyn, Lick Creek, and Poke Patch. He defied slavery and organized churches in the South and ordained ministers in New Orleans a decade before the Civil War. His life intersected with many of the country's most zealous and radical thinkers of various denominations—Martin Delany,

Henry Highland Garnet, and Lewis Tappan along with his friends, Lewis Woodson and Willis Revels.

Quinn was beaten, was robbed, and faced numerous dangers "while searching for souls in the wilderness," no doubt observing the horrors of slavery and the conditions pertaining to free people of color across his vast conferences. Elaine Welch notes, "He was untiring in his efforts against slavery, and helped many slaves to escape from their masters, and to find an asylum in the north . . . Being a man of resourcefulness, he was expert in smuggling slaves, and could on the spur of the moment form a ruse, by which the slave owner could be misled."[59] The "Pioneer of the West" left a legacy of radical activism that began early in his life as a preacher in New York and Pennsylvania.

From Bethel AME Church in New Jersey through Pennsylvania, Maryland, and into Ohio, Indiana, and Illinois, the states of the Old Northwest, extending to Kentucky, Missouri, and farther west into Iowa and Kansas, and north into Canada, Bishop Quinn's name is consistently linked to escape from slavery and Underground Railroad churches.[60]

## Mapping Black Settlements and Churches

Mapping Black settlements visually clarifies and exposes the relationship between African American churches, settlements, and historic Underground Railroad routes. Following Blacks as they moved toward freedom and plotting the sites associated with their involvement in the Underground Railroad graphically locates Black life at the edges of freedom. Identifying and mapping Black settlement sites constitute essential components of the geography of resistance for understanding routes and operations of the Underground Railroad.

Examining Black settlements in Indiana, Emma Thornbrough observed that in nearly every instance, free Black communities were located on one of the routes of the Underground Railroad, suggesting that runaways either tended to seek out members of their own race or remained in Indiana rather than fleeing farther northward.[61] A map of Black churches drawn by local Indiana historian Coy Robbins and Xenia Cord's map of Black settlements in Indiana provide the foundations for a revised Underground Railroad map that supports Thornbrough's assertion (map 5).[62]

Routes connecting African American communities along known Underground Railroad lines connected with Quaker and other abolitionist settlements. When Wilbur Siebert mapped the Underground Railroad in Indiana, for example, he identified Friends communities near both the Beech and Roberts neighborhoods, which were active stations on the Black Underground (map 5).

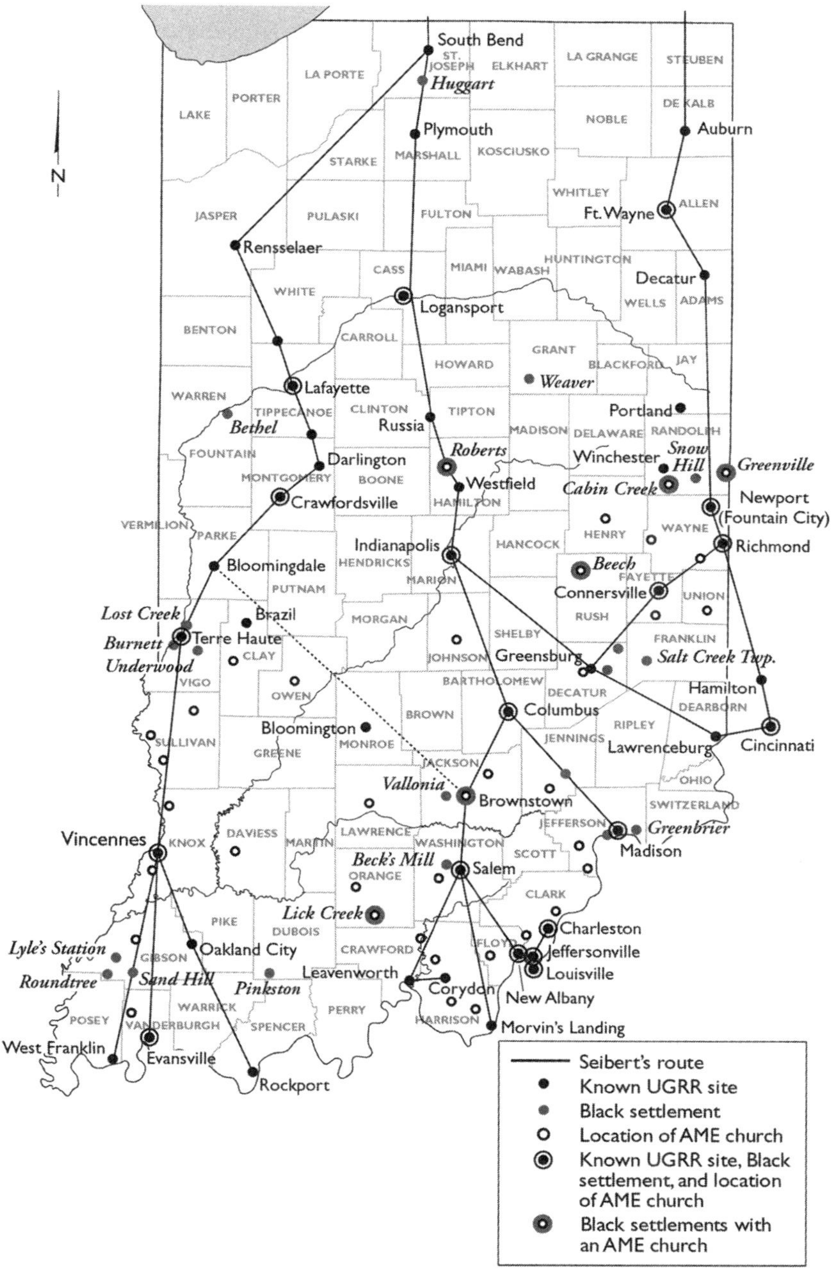


*Map 5.* Unified Underground Railroad map of Indiana 1840–50. Map connects Siebert's routes, locations of AME churches, and Black settlements.

However, Siebert routinely failed to recognize the African American correlates in the landscape paralleling and often overlapping the Quaker settlements.

Black settlements and churches coincided with Quaker and other abolitionist centers. Juxtaposing maps of Black churches and settlements with Underground Railroad maps visually communicates the proximity and the parallels between the two types of routes, one primarily African American and hidden, the other well known and dominated by White abolitionists. The revised map deciphers the mechanisms of African American involvement in the Underground Railroad (map 5).[63]

Several Black settlements and their Quaker counterparts predate formation of the Underground Railroad. Paths formed around and linked to these early sites. For example, in Gloucester County, New Jersey, where extensive maps of Black churches and settlements exist, Emma Marie Trusty notes, "When URR cars rumbled into Woodbury in the late 1700's an existing small, free black community received the 'baggage on board.'" After 1816, when the church at Woodbury aligned with AME, Richard Allen and William Paul Quinn assumed organizational roles.[64]

Escaping slaves had few contacts in the North, particularly in the early years before the Underground Railroad was formally organized, and generally first relied on help from family, friends, and those of their own race. Often, Blacks made the initial contact, providing shelter and assistance, while nearby sympathetic Whites or those farther up the line provided money, clothes, transportation, and legal services.

In the treacherous southern portions of Illinois, Indiana, and Ohio, the few well-worn routes leading out of the southern portions of the states come closest to merging Black settlements with the nearby abolitionist centers. Routes branched into a lattice-like pattern of intersecting and transecting paths to freedom as they extended northward. Nineteenth-century Black settlements across the country functioned as conduits to freedom, offering some form of sanctuary to those escaping slavery, independent of yet entwined with, White abolitionist centers.

Maps of Black communities and their churches exist for New Jersey, Ohio, and Indiana. I first recognized the correlation for this study relying on Coy Robbins and Xenia Cord's map of black settlements in Indiana (see map 5). The map of Underground Railroad routes in New Jersey in 1860 conveys the same relationship. The Salem circuit in New Jersey and the Underground Railroad Greenwich route are examples of the geography of resistance in action. Each route or circuit has been largely analyzed within its own discrete sphere. Yet, when taken together, the distinctions between the Greenwich Underground Railroad line and the Salem AME circuit blur (map 6). Archaeologist Chris Barton found that all the locations of free

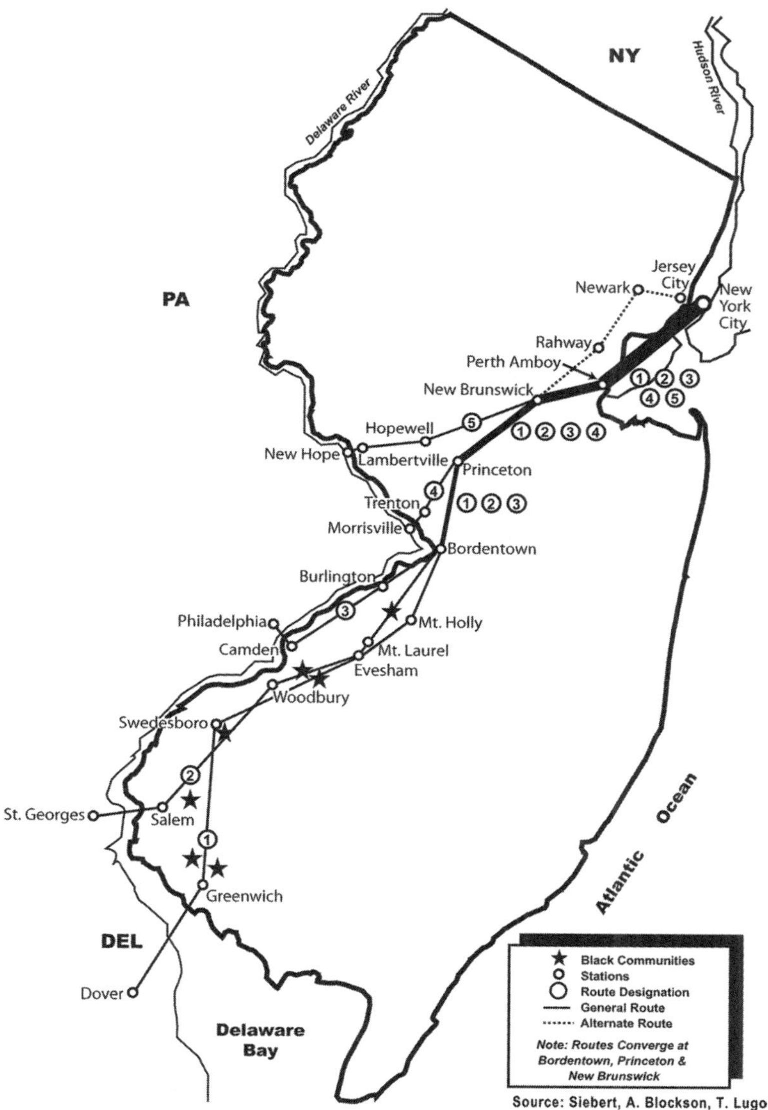


*Map 6.* Greenwich Line of the Underground Railroad in New Jersey, 1860. Map depicts the convergence of known Underground Railroad escape routes and Black settlements. Source: Giles R. Wright, *Afro-Americans in New Jersey: A Short History* (Trenton: New Jersey Historical Commission, 1988), 40.

African American communities that existed in South Jersey prior to the abolition of slavery were located in close proximity to Quaker centers of abolition.

Black communities of Small Gloucester and Cootstown sat outside of Swedesboro in Gloucester County. Guinea Town of Salem County was located a little beyond Salem. Gouldtown and Springtown, early Black communities, developed a few miles away from Greenwich in Cumberland County. Saddlertown and Snowhill (later called Free Haven and in 1887 Lawnside) stood near Haddonfield in Camden County.[65] Again, although the connection is generally not drawn, most of the Black towns were known to have had AME churches and were active on the Underground Railroad. Rev. Quinn held connections to the New Jersey churches as well. During the early days of his ministry in the 1820s, he pastored in Gouldtown, Springtown, and Salem, New Jersey, among other places.[66]

Mapping routes has been a staple of the Underground Railroad genre since Siebert introduced his iconic route map in 1898. Modern authors provide local maps of Underground Railroad routes. Major contributions archaeology can make to Underground Railroad research are surveying, identifying, and mapping sites and defining spatial relationships between Black communities and churches and the Underground Railroad. Mapping the pre–Civil War landscape would emphasize the geography of resistance that shaped the pathways to freedom.

CHAPTER 8

# Faith and Fraternity

## Black Organizations and Interracial Cooperation

Black convention meetings and fraternal societies fused activists and free people of color together with childhood friends, schoolmates, and former slaves. Prominent participants representing Black churches or the Free and Accepted Masons routinely interacted with Underground Railroad operatives at Black conventions and major gatherings, providing information connecting rural families to the larger world. The nation's prominent Black abolitionists and Underground Railroad activists maintained family ties to the rural settlements or had an acute understanding of what it took to escape from slavery. Several among them had gotten themselves out of captivity years before.

Beginning in the 1840s, the names and influences of Black abolitionists weave through Underground Railroad narratives. The organizations to which these early Black activists belonged such as Vigilance Committees and meetings they attended accomplished much of the unseen work of the Underground Railroad. Through the participation of its ministers and lay leaders, the Black church silently collaborated with numerous interracial organizations: the American Missionary Association, the American Home Missionary Society, Friends yearly meetings, the state and national Black convention movement, Vigilance Committees, and Anti-Slavery Societies.[1] These organizations frequently claimed among their attendees, activists, both discreet and fiery, with ties to the Underground Railroad. Martin Delany, Lewis Tappan, Frederick Douglass, and Henry Highland Garnet seemed to be everywhere. Quinn's friend, Lewis Woodson, was active in both the AME Church and the Black convention movement. Seeking to relieve the plight of people of color participants labored on the Underground Railroad in some capacity.

Interracial cooperative associations developed. Like-minded women and men created opportunities to congregate and strategize beyond the business at hand. The interracial component of the Underground Railroad movement emerged as part of the political and equal rights movements, or through moral reform and religious principle. Interdenominational cooperation among Blacks and Whites was less common than interracial cooperation between these groups. Within the Underground Railroad, cooperation between African Americans and Quakers overshadowed all other cooperative ventures. If interracial and interdenominational cooperation did occur, it was frequently in antislavery societies or organizations such as the AMA.

Underground Railroad routes often mirrored the religious denominations of participants. AME and Black Baptist members worked within their religious lines; the Presbyterians of Southern Illinois labored within a Presbyterian network in the familiar pattern of the Quaker tradition.[2] Denominational affiliation of abolitionist and antislavery workers formed vital links along the Underground Railroad. Quakers and African Americans lived near and among each other, giving shape to Underground Railroad paths to freedom.

Various sects and denominations commonly held organizational gatherings at yearly meetings, conventions, or synods. Members from distant locales intermingled and perhaps formulated strategies. Further unraveling the mysteries of how the Underground Railroad operated, antislavery annual meetings, and the Black national and state conventions, in addition to religious conferences, were ideal opportunities for working out Underground Railroad business, affording the more radical participants convenient and justifiable access to one another.

## Black Conventions, Meetings, and Societies

Free Black men, representing the elite from the various Black communities, met together at a range of organizations and societies, conventions and conferences. A bold and daring spirit launched the first convention of the colored people of the United States in 1830. Many of those attending the extraordinary meetings read like the who's who of the Underground Railroad. J. W. C. Pennington, author of *The Fugitive Blacksmith*, attended the convention a mere two years after his escape from slavery in Maryland. His first encounter with White abolitionists William Lloyd Garrison, Simeon Jocelyn, and Lewis Tappan occurred at the annual convention in Philadelphia in 1831. The men came to discuss establishing a college in New Haven for educating young men of color.[3]

Abraham D. Shadd, patriarch of his Underground Railroad family in Wilmington, Delaware, and West Chester, Pennsylvania, attended the first four national conventions and presided over the third in Philadelphia in 1833. Noted Underground Railroad operatives Robert Purvis, Pennington, and David Ruggles were present. Conventioneers organized a committee formed to "report whether any and how far encouragement ought to be given to the settlement in Upper Canada."[4] Shadd eventually moved to Canada with his family after passage of the Fugitive Slave Bill in 1850. His consistent dedication and militant advocacy on behalf of Black causes led him to serve as a delegate to Pennsylvania's 1841 and 1848 Black state conventions as well.

Education stood out as a constant concern whether among the small Black settlements that established schools in their little churches or at the national level where abolitionists unsuccessfully attempted to establish a college for Blacks in Connecticut.

The Phoenix Society, the literary society established by and for Blacks, counted among its members some of the wealthiest and most talented men in New York City, Black and White. The society began as an outgrowth of the colored conventions and connected AME minister W. Paul Quinn to the movement. The society aimed to unite colored people into a fraternity for self-improvement. Members sponsored day and evening adult schools, operated libraries and reading rooms, encouraged vocational training for city Blacks, and imparted a message of general mental and moral uplift. In his youth, Henry Highland Garnet, arguably one of the fieriest militant thinkers of his time, used the Phoenix Society to train as a public speaker.

As a director of the society, Quinn fraternized among leading abolitionists and thinkers, with Peter Williams, Thomas Downing, and Simeon Jocelyn. Alexander Crummell and his father, Boston, participated. When the fourth national Black convention met in Asbury Church in New York in 1834, Phoenix Society members were honored with a special commendation for their outstanding work. Quinn's role as one of the society's directors placed him in contact with its officers, including President Christopher Rush, First Vice President Theodore S. Wright, and Treasurer Arthur Tappan. Black abolitionists David Ruggles, Charles B. Ray, and Samuel Cornish served on the board of directors.[5] Several among these same men also came together in the American Missionary Association that had been so active in Miller Grove. Christopher Rush, second bishop of the African Methodist Episcopal Zion Church (AMEZ), worked along with Rt. Rev. Morris Brown, who later became the second bishop of the AME Church. Ohio's well-known Underground Railroad leader Presbyterian Rev. John

Rankin crossed racial barriers and denominational lines to serve the AMA. Simeon Jocelyn, White pastor of a Black Congregational church in New Haven, acted as corresponding secretary. Officers included Black abolitionist Theodore S. Wright and Rev. Samuel Cornish. Reverend Daniel A. Payne, who led AME as its third bishop, and Rev. Lewis Woodson served among a forty-three-man interracial, interdenominational group representing at least five states. New York City's Charles B. Ray was involved alongside Henry Highland Garnet and Jermain W. Loguen, both of whom had escaped slavery years before. These same names and more reappear as part of the state and national Black convention movement and surface again and again as Underground Railroad activists. Black Congregationalist minister Amos Beman, for example, frequently risked his position and standing by harboring men and women in Connecticut who had escaped slavery. Lewis Tappan and Simeon Jocelyn were known to aid runaways; Tappan had worked with David Ruggles of the New York Vigilance Committee since its founding in 1836.[6]

The Underground Railroad had no meeting schedule for its members. The movement operated inside of other organizations. The Phoenix Society brought together identified Underground Railroad agents and sympathizers. Members such as Thomas Downing, in cooperation with his son, George, were Underground Railroad operatives whose famed Oyster House in Lower Manhattan was a station for thirty years. Amid lively dinners and crowds of distinguished diners, George used the basement to shelter escapees from kidnappers and bounty hunters.[7] Wilbur Siebert identifies both David Ruggles and Charles B. Ray as Underground Railroad operators, although he misidentifies Ray as White.[8] Theodore Wright actively worked for the New York Vigilance Committee and the AMA. David Ruggles, whom William Wells Brown identified as "one of the founders of the celebrated Underground Railroad," served as secretary.[9]

National Black convention meetings bound the eastern and western activists. The reach of the convention movement expanded as it moved westward. The brilliant and outspoken William Lambert, known as the "president of the Michigan Underground Railroad," helped organize Michigan's first State Convention of Colored Citizens and served as its chairman in 1843. The convention urged direct participation in the struggle for freedom and equality.[10]

Consider the convergence of so many Underground Railroad operatives at the National Colored Convention held at the Liberty Street Church, Troy, New York, in October 1847. Connecticut's James W. C. Pennington, "the fugitive blacksmith," served as one of the vice presidents. Congregational minister and Underground Railroad conductor Amos G. Beman also represented Connecticut. Editor of *The Colored American*, Charles B. Ray, of New York City and William C. Nell of Boston served as secretaries. Escaped slaves Frederick Douglass and William Wells Brown together represented Massachusetts. Alexander Crummel chaired the Committee of Education. The searing minister and abolitionist Henry Highland Garnet acted as chair of the Business Committee, alongside Michigan's Lewis Hayden. Hayden had escaped slavery in Kentucky, making his way to Detroit before moving on to Boston, where he and his wife turned their home into a haven for the Underground Railroad. It was to Lewis Hayden that Harriet Beecher Stowe turned for facts for her *Key to Uncle Tom's Cabin* to corroborate and quell criticism of her astonishing book.[11] Likewise, Ray opened his New York home for great and earnest interracial exchanges among advocates of freedom such as Lewis Tappan and Simeon Jocelyn. Whenever Ray needed immediate and practical assistance with urgent Underground Railroad business, however, he turned to Stowe's brother, Henry Ward Beecher, minister of Brooklyn's Plymouth Church.[12]

W. Paul Quinn served among these Black abolitionists before he assumed greater responsibility for growing the AME Church in the West in 1844. Ten years later, he represented Pittsburgh in the largest delegation at the National Emigration Convention in Cleveland. Those opposed to emigrating (in contrast to being essentially deported by the colonizationists) from the racist society of the United States were neither invited nor welcomed. Quinn served as a vice president. Emigration to Central America, Haiti, and Africa's Niger Valley were the proposed destinations.[13] The convention endorsed emigration to the Caribbean via Canada, which was expected to function as a way station in preparation for "an empire of the colored peoples in the tropical areas of the Western Hemisphere."

The National Convention of Colored Freemen convened in Cleveland in 1848, chaired by Chicago's John Jones. Of the five delegates appointed by the chair, two, Frederick Douglass and Henry Bibb, had escaped slavery and brought direct knowledge of the plight of freedom seekers. Ohio's Dr. Charles Henry Langston held several committee responsibilities at both state and national conventions. Demonstrating concern for those still suffering under the yoke of oppression, Langston delivered an impromptu speech to the convention condemning those who refused to help fugitive slaves. By 1858, Langston would back up his words with action, operating as one of the rescuers in the widely publicized Oberlin-Wellington rescue. Langston was tried for his role in the rescue of John Price, who was liberated from custody and sent to freedom in Canada.[14]

Several of Alton's prominent African American men at the forefront of establishing the Black churches in the Alton area represented Madison County at the First Convention of Colored Citizens of Illinois held in Alton in 1853. Chicago's prominent Underground Railroad agent and former Alton resident John Jones took a leading role. Jones was deeply involved in the Underground Railroad in Chicago and would have understood the routes and participants from the Rocky Fork, Alton, and Brooklyn area quite well. Convention meetings regularly brought together active Underground Railroad agents who assembled to work on the apparent matters at hand.

Underground Railroad agent Martin Delany went on to work with John Brown on the 1858 Constitutional Convention for the Oppressed People of the United States, held in Chatham, Canada.[15] Brown's plan involved ousting Canada as the main terminus of the Underground Railroad, forcibly replacing it with Kansas, where a new sovereign state would come into existence. Richard J. Hinton, a supporter of John Brown's cause, indicated that Brown was intent on taking advantage of the secret organization of the Black network to freedom. Since his childhood days in Ohio, Brown had watched his father offer aid to escapees and followed in his footsteps. Later as an adult in western Pennsylvania, New York, and Kansas, John Brown found acceptance through his experiences as an Underground Railroad activist, strategizing for militant liberation among like-minded African American escapees. Brown met with Frederick Douglass, William Still, Henry Highland Garnet, William Lambert, Harriet Tubman, and other Black abolitionists. He found inspiration in Garnet's outspoken, radical "Address to the Slaves." So much so that he published Garnet's "Address" at his own expense. Garnet's stand advocating violence when necessary and political abolition stood firmly on the foundation of David Walker's *Appeal*.[16]

W. E. B. Du Bois also refers to the "Liberty League whose duty it was to help the slaves to escape to Canada." After the passage of the Fugitive Slave Law, John Brown formed the U.S. League of Gileadites nine years before his assault at Harpers Ferry. The Gileadites were an armed Black self-defense group of forty-four men and women organized in an effort at systematic resistance to the enforcement of the law. Du Bois observes, "The co-operation in rescuing fugitive slaves just before the war was due in considerable degree to this organization and others like it in different places."[17]

John Brown needed to tap into these leagues and understand Underground Railroad routes and stations. He scrutinized census records to study the distribution of Blacks and their settlements and made maps of escape routes, noting roads, plantations, and supplies. Brown decided to travel along the Appalachian Mountains, which ran along a south-north axis. Brown focused on an escape route through the Shenandoah Valley known as the Great Black Way, which had been suggested to him by Harriet Tubman. Along the way, he garnered support from a number of small Black communities in close proximity to Harpers Ferry. The area was active in the Underground Railroad and connected to the region's iron furnaces.[18]

According to Du Bois, John Brown had been looking for ways to tap into the Black organizations and their networks to freedom. The "League of Freedom," "Liberty League," or "American Mysteries," in addition to "Order of the Men of Oppression," systematized the escape along the Underground Railroad.[19] By this time, the Underground Railroad contained sufficient structure and organization for Brown to conceptualize it on a national level, beyond the narrow, local workings of individual conductors and regional and state escape routes.

After Brown's unsuccessful raid on the federal arsenal at Harpers Ferry, Underground Railroad stalwart William Still bravely sheltered some of Brown's men and helped them elude capture. At the hour of Brown's death, Still and his wife opened their home and hearts to attend to Brown's grieving widow, Mary, who in return sent a lock of his hair in gratitude.[20] Such were the politics of the people connecting the tentacles of Bishop Quinn's political and religious life. The involvement of Quinn in the 1854 emigration convention in addition to his use of David Walker's *Appeal* ties the AME Church to a radical tradition. The small churches Quinn founded in the rural areas of Ohio, Illinois, and Indiana, among several other states, as well as the ministers he ordained fused the larger Black Atlantic world by their associations with the Underground Railroad.

## Prince Hall Free and Accepted Masons

Prominent ministers and Underground Railroad operatives joined the Prince Hall Order of Free and Accepted Masons. The connections among the Masons, the Underground Railroad, and the Black church are well concealed, however. The Masons participated in a secret society; the Underground Railroad succeeded as a clandestine operation; and Black churches harbored escaped captives. Of the three, the Masons have proved the most difficult to tie to the Underground Railroad.

For more than thirty-five years, Prince Hall, the founder of the Masonic Order, was revered in African American protest circles. The organization he founded encouraged mutual protection and community action.[21] In 1775, during the Revolutionary War era, Prince Hall imprinted the powerful influences of Freemasonry on Black America. Early lodges were established in Boston and Philadelphia.

W. Paul Quinn, following in Allen's footsteps, operated within this tight-knit fraternal environment. Quinn's hidden hand extended to the Prince Hall Masonic movement. Reportedly, the Masonic lodge located in Richmond, Indiana, the site of Quinn's home in later years, retains a copy of his enrollment certificate from a New York lodge. Quinn was not the sole Mason among the AME bishops and church leadership, however.

Ten years after Richard Allen and Absalom Jones united to lay the foundations of Methodism among people of color, the two men again joined forces, organizing the first Masonic lodge among men of color in Pennsylvania and the second in the United States. Absalom Jones served as the first Worshipful Master; Allen acted as treasurer, cementing the strong bond between the church and Freemasonry from the beginning. With the exception of Bishop Payne, the majority of nineteenth-century bishops and many church ministers were Prince Hall Masons.[22]

In Freemasonry, Richard Allen and the subsequent bishops found a vehicle for the continued adoption of middle-class values within Black society—racial uplift, self-help, and solidarity—deemed necessary for Black success.[23] Senator Hiram Revels, Willis Revel's younger brother and an AME minister in Kentucky, Indiana, and Maryland, took Masonry with him when he served as the nation's first Black senator after the Civil War. The clergy spread Freemasonry as they spread the word of God, and it increasingly appears, with African American involvement in the Underground Railroad.

Rev. Jordan W. Early, one of the original western AME pioneers, spent much time in the city of New Orleans, where he began planning for the establishment of the AME Church in 1842. While there, he aligned with a number of men who were members of the Masonic fraternity, seeking their wisdom and counsel about the best methods for establishing a church in that deeply southern city. His Masonic brother, James Hunter, prevailed upon a member of the Louisiana state legislature to bring forward a bill seeking permission to establish the AME church. The legislation passed, stipulating that the church had to meet between sunrise and sunset.

Rev. Early repeatedly demonstrated his willingness to rely on the privileges of his Masonic ties. Early suffered through an attempt to brand him as a fugitive from slavery while riding his Shawneetown circuit in the Miller Grove region. Using his Freemasonry connections to claim his freedom, he recounted his strategy for escaping his well-armed captors. "While they went out to regale themselves with a fresh drink, I gave the squire the sign of the Masonic fraternity, which he acknowledged, and I showed him my papers both from the government and my native state." Early was permitted to go about his business.[24]

The spread of Prince Hall Masonry into Canada has roots in the United States. Noted abolitionist and Underground Railroad operative Abraham Shadd influenced the establishment of Freemasonry in Canada West. The union of New Jersey Grand Master George Shreve to Elizabeth Shadd, another of the daughters of A. D. Shadd, cemented the marriage between Freemasonry and abolitionism and between Masonry in the United States and Masonry in Canada. The Shreve family followed the Shadd family and moved to Canada West in 1852. Prior to the move, George Shreve of the Union Grand Lodge in New Jersey authorized a lodge in Hamilton, Canada West. Conveniently situated near the U.S. border in Niagara Falls, the lodge became a "way-station for the refugees from slavery."[25] Subsequent lodges established in St. Catharine's and Windsor sat closely and conveniently to the U.S. border. These sites had large numbers of refugees from slavery among their membership.[26]

Among those associated with AME and Freemasonry in Canada, Martin Delany, Abraham Shadd, and AME minister Josiah Henson have the clearest ties to the Underground Railroad. Delany, an early Masonic historian and Worshipful Master of the St. Cyprian Lodge in Pittsburgh, found strength and camaraderie in his Masonic bonds linking him to other fighters for Black freedom.[27] Delany used his Pittsburgh home to shelter escapees and sent them north to Chatham, Canada, and maintained contact with another Underground Railroad operative and fellow Mason in Canada, AME minister Josiah Henson.[28] Speaking of his work on the Underground Railroad, Henson admitted, "I was glad to help such of my old friends as had the spirit to make the attempt to free themselves; and I made more than one trip . . . to Maryland and Kentucky, with the expectation, in which I was not disappointed, that some might be enabled to follow in my footsteps. I knew the route pretty well, and had much greater facilities for travelling than when I came out of that Egypt for the first time."[29] He knew the route because he had traveled it with his family during their escape.

Throughout the years before the Civil War, Black Masons promoted education, protested illegal kidnappings, and agitated for an end to slavery. Oral and historical narratives assert that lodges served as stations on the Underground Railroad.[30] Prince Hall Masons were labeled as dangerous and placed in the same category as free Blacks in general. One writer expressed the fears that were surfacing after Nat Turner's 1831 attack. The writer believed "that a plan has been maturing for many years by the better informed free blacks at the north, most of whom are Free Masons, for the final liberation of the slaves of the south." The writer was convinced that those plans had been made "in the dark recesses of the African Lodges." "If there was to be devised a scheme for organizing and preparing the Southern blacks for insurrection, none that I can conceive of is so admirably calculated for the purpose as Free Masonry introduced among free Negroes. They of all others are most forward in promoting the spirit of revolt among slaves." The writer sounded the alarm that the means of preparing the minds of southern slaves and turning them into a confederated band of insurgents was started, ripened, and executed inside these same lodges. In his view, secret organizations among Blacks were the means by which "free Blacks of the north hold a direct communication with the slaves of the south."[31]

## Faith, Fraternity, and the Seeds of Rebellion

Demands by people of color to be released from slavery and its concomitant evils first drove slaveholders and politicians to enact a series of fugitive slave laws that increasingly fueled the fires of rebellion and war.[32] In the end, numerous tactics combined to destroy the "many headed hydra" that slavery had become. The Civil War ended a long strategic continuum among abolitionists and antislavery workers. Harriet Tubman relied on the skills she developed in guiding multitudes of captives out of slavery to aid the Union army.[33] Bishop Quinn traveled to Kansas and ministered to freedmen who crossed the lines into Union territory.[34] Kansas had become another destination offering freedom's refuge. Between 1860 and 1865, the Black population of Kansas swelled from 627 to 12,527.[35]

Escapees, with help from Black participants, fled from behind enemy lines retracing the footsteps to freedom along Underground Railroad routes. Reaffirming the effectiveness of the clandestine effort, the "railroad" became a silent partner in the Union war effort.[36] By the time of the Civil War, the Underground Railroad had gained sufficient notoriety for Martin Delany to propose a plan to President Lincoln. Blacks of the North, combined with armed Blacks from the South, would help defeat the Confederacy "through the medium of the *Underground Railroad*." Lincoln was enthusiastic enough about the plan to name Delany the first Black major in the Union army.[37]

Joining the U.S. Colored Troops (USCT) represented an additional component of a multi-pronged antislavery tactic. The approaching reality of the Civil War moved Chicago's noted Underground Railroad worker John Jones to capitalize on the respect he enjoyed in the Black community. Jones recruited and enlisted Black soldiers, as did Martin Delany and Mary Ann Shadd, both of whom were in Canada.[38] Frederick Douglass's famed connection with the 54th and 55th Massachusetts regiments represented only the most noted example of widespread recruitment in support of the war. AME preacher and physician Willis Revels lent his support by helping out-of-state recruiters and serving as a recruiting officer for Indiana. His brother Hiram recruited two regiments, the 4th and 39th USCTs, from his Baltimore pulpit.[39] Underground Railroad activists geared up for their final push toward freedom. Henry Highland Garnet encouraged Black men to enlist with the Union army and volunteered his services as a chaplain to Blacks in New York troops.[40] Transplanted Canadian Blacks returned to the land of their birth to join the fight for freedom.

Siebert proclaimed, "The Underground Railroad was one of the greatest forces which brought on the Civil War and thus destroyed slavery" and modern scholars agree. In his second inaugural address, President Lincoln pinpointed slavery as the cause: "These slaves constituted a peculiar and powerful interest. All knew that this interest was somehow, the cause of the war."[41] The end of the Civil War, however, did not signal the end of the fight against slavery and oppression. Black abolitionists were clear that enfranchisement, civil and political equality, and economic opportunity had been and remained key Black abolitionist agendas.[42] J. W. C. Pennington, echoing the view of fellow Black activist Henry Highland Garnet, declared, "The battle has just begun."[43]

In an 1865 speech delivered before the annual meeting of the Massachusetts Anti-Slavery Society five years before the ratification of the Fifteenth Amendment, Underground Railroad icon Frederick Douglass called for the "immediate, unconditional, and universal enfranchisement of the Black man, in every state in the Union."[44] Ratification of the Fifteenth Amendment granting Black men the right to vote fulfilled Douglass's dream.[45] Blacks wrote speeches and composed songs. Frances Watkins Harper expressed her joy in her poem, "The Fifteenth Amendment," "Ring out! Ring out! Your sweetest chimes / . . . / Let every heart with gladness thrill / . . . / Shake off the dust, O rising race! / Crowned as a brother and a man; / Justice to-day asserts her claim."[46]

CHAPTER 9

# Destination Freedom

Free Blacks carried out much of the clandestine work of the Underground Railroad as they probed the meaning of freedom in pre–Civil War America. Covert works of African Americans drove the efforts inside one of the world's most successful resistance movements. Placing the Underground Railroad inside Black communities sheds a different light on the culminating phase of more than two centuries of escapes by people of color. Whether urban or rural, Black settlements positioned at the borders between northern and southern states or at other critical junctures acted as the first line of freedom while simultaneously offering sanctuary to escaping captives.

Each of the sites in this study contains different landscape features that define the geography of resistance. The communities of Rocky Fork, Brooklyn, and Alton reflect the nature of the Underground Railroad along the Mississippi River in south-central Illinois. The geography of resistance brings the history and Underground Railroad activities in the little Black settlements out from the shadows of the more flamboyant, better-documented abolitionist havens nearby. The geographic and religious relationship between Brooklyn, Rocky Fork, and Alton positions the communities within an Underground Railroad zone.

Rocky Fork's strategic accessibility along waterways, its location among Quakers and sympathetic Whites, combined with oral narratives and the history of the radical AME Church sum up the factors indicating how the geography of resistance influenced Underground Railroad activity. The history of the enclave exposes the importance of family and friendships, institution building and self-reliance, landownership and economic stability among pre–Civil War African American communities.

The caves and iron furnaces along Underground Railroad routes in Miller Grove or Poke Patch contribute to the list of Underground Railroad spaces distinguished in a geography of resistance approach to the landscape. As small rural Black communities such as Miller Grove, Lick Creek, and Poke Patch are mapped and a cartographic signature established, vital associations between the smaller Black settlements and the better-known White abolitionist centers sharpen into focus. Blacks exploited the landscape to stake a claim for freedom within the Underground Railroad movement even as one law after another attempted to thwart escapes. Moving through the land as a method of securing freedom typified the Underground Railroad movement from the beginnings of enslavement until after the end of the American Civil War. Escape and reliance on the land lingered to the last.

The devotion to freedom found in the world's maroon communities and its later versions in free Black settlements further extended to Black Canadian communities. Whether in maroon communities or within the Underground Railroad movement, freedom has been as much about place as it has been about liberty. The history of African Americans written in the land reveals the pragmatic uses of the terrain.

The landscape evokes the memory of Black rural communities once dotting the countryside. Elements of the landscape provide a few more pieces of the puzzle that fill the gaps between the escapees' flight from slavery and the reemergence of the successful few who made it out of the South. The silent moments between escape and freedom, the exposing days and the desolate nights between Underground Railroad stations surface as the most difficult to understand or document. Leaving southern plantations and slave states, escapees found aid where they could in kitchens and cabin quarters.

During the period of the traditional Underground Railroad, individual escapes such as that of J. W. C. Pennington or Harriet Tubman were acts of single-minded personal liberation and courage. Yet, each relied on community support. As the slavery crisis deepened, the mechanisms of escape extended from lonely singular escapes to groups and families attempting to free themselves from bondage, and finally to armed conflict in the name of freedom. Through two wars with a third looming on the horizon, Blacks fought in the military, siding with whoever seemed more likely to grant the freedom and liberty the country espoused.

The story shifts over time and geography from sheltered and sequestered rural spaces to bold public action, culminating in daring, dramatic rescues in major northern cities such as Boston, Syracuse, Detroit, Oberlin, Ohio, and Troy, New York. Within the urban landscape, the Underground Railroad history of a host of major U.S. cities is as much about the history of communities in action as it is about individuals. Across the country, cities, towns, counties, and regions maintained distinctive identities along the pathways to freedom.

Migration shaped families and communities. From American Colonization Society plans and Black Nationalist emigration initiatives, to Quaker emigration ventures, to Canadian settlements, international lands appeared as remedies for American domestic policies. True freedom could not exist as long as slavery persisted anywhere in the country. Rather than abandon their homes and flee to foreign soil, a tactic that reached its height after passage of the Fugitive Slave Law of 1850, many escapees took their chances, defied the law, and remained in one of the free states. Urban Blacks, joining forces with White abolitionists, became increasingly militant in their attempts to stave off slave catchers and ban together to rescue their brethren.

AME Zion minister Jermaine Loguen refused to leave the country. He stubbornly defied the Fugitive Slave Law, saying, "The time has come to change the tones of submission into tones of defiance—and to tell Mr. Fillmore and Mr. Webster, if they propose to execute this measure upon us, to send on their blood-hounds." In other words, escape in defiance of the law. Loguen stubbornly resisted purchasing his freedom or having others pay slavery's ransom for him.[1]

Although legislation presents a "Blacks as nuisance" perspective, the zeal with which state and federal governments sought to rid themselves of free Blacks through enforcement of draconian Black Codes and Fugitive Slave Laws tacitly affirms Black humanity and power. The mere necessity for such laws exposes slavery as deficient, an unnatural social institution that required constant renegotiation, legislation, and vigilant, violent reinforcement. Moreover, no matter how humble or meager circumstances may have been, free Blacks demonstrated the possibility of a life of freedom.

The roots of pre–Civil War African American community networks often grew deep into the southern states from which the original settlers migrated and branched into Canada where many escapees eventually found safe haven. The Underground Railroad actually surfaces toward the end of a centuries-long progression of escape, connecting geographically unrelated, yet politically connected, philosophically aligned sites, interconnected by families as well as individuals in their relentless insistence on freedom.

The personal details of family histories signify the future of African American history. Tracking pre–Civil War Black churches and particularly their cemeteries leads to the residue of black communities that can provide new details about Underground Railroad routes. Material culture specialists consider surviving headstones optimal objects of authenticity. Primary sources of information gathered from geographically anchored cemeteries and gravestones allow confidence in assigning cultural complexity and interpretation to former communities.[2] Remnants of rural African American settlements and their associated cemeteries contain the stories of migration, community, and family that are central to the African American experience. Cemeteries, particularly those connected to pre–Civil War Black communities, are among the country's most precious historical resources and the most threatened. The historical wealth contained in these community burying grounds remains largely unrecognized, however. This important resource is quietly disappearing from the documentary record—their inhabitants, along with their history, silently buried.

Driven by the ever-increasing sophistication and resourcefulness of genealogists and the intertwining of family accounts, community studies and Black church histories rest at the center of research into the historic period of the Underground Railroad. Tracing family lines, genealogical connections, and the work of Black ministers, particularly the itinerant preachers who linked rural settlements together, form effective research strategies in addition to mapping Black settlements. The resulting evidence supports the conclusion that nineteenth-century Black settlements across the country, city or rural, functioned as conduits to freedom, offering some form of sanctuary to those escaping slavery, independent from, yet often in partnership with, White abolitionist activities.

At these African American communal sites, free Blacks blunted the economic oppression and the political shackles of slavery. Blacks sought refuge and anonymity within the free Black communities and employment where it could be found. By purchasing and cultivating farmland, by establishing Black churches that served as the institutional, social, and political center of their world, or by purchasing their own freedom as a form of economic emancipation from slavery, many Blacks finally realized their dream of liberty if not the goal of racial equality.

Identifying the networks that are the backbone of the Underground Railroad requires careful scrutiny of the relationships between Black abolitionists, Black church leaders, and the geographic proximity between Black settlements and religious groups such as Quakers, Presbyterians, and Methodists. Caves and iron furnaces must be added to the list of Underground Railroad spaces. Approaching the historic period of the Underground Railroad focused on combined efforts across multiple groups and new terrain should lessen the perpetuation of stilted, romanticized stories while simultaneously recognizing romanticized legends as part of the genre.

Moving outside Underground Railroad literature, connecting annual meeting participants apart from their civic or religious associations, and diagramming relationships among Black communities and Black activists will remove the shroud from the elusive understanding of African American participation. Following the long reach of Lewis Woodson or William Paul Quinn, for example, and mapping their relationships with other Underground Railroad participants across race, space, and time will bring new insights to old stories.

The activism of the convention movement, the focus of literary societies and fraternal organizations, and the aim of the church beyond spreading the gospel arched toward freedom and equality. Ultimately, southern slaveholders were unable to suppress the enslaved's constant longing for freedom, whether through flight or self-purchase. Neither violence nor terror, neither coercion nor religious indoctrination, extinguished the light of liberty.

Homes of prominent abolitionists form the most tangible and the most popular components of the landscape of Underground Railroad history. Well-known Underground Railroad stops made famous by men such as Levi Coffin and John Rankin, and conductors such as Harriet Tubman and John Parker, dominate understanding of Underground Railroad operations. Although the home of William Paul Quinn is an exception, African American family homes in black settlements connected to the Underground Railroad rarely survive. Black community stories reside in the domain of family histories, personal narratives, and oral accounts, and if we are fortunate, newspaper articles—sources that tend to make historians queasy. As a fundamental historical unit, the Black family comes forward as foundational to both the Black community and the Black church, providing refuge within hostile environments through which the Underground Railroad operated. Church, community, and family coexisted, entwined in interdependent and inseparable ways.[3]

Increasingly, however, archaeology will help identify new networks, routes, and previously unidentified participants. In so doing, archaeological investigations should receive equal consideration in tandem with oral history, mapping, and historical documentation as necessary components within an expanded reclamation process. Archaeology furthers the ability to identify and map Black settlements and to define spatial relationships between families and institutions.[4]

Frequently, due to preservation policies, remnants of African American presence in the land remain solely as archaeological resources. Identifying and then mapping pre–Civil War African American communities delineates the close association between Black settlements, the Black church, and their White Quaker or Presbyterian counterparts, or other neighbors and collaborators involved with abolitionism and the Underground Railroad (see map 5).

This work conceptualizes the historic period of the Underground Railroad through the geography of resistance, relying on distinct regional considerations, including landforms, proximity to water, distance from southern states, and the overall political position of the surrounding community. Mapping visually defines the relationship between African American settlements and historic Underground Railroad routes. As progress and development continue to take their toll on historic African American sites, mapping ranks as one of the most crucial aspects for discovering new Underground Railroad pathways and preserving the existing ones. For those struggling to document or preserve Underground Railroad sites, looking at the Black involvement through the lens of the geography of resistance applies badly needed theory to a topic surrounded by myth, legend, and lore. Therefore, *The Geography of Resistance* expands preservation methods and theories in its approach to historical memory. African Americans, their sites and their history, were not seen as part of the American collective identity, which justified a lack of preservation efforts.[5] Where the written record is barren, turning to the landscape as evidence of the day-to-day interactions of free Blacks living in community enlivens our understanding.[6]

As Lick Creek, Miller Grove, and Rocky Fork demonstrate, archaeology can be useful in supporting new sites and expanding the narrative beyond the 150 years of oft-repeated stories. However, the ambiguous, confusing, and nonspecific nature of the results, coupled with a lack of definitive historical documentation, can place researchers working with new Underground Railroad sites on a slippery slope where rigor, authentication, and interpretation are paramount challenges.

The archaeological signature of the Underground Railroad may well turn out to be the footprint of the Black church rather than the tunnels and subterranean places of concealment that have been the very limited focus of the discipline.[7] Using the geography of resistance alerts archaeologists, researchers, preservationists, and other historians to hidden, overlooked dimensions in the terrain that situate free Black communal sites within one of the world's most important freedom struggles.

The powerful story of Blacks and the Underground Railroad is not meant to ignore the valiant work of Quakers or the harrowing, dedicated work of White abolitionists. Indeed, Calvin Fairbank, who delivered Lewis Hayden, his wife, Harriet, and her son, Joseph, out of slavery in Kentucky, spent seventeen years in prison for his efforts. Schooner owner William Baylis served six years of a forty-year prison sentence for his offenses. Seth Concklin lost his life in his efforts to rescue Peter Still's family from Alabama. Fines imposed on Thomas Garrett forced him to the brink of financial ruin. Other stories of the suffering of White antislavery workers are well-documented. This study highlights an alternative narrative.[8]

Relationships among Black abolitionists were crucial to the success of the Black underground. Agents moved across the country selling black newspapers, preaching, or visiting settlements. Underground Railroad operatives met at conventions and annual meetings. Over his long and influential life, Bishop William Paul Quinn formed lasting ties to the little settlements and churches while maintaining his connection with many of the country's most ardent and radical thinkers—Martin Delany, Henry Highland Garnet, and Lewis Tappan along with his friends Lewis Woodson and Willis Revels to name but a few Underground Railroad ties revealed through his ministry.

African Americans working together in communities embodied the Black community's expanding commitment and its growing independence. People of color shared "both the promise of America and the burden of its hypocrisy."[9] Self-determined Blacks forced alternatives to untenable situations by challenging the existing injustices of American society. As a group, the country had failed these men and women as it had failed people of color in general. A communicating, determined Black community connected over a wide social network and geographic region would have been unthinkable for many nineteenth-century White Americans.

Pulitzer Prize–winning historian Annette Gordon-Reed and other historians have cautioned against "painting too rosy a picture of plucky slaves prevailing against all odds."[10] Withering betrayals, petty infighting, egoism, and devastating mistrust plagued escapees. Likewise, Berlin draws attention to the "distant prospect" freedom was for even the most determined fugitive.[11] Too often free Blacks "crossed the strongly fortified border into freedom only to see the American dream still besieged."[12] Jermain Loguen described his initial jubilance upon crossing the Ohio and reaching Indiana. His joy quickly turned to despair however, after a Black man informed him, "There is no place in the States where you can be safe. To be safe, you must get into Canada. I am sorry to say that the only power that gives freedom in North America, is in England."[13]

Underground Railroad workers took advantage of weaknesses by exploiting lapses and defying convention. Hundreds of years after the fact, secluded, wooded rural enclaves rival the homes of abolitionists as Underground Railroad spaces. The connections between Blacks in country areas and their counterparts in better-known urban centers forged the wider community. For the Underground Railroad, no artifact or document more thoroughly expresses this great quest for freedom and social justice than the landscape of freedom within free Black communities.

# APPENDIX

This preliminary chart shows the denominations of African American ministers who also participated in the Underground Railroad movement. Their role as ministers is not always recognized when their Underground Railroad work is being highlighted.

| Minister | Denomination | Location | Date | Formerly Enslaved? | Free Mason |
|---|---|---|---|---|---|
| Richard Allen (founder) | AME Bishop | Mother Bethel AME, Philadelphia | 1816–1831 | Y | Y |
| Duke William Anderson | AME/Baptist | Wood River, IL | | | |
| Amos Gerry Beman (son) | AME Zion/Congregational | Temple Street African Congregational, New Haven, CT (later Dixwell Ave. Congregational) | 1839–1857 | | |
| Jehiel Beman (father) | AME Zion (Freedom Church) | Cross Street, Middletown, CT/Boston | 1830- | | |
| Morris Brown | AME Bishop | Charleston/ Mother Bethel, Philadelphia | 1818–1844 | | ? |
| Samuel E. Cornish (founder) | Black Presbyterian | First Colored Presbyterian Church, NY, NJ (later Shiloh) | 1822 | | Y |
| Alexander Crummell | Episcopalian | St. Matthew's, NYC; RI, PA, DC | 1842–1851 | | Y |
| Moses Dickson | AME | Olive Chapel, Kirkwood, MO | 1866 | | Y |
| Amos N. Freeman | Congregational | The Abyssinian Church/Meetinghouse Portland, ME | 1841–1851 | | |
| | Presbyterian | Siloam Presbyterian, Brooklyn, NY | 1852–1881 | | |
| Henry Highland Garnet | Presbyterian | Liberty Street Presbyterian Church, Troy NY | 1839–1848 | Y | Y |
| | | Jamaica, WI | 1852–1855 | | |
| | | First Colored Presbyterian (Shiloh) NYC | 1856–1864 | | |
| | | Fifteenth Street Presbyterian, WDC | 1864–1866 | | |
| | | (founder) Grace Memorial Presbyterian, Pittsburgh, PA | 1867–1868 | | |
| John Glouster (founder/father) | Black Presbyterian | First African Presbyterian Church, Philadelphia | 1807–1822 | Y | |
| Jeremiah (son) | Black Presbyterian | Second African Presbyterian Church, Philadelphia | 1822 | Y | |
| John (son) | Black Presbyterian | | | Y | |
| Stephen (son) | Black Presbyterian | Third African Presbyterian Church, Philadelphia | 1844 | Y | |
| James (son) | Black Presbyterian | Baltimore | 1849 | Y | |
| | | Siloam Presbyterian, Brooklyn, NY also Buffalo | | | |
| Leonard Grimes | Baptist | Twelfth Baptist Church, Boston (The Fugitive Slave Church) | 1848–1874 | | |
| Prince Hall | AME | Boston | | | Y |
| Lemuel Haynes | Congregationalist | Rutland, VT | 1785–1818 | | |
| Joshiah Henson | ME/AME/ British Methodist Episcopal | Dresden, Ontario, CA | 1828–1883 | Y | Y |
| J. Theodore Holly | Protestant Episcopal | St. Luke's, New Haven, CT | 1856–1861 | | |
| George Liele (Left with British 1783) | Baptist | Georgia/Kingston, Jamaica | 1772–1828 | Y | |

| Minister | Denomination | Location | Date | Formerly Enslaved? | Free Mason |
|---|---|---|---|---|---|
| Jermaine Loguen | AME Zion Bishop | Syracuse/Binghamton/Bath/ Ithaca/Troy, NY | 1842–1872 | Y | |
| William M. Mitchell | Baptist | Ohio and Teraulay (Bay) Street Baptist, Toronto, CA | | | |
| James Oliver | AME | Camden, NJ ? | | | |
| Benjamin Paul (brother) | Baptist | Albany, NY | | | |
| | | Abyssinian Baptist, NYC | 1824 | | |
| | | First African Baptist, Wilberforce, Canada | 1831 | | |
| Nathaniel Paul (brother) | Baptist | First African Baptist, Albany | 1820 | | |
| | | First African Baptist, Wilberforce, Canada | 1831 | | |
| | | Hamilton Street Baptist Church, Albany | 1836 | | |
| Thomas Paul, Sr. (brother) | Baptist | African Meeting House, Boston | 1806 | | Y |
| | | Abyssinian Baptist, NYC | 1808 | | |
| J. C. Pennington | Congregational | Temple Street African Congregational, (later Dixwell Ave.) New Haven, CT | 1837 | | |
| | | Talcott Street Church, Hartford | 1840 | | |
| | Presbyterian | Shiloh Church, NYC | 1847 | Y | |
| | | First Colored Presbyterian (Shiloh/ Prince Street) | 1848–1856 | | |
| William Paul Quinn | AME Bishop | United States and Canada | 1817–1873 | | Y |
| Charles B. Ray | Congregational | Bethesda Church, NYC | 1845 | | |
| Hiriam Revels (brother) | AME | Wylie Avenue Church, Pittsburgh, PA/ Richmond, IN also MD, IL, OH, TN, MO, KS | ca. 1845–1901 | | |
| Willis Revels (brother) | AME | Bethel AME, Indianapolis, IN also Lick Creek, IN/Quinn Chapel, Louisville, KY | 1842 | | |
| Christopher Rush | AME Zion | New York City | 1822–1873 | | |
| Peter Spencer (founder) | African Union Methodist | African Union Methodist Protestant Church, Wilmington, DE | 1813–1843 | Y | Y |
| Samuel Ringgold Ward | Presbyterian/Congregational | New York/Jamaica | 1841–1866 | Y | |
| Peter Williams, Sr. (father) | AME Zion | New York City | 1798 | Y | |
| Peter Williams, Jr. (son) | Black Episcopalian | St. Philip's Episcopal, NYC | 1818–1840 | | |
| Hiram Wilson | Colored Presbyterian | Canada | 1836 | | |
| Thomas Woodson (father) | AME | Ohio | | Y | |
| Lewis (son) | AME | Pittsburgh | 1830s | | |
| Thomas, Jr. (son) | AME | Ohio | | | |
| John (son) | AME | Ohio | | | |
| Theodore S. Wright | Presbyterian | First Colored Presbyterian (Shiloh), NYC | 1833–1847 | | |

# NOTES

## Preface

1. Fruehling and Smith, "Subterranean Hideaways"; Weik, *The Archaeology of Antislavery Resistance.*

2. Griffler, *Front Line of Freedom.*

3. Hodges, *David Ruggles*, 4–5.

4. National Park Service, *Exploring a Common Past*, 3.

5. Herbert, "National Park Service."

6. Henry Highland Garnet, *The Past and Present Condition, and the Destiny of the Colored Races: A Discourse* (Troy, NY: Kreeland, 1848), 19.

7. De Boer, "The Role of Afro-Americans," 189.

## Introduction

1. Larry Gara, "William Still and the Underground Railroad," in *Blacks in the Abolitionist Movement*, ed. John H. Bracey, August Meier, and Elliot Rudwick (Belmont, CA: Wadsworth Publishing Co., 1971), 44.

2. Shackel, *Memory in Black and White.*

3. P. Lewis, "Common Landscapes as Historic Documents."

4. Douglass, "The Present Condition and Future Prospects of the Negro People."

5. Chapman, *Black Voices*; H. Wilson, *History of the Rise and Fall of the Slave Power in America*; Charles Eric Lincoln, *The Negro Pilgrimage in America* (New York: Bantam Books, 1967); Simpson, *Under the North Star.*

6. McDougall, *Fugitive Slaves (1619–1865).*

7. *The Granite Freeman*, May 22, 1845; Nash, *Forging Freedom.*

8. Siebert, *The Underground Railroad*, 38; "An Act to authorize the people of the Missouri territory to form a constitution and state government, and for the admission of such state into the Union on equal footing with the original states, and to prohibit slavery in certain territories" (*A Century of Lawmaking for a New Nation: U.S. Congressional Documents and Debates, 1774–1875*, 548, Statutes at Large, 16th Congress, 1st Sess.).

9. "The Albany Forwarding Trade," *Emancipator and Republican*, April 20, 1843, 199.

10. "New York State Vigilance Committee," *The North Star*, May 19, 1848, 2.

11. Starling, *The Slave Narrative*, 193.

12. Moses Roper, 1838; Lewis Clarke, 1845; William Wells Brown, 1847; Josiah Henson, 1849; and Henry Bibb, 1849, all wrote of their escapes from slavery. J. W. C. Pennington, 1849; Samuel Ringgold Ward, 1855; Jermaine Loguen, 1859; and William and Ellen Craft, 1860, outlined their escapes from slavery. This is not a complete list of narratives of escape.

13. Moses Roper, *Narrative of the Adventures and Escape of Moses Roper, from American Slavery. With an Appendix, Containing a List of Places Visited by the Author in Great Britain and Ireland and the British Isles, and Other Matter* (Berwick-upon-Tweed: Published by the Author, 1848), 52.

14. Henry Bibb, *Narrative of the Life and Adventures of Henry Bibb, An American Slave, Written by Himself* (New York: Published by the Author, 1849), 15–16.

15. Pennington, *The Fugitive Blacksmith*.

16. *Ohio Statesman*, June 25, 1850, 2.

17. An Act to Organize the Territories of Kansas and Nebraska, in *A Century of Lawmaking for a New Nation, U.S. Congressional Documents and Debates, 1774–1875*, Statutes at Large, 33rd Congress, 1st Sess., sec. 9 and 10.

18. "The Schism of 1861."

19. W. W. Brown, *Rising Son*, 329.

20. Drew, *A North-side View of Slavery*.

21. W. Mitchell, *The Underground Railroad*, v.

22. Dyson, "Gerrit Smith's Effort," 354.

23. W. Mitchell, *The Underground Railroad*, 14.

24. Still, *The Underground Railroad*.

25. Siebert, *The Underground Railroad*, 32.

26. L. Coffin, *Reminiscences of Levi Coffin*.

27. Siebert, *The Underground Railroad*. Although this quote is from a 1939 Winston Churchill radio broadcast, Underground Railroad writers have appropriated the apt description. Bartlett, *Bartlett's Familiar Quotations*, 743:17.

28. Christopher Densmore, "Introduction," in Smedley, *History of the Underground Railroad*, viii.

29. Smedley, *History of the Underground Railroad*, 26–27.

30. "The Underground Railway" and "Knights of Liberty," *The Freeman* (Indianapolis), February 24, 1900.

31. Cockrum, *History of the Underground Railroad*, 18.

32. Cockrum, *History of the Underground Railroad*, 21.

33. Ronald L. Baker, *Homeless, Friendless, and Penniless: The WPA Interviews with Former Slaves Living in Indiana* (Bloomington: Indiana University Press, 2000), 25, 205.

34. Gara, *The Liberty Line*, preface.

35. Gara, *The Liberty Line*.

36. Blockson, "Escape from Slavery," 3–39; Blockson, *The Underground Railroad in Pennsylvania*; Blockson, *The Underground Railroad*; Blockson, *Hippocrene Guide to the Underground Railroad.*

37. Franklin and Schweninger, *Runaway Slaves*, 69.

38. Rael, ed., *African-American Activism before the Civil War.*

39. Hodges, *David Ruggles*, 2.

40. Bradford, *Scenes in the Life of Harriet Tubman*; Bradford, *Harriet Tubman*; Conrad, *Harriet Tubman*; Hodges, *David Ruggles*, 2; Newman, "Protest in Black and White," 197–98; Jeremiah Wilson, *The Golden Age of Black Nationalism, 1850–1925* (New York: Oxford University Press, 1988). For recent works on Tubman, see Humez, *Harriet Tubman*; Larson, *Bound for the Promised Land*; Catherine Clinton, *Harriet Tubman: The Road to Freedom* (New York: Little, Brown and Company, 2004); Milton C. Sernett, *Harriet Tubman: Myth, Memory, and History* (Durham: Duke University Press, 2007).

41. Trusty, *Underground Railroad.*

42. Cha-Jua, *America's First Black Town*, 40.

43. Glasco, *WPA History of the Negro*, 112.

44. Ginsburg, "Escaping through a Black Landscape."

45. Griffler, *Front Line of Freedom*, xii.

46. Griffler, *Front Line of Freedom*, xii, xi; LaRoche, "On the Edge of Freedom," 18.

47. Griffler, *Front Line of Freedom*, 43–44; LaRoche, "On the Edge of Freedom."

48. Ernst, *A Nation Within a Nation.*

49. Carl L. Spicer, "The Underground Railroad in Southern Illinois," unpublished manuscript, The William H. Siebert Underground Railroad Collection, Ohio Historical Society, n.d. The interdenominational character of antislavery societies was a major factor in the Quaker schism; Hodges, *David Ruggles.*

50. *Syracuse Standard*, June 22, 1857.

51. For example, see "Rev. J. W. Loguen," *Frederick Douglass' Paper*, February 1, 1856, 3.

52. Baldwin, *"Invisible" Strands in African Methodism*, 38.

53. *The Morning News*, August 26, 1889, 1, 8.

54. Baldwin, *Peter Spencer*, 84.

55. Curry, *The Free Black*, 194.

56. R. Wright, *Centennial Encyclopaedia*, 5.

57. Walls, *The African Methodist Episcopal Zion Church.*

58. Carter G. Woodson, *The Negro Church*, 2nd ed. (Washington, DC: Associated Publishers, 1921), 148–49.

59. Gayraud S. Wilmore, *Religion and Black Radicalism: An Interpretation of the Religious History of African Americans* (Maryknoll, NY: Orbis Books, 1998).

60. Taylor, *The Black Churches of Brooklyn*; Raboteau, *Canaan Land*; Melton, *A Will to Choose.*

61. Weik, *The Archaeology of Antislavery Resistance.*

## Chapter 1. Rocky Fork, Illinois

1. For research purposes, sections 20, 21, 22, 27, 29, 30, and 33 are also associated with the settlement. The site can be reached from State Street in Alton, Illinois, 2.1 miles west on Illinois Route 3 (formerly Route 100 Delmar Avenue) to Boy Scout Lane, north on Boy Scout Lane 0.6 mile to Rocky Fork Road, west on Rocky Fork Road 0.4 mile to Rocky Fork Cemetery. "Scout Camp Spot Rocky Fork Is Historic Spot," *Alton Evening Telegraph*, May 28, 1921.

2. Holmes and Arnold, 1861 Map of Madison County, Illinois, Civil Engineers and Map Publishers, Buffalo, New York; Timmermiere, "History of New Bethel AME Church Rocky Fork."

3. Buchanan, *Black Life on the Mississippi*; Dunphy, *Abolitionism and the Civil War*.

4. C. Johnson, "Underground Railroad Network."

5. Listed in the 1860 Madison County Census as Andrew F. and Hellen M. Hawley; *History of Madison County, Illinois, Illustrated, with Biographical Sketches of Many Prominent Men and Pioneers* (Edwardsville, IL: W. R. Brink & Co., 1882).

6. Vincent, *Southern Seed*.

7. Mr. Townsend was born November 8, 1908. LaRoche interview, June 2000.

8. Middleton, *The Black Laws*, 293.

9. Hindman as cited in Thornton, "New Bethel Church"; "Scout Camp Spot Rocky Fork Is Historic Spot," *The Alton Evening Telegraph*, May 28, 1921.

10. Interview with Charlotte Johnson, committee member, Committee on Black Pioneers, Alton Museum of History and Art, Alton, Illinois. Tape recording, conducted by Cheryl LaRoche, Wood Station, Illinois, June 2000.

11. Interview with Charles B. Townsend. Tape recording, conducted by Cheryl LaRoche, Alton, Illinois, June 2000; Charlotte Johnson interview.

12. London Parks to Peter Baker, 1856, sec. 29, Land Transfer records, Madison County Courthouse, Edwardsville, Illinois.

13. Leighty, "Old Rocky Fork."

14. Charlotte Johnson interview.

15. Townsend interview.

16. Thornton, "New Bethel Church."

17. Charlotte Johnson interview. Oral sources report the existence of a letter that I have yet to locate in which Quinn mentions Rocky Fork.

18. Singleton, *The Romance of African Methodism*; LaRoche and Palmer, "The Look of Eagles"; Welch, *William Paul Quinn*.

19. Welch, *William Paul Quinn*, 6.

20. Cha-Jua, *America's First Black Town*; R. Wright, *Centennial Encyclopaedia*; Yancey and Galloy, "Mother Baltimore's Freedom Village."

21. Cha-Jua, *America's First Black Town*; Yancey and Galloy, "Mother Baltimore's Freedom Village"; Singleton, "Following the Trail of the Fathers," 3–5.

22. Beckly, "The African Methodist Episcopal Church."

23. Harris, *The History of Negro Servitude*; Cha-Jua, *America's First Black Town*; Minutes of the 7th General Conference of the AME, Pittsburgh, Pennsylvania, 1844; Payne, *History of the African Methodist Episcopal Church*, 170–71.

24. Demczuk, "Unionville." Hindman is variously spelled Hyndman, Heinman. I have followed the spelling associated with each citation.

25. Forty-eight-year-old Parks is listed in the 1845 census of Madison County. Lundun (this is a variation on the spelling on London) had four "free males" and "three free females" living with him in Alton (Township 5 N R10W) at the time.

26. Spaulding Account Books, Box 1, Illinois State Historical Library, Springfield, and Ledger in the possession of John Matlock Jr.; *Alton Evening Telegraph*, May 28, 1921.

27. Interview with John Matlock Jr. Tape recording, conducted by Cheryl LaRoche, Rocky Fork, Illinois, June 2000; UGRR Network to Freedom Application, Camp Warren Levis.

28. Black Pioneer Files, Alton Museum of History and Art, Alton, Illinois; Goers, "Rocky Fork," 8.

29. "Scout Camp Spot Rocky Fork Is Historic Spot," *Alton Evening Telegraph*, May 28, 1921; Dunphy, *Abolitionism and the Civil War*.

30. Black Pioneer File, Alton Museum of History and Art, Alton, Illinois. This is a constant problem with the imprecision of oral narratives, which often use updated contemporary landmarks to refer to historical events, and highlights the problem of change over time. The site remained the same but the historical landmarks are often destroyed, leaving the oral record bereft of anchoring points.

31. "The Underground Line. Railway of the Olden Time, without Rails, Road-Bed, or Visible Apparatus," *The Inter Ocean*, February 20, 1875; Dunphy, *Abolitionism and the Civil War*; Hoffman, *God's Portion*; "Death of John Jones," *The Inter Ocean*, May 22, 1879.

32. Hoffman, *God's Portion*, 46.

33. Siebert, *The Underground Railroad*; Blockson, *The Underground Railroad*; Blockson, *Hippocrene Guide to the Underground Railroad*.

34. Dunphy, *Abolitionism and the Civil War*; Hoffman, *God's Portion*; Charlotte Johnson, "Underground Railroad Network." "Depot" is another Underground Railroad term that refers to a station.

35. Lymann Goodnow, "Recollections," 1880, unpublished manuscript, The State of Wisconsin Collection; John Nelson Davidson, *Negro Slavery in Wisconsin and the Underground Railroad* (Milwaukee: Parkman Club Publications 18, 1897).

36. The word "friends" can be difficult to interpret. Not all writers adhere to the convention that when referring to the Society of Friends the word is capitalized. In places such as Southern Illinois, where Presbyterians, Methodists, and Scotch Covenanters rather than Quakers formed the antislavery "bonds of Christian brotherhood" found along the Underground Railroad, the word "friends" may be literally understood to refer to friends of the escapees; Spicer, "The Underground Railroad in Southern Illinois"; Gara, "The Underground Railroad in Illinois."

37. Cha-Jua, *America's First Black Town*, 44.

38. W. W. Brown, *The Travels of William Wells Brown*; G. Turner, *The Underground Railroad in Illinois*.

39. Blockson, *Hippocrene Guide to the Underground Railroad*; W. W. Brown, *The Travels of William Wells Brown*.

40. Demos, "The Antislavery Movement"; James G. Birney as quoted in L. Coffin, *Reminiscences of Levi Coffin*, 66.

41. Twelvetrees, ed., *The Story of the Life of John Anderson*; Craft and Craft, *Running a Thousand Miles for Freedom*, 36.

42. Now 1828 W. Delmar Avenue in Godfrey Township, Madison County. A. T. Hawley did not register the farm name Lilac Lodge until December 13, 1916. Index to Farm Names, Register of Farm Names Madison County, Madison County Courthouse, Edwardsville, Illinois; The spelling of Hyndman's name alternated among Hindman, Hineman, and Hyndman.

43. "Scout Camp Spot Rocky Fork Is Historic Spot," *Alton Evening Telegraph*, May 28, 1921, 4; personal communication, George Wadleigh, September 2, 2000; Goers, "Rocky Fork," 8.

44. *Alton Evening Telegraph*, January 26, 1907.

45. Timmermiere, "History of New Bethel A.M.E. Church Rocky Fork."

46. Leighty, "Old Rocky Fork."

47. Thornton, "New Bethel Church," AA5; Timmermiere, "History of New Bethel A.M.E. Church Rocky Fork."

48. *St. Louis Post Dispatch*, December 12, 1988.

49. Goers, "Rocky Fork"; Schmidt, "Blaze Destroys Rocky Fork Again."

50. Woods, *Development Arrested*, 12.

51. Much of the information contained in this report was taken from text panels, Alton Museum of History and Art, compiled by Charlotte Johnson, Committee on Black Pioneers, Black History Commission.

52. Charlotte Johnson, "Underground Railroad Network."

53. Titcomb, "Rocky Fork," 12–13; Pierce, "Proposal for Crosstown Highway."

## Chapter 2. Miller Grove, Illinois

1. McCorvie is from the Murphysboro Ranger Station; McNerney, "A Thematic Study of Rural Historic Farmsteads."

2. Annable, *Pope County Illinois*.

3. National Forest Service, "Miller Grove."

4. Final Decree, Peter Singleton.

5. Mary McCorvie, "Archeological Griots: An Environmental History Program at Miller Grove, a Free Ante-Bellum African American Community in Southern Illinois," *African Diaspora Archaeology Network Newsletter*, December 2005, www.diaspora.uiuc.edu/news1205/news1205.html#1; Final Decree, Peter Singleton.

6. West to Jocelyn, July 5, 1859, American Missionary Association Archives, Tulane University, New Orleans (hereafter AMAA) 31453.

7. Annabel, *Pope County Illinois.*

8. Will of Henry Sides.

9. Annable, *Pope County Illinois*; marriage certificate of Edward Dabbs and Dolly Sides; marriage certificate of Edward Dabbs and Clarissa Fields.

10. Marriage certificate of Edward Dabbs to Dolly Sides, April 1, 1848.

11. State of Illinois, sale bill, estate of Edward Dabbs, filed July 30, 1866, on file, Pope County Clerk's Office, Golconda, Illinois.

12. Cornish, Wright, and Garnet were Presbyterian ministers; Pennington, Beman, Ward, and Ray were Congregational clergymen. De Boer, "The Role of Afro-Americans," 77. Pennington would later become an itinerant preacher for the AME Church in Natchez as cited in Ripley, ed., *The Black Abolitionist Papers*, vol. 5, 394 (hereafter *BAP*).

13. West to Jocelyn, June 1, 1857, Amistad Center, AMAA 30582.

14. Muelder, *Fighters for Freedom*, 207.

15. *BAP*, vol. 2, 116n.

16. Fuller, "Miller Grove."

17. Annable, *Pope County Illinois.*

18. West to Tappan, Gilbert, Whipple, and Joslin, July 16, 1856, AMAA 30133.

19. Raines, *Abolitionists and Anti-Slavery Men*, 12; West to Jocelyn, July 18, 1859, AMAA 31569.

20. Lewis Tappan Antislavery Library Catalogue; Bradford, *Harriet Tubman.*

21. *Acts of the General Assembly of the State of Georgia, 1829*, 168–75; Eaton, "A Dangerous Pamphlet," 329. North Carolina passed a bill in late 1830 to prevent all persons from teaching slaves to read or write. The issue of the education of the slaves once again became a vital Quaker concern as well. Hatcher, "North Carolina Quakers," 92.

22. Raines, *Abolitionists and Anti-Slavery Men*, 13.

23. Berry and Blassingame, *Long Memory*; Litwack, *North of Slavery*, 57.

24. Hinks, *To Awaken My Afflicted Brethren*, 115.

25. Wyatt-Brown, "The Abolitionists' Postal Campaign of 1835."

26. West to Jocelyn, monthly statement to the AMA, June 1–July 15, 1857, AMAA 30630.

27. De Boer, "The Role of Afro-Americans," 67.

28. De Boer, "The Role of Afro-Americans," 192.

29. Wyatt-Brown, *Lewis Tappan*, 300.

30. Testimony of William H. Collins, January 13, 1896, as cited in Spicer, "The Underground Railroad in Southern Illinois."

31. West to Jocelyn, June 1, 1857, AMAA 30582.

32. Presumably, this is a copy of Fredrick Douglass's *My Bondage and My Freedom*, published in 1856. James West Colporteur's report, AMAA 31018.

33. West to Jocelyn, monthly statement to the AMA, July 2–August 1, 1860, AMAA 32076.

34. De Boer, "The Role of Afro-Americans," 231.

35. West to Jocelyn, June 1, 1857, AMAA 30582.

36. Fee, *Autobiography of John G. Fee*, 147; Muelder, *Fighters for Freedom*, 308; Beard, *A Crusade of Brotherhood*, 100–103; Fee, *Autobiography of John G. Fee*, 147.

37. Fee, *Autobiography of John G. Fee*; Galesburg *Free Democrat*, September 14 and November 16, 1854, as cited in Muelder, *Fighters for Freedom*, 307; Fee, *Autobiography of John G. Fee*; Gara, *The Liberty Line*, 86.

38. De Boer, "The Role of Afro-Americans," 78, 219; West to Jocelyn, monthly statement to the AMA, September 7–October 11, 1860, dated October 15, 1860, AMAA 32209.

39. West to Jocelyn, April 16, 1860, AMAA 31917.

40. Raines, *Abolitionists and Anti-Slavery Men*, 22.

41. West to Jocelyn, monthly statement to the AMA, October 15, 1860–January 11, 1861, AMAA 29.

42. De Boer, "The Role of Afro-Americans," 92.

43. Raines, *Abolitionists and Anti-Slavery Men*, 2; Spicer, "The Underground Railroad in Southern Illinois."

44. West to Jocelyn, monthly statement to the AMA, June 1–July 15, 1857, AMAA 30630.

45. Illinois WPA Narratives, "The Negro In Illinois," Box 7, Folder 7, Dr. Charles Volney Dyer, Chicago Public Library. Also see Still, *The Underground Railroad*; Illinois WPA, 4-The Underground Railroad, Box 7, Folder 1.

46. West to Jocelyn, monthly statement to the AMA, September 19, 1859, AMAA 31633.

47. Griffler, *Front Line of Freedom*; Conklin quoted in Pickard, *Kidnapped and the Ransomed*, 284–85.

48. S. Early, *Life and Labors of Reverend Jordan W. Early*, 50.

49. Bryce Crawford, Sparta, to AMA, January 16, 1854; Eden W. Holmes to Jocelyn, April 20, 1860, May 12, 1860; A. L. Rankin, Chicago, to Jocelyn, March 1, 1861, AMAA, quoted in Raines, *Abolitionists and Anti-Slavery Men*, 2, 19.

50. Gara, *The Liberty Line*, 55.

51. Raines, *Abolitionists and Anti-Slavery Men*, 18.

52. West to Tappan, Gilbert, Whipple, and Joslin, July 16, 1856, AMAA 30133.

53. Drew, *A North-side View of Slavery*, 317–18.

54. Drew, *A North-side View of Slavery*.

55. Tregillis, *River Roads to Freedom*, 31–32.

56. Personal communication to Mary McCorvie, National Forest Service, and Cheryl LaRoche, University of Maryland.

57. Spicer, "The Underground Railroad in Southern Illinois"; Cooley, "Illinois and the Underground Railroad."

58. Raines, *Abolitionists and Anti-Slavery Men*, 7, 10–11.

59. Siebert, *The Underground Railroad*, 32.

60. Cooley, "Illinois and the Underground Railroad"; Spicer, "The Underground Railroad in Southern Illinois."

61. Dearinger, "Miller Grove."

## Chapter 3. Lick Creek, Indiana

1. See Stout, *History of Orange County, Indiana.*

2. Krieger, Initial Report of Phase I Survey. African Americans are known to have owned land in T1N, R1E sections 10, 12, 14, 20, 21, 22, 23, 27, 28, 29, 32, 33; T1S, R1E section 4; and T2N, R1E, section 27.

3. National Forest Service, CD Rom.

4. Robbins, *Forgotten Hoosiers.*

5. National Forest Service, CD Rom with power point overview of the three Forest Service sites provided by Angie Krieger; Robbins, *Forgotten Hoosiers*; "Lick Creek," www.fs.fed.us/r9/hoosier/docs/history/lick_creek.htm.

6. Robbins, *Forgotten Hoosiers*; Cord, "Indiana Applications."

7. Jonathan's sister married Joshua Hadley. From William Wade Hinshaw, "North Carolina Yearly Meeting of Friends," in *Encyclopedia of American Quaker Genealogy*, 6 vols. (Ann Arbor: Edwards Brothers, Inc, 1936–50), vol. 1, 358. Lindley attended the Cane Creek monthly meeting. Distance between Cane Creek and New Garden is thirty miles.

8. Kroupa, *Slave Revolts*, 19.

9. Dungy, "A Friend in Deed."

10. *Book of Meetings*, 58–59.

11. Hamm et al., "Moral Choices"; Woodson, *A Century of Negro Migration*, 58.

12. Robbins, *Forgotten Hoosiers.*

13. Robbins, *Forgotten Hoosiers.*

14. Thornbrough, *The Negro in Indiana before 1900*; Robbins, *Forgotten Hoosiers.*

15. Robbins, *Forgotten Hoosiers*; National Forest Service, www.fs.fed.us/r9/hoosier/docs/history/lick_creek.htm.

16. Robbins, *Forgotten Hoosiers*; National Forest Service, www.fs.fed.us/r9/hoosier/docs/history/lick_creek.htm.

17. Vincent, *Southern Seed*, 10.

18. Weeks, *Southern Quakers and Slavery*, 261.

19. Cox, "The Peace and Social Concerns of Wrightsborough Friends," 7.

20. Soderlund, *Quakers & Slavery*; Meaders, "Kidnapping Blacks in Philadelphia," 2, 8; Hiram H. Hilty, "North Carolina Quakers and Slavery" (Ph.D. dissertation, Duke University, 1969). Guilford County Friends meetings during 1830s were New Garden, Deep River, Dover, Center, Hopewell, and Springfield. A tide of emigration flowed from Guilford and Randolph County; Dungy, "A Friend in Deed"; Cox, "The Peace and Social Concerns of Wrightsborough Friends"; Hatcher, "North Carolina Quakers"; Weeks, *Southern Quakers and Slavery,* 224.

21. Hilty, "North Carolina Quakers and Slavery," 167. See Algie I. Newlin, *The Newlin Family, Ancestors and Descendants of John and Mary Pyle Newlin*, Guilford College, Greensboro, North Carolina, 57–58, for a description of Jim Guthrie (Black Jim) and his manumission; Robbins, *Forgotten Hoosiers.*

22. Franklin, *The Free Negro in North Carolina.*

23. Franklin, *The Free Negro in North Carolina*; L. Coffin, *Reminiscences of Levi Coffin*, 113, 75, 76.

24. Weeks, *Southern Quakers and Slavery*, 229–30.

25. Hamm et al., "Moral Choices," 117–54.

26. Berlin, *Slaves Without Masters*, 20.

27. Robbins, *Forgotten Hoosiers*.

28. Vincent, *Southern Seed*; R. Wright, *Centennial Encyclopaedia*; Jenifer, *Centennial Retrospect*, 29.

29. Robbins, *Forgotten Hoosiers*; National Forest Service, www.fs.fed.us/r9/hoosier/docs/history/lick_creek.htm.

30. Drake, *Quakers and Slavery in America*; Child, *Isaac T. Hooper*.

31. Payne, *History of the African Methodist Episcopal Church*.

32. Hiram Revels was the first person of color to serve in the U.S. Senate. He also served later as the first president of Alcorn State University.

33. "Allen Chapel AME Church," *Wabash Valley First Profiles*, Vigo County Historical Society; "Allen Chapel African Methodist Episcopal Church," National Register of Historic Places, National Park Service; Payne, *History of the African Methodist Episcopal Church*.

34. *Provincial Freeman*, December 23, 1854, Toronto, Canada West; Payne, *History of the African Methodist Episcopal Church*; Hudson, *Fugitive Slaves*, 109.

35. Payne, *History of the African Methodist Episcopal Church*; Mabee, *Black Freedom*, 402, n. 17; Robbins, *Forgotten Hoosiers*.

36. C. Smith, *A History of the AME Church*, 17; R. Wright, *Centennial Encyclopaedia*; Thornbrough, *Negro in Indiana*; Peters, *The Underground Railroad in Floyd County, Indiana*, 187, n. 38; Welch, *William Paul Quinn*.

37. Thornbrough, *The Negro in Indiana before 1900*.

38. Goodspeed, Goodspeed, and Goodspeed, *History of Lawrence, Orange and Washington Counties*.

39. National Forest Service, www.fs.fed.us/r9/hoosier/docs/history/lick_creek.htm.

40. Peters, *The Underground Railroad in Floyd County, Indiana*; National Forest Service, CD Rom.

41. Hudson, *Fugitive Slaves*, 93–94.

42. Henson, *"Uncle Tom's" Story*, 82, 86.

43. Josiah Henson, *Truth Is Stranger Than Fiction: Father Henson's Story* (Boston: John P. Jewett and Company, 1858), 144, 158, 120; Karolyn Smardz Frost, *I've Got a Home in Glory Land: A Lost Tale of the Underground Railroad* (New York: Farrar, Straus and Giroux, 2007).

44. L. Coffin, *Reminiscences of Levi Coffin*.

45. Morris, *The Underground Railroad*; Vincent, *Southern Seed*; L. Coffin, *Reminiscences of Levi Coffin*.

46. Forstchen, "The 28th United States Colored Troops: Indiana's African-Americans Go to War," 73.

47. "Allies for Freedom"; Forstchen, "The 28th United States Colored Troops"; Rhodes, *Mary Ann Shadd Cary*.

48. "Lick Creek," www.fs.fed.us/r9/hoosier/docs/history/lick_creek.htm.

49. Dunn, *Iron Men, Iron Will*, 229–30; personal communication, Harry Hunter, Smithsonian Institution; Angie Krieger, Hoosier NFS; April 3, 1918, obituary provided by Hunter, no citation beyond date.

50. Jordan, *Black Confederates and Afro-Yankees*, 276–78; Robbins, *Forgotten Hoosiers*; See Glatthaar, *Forged in Battle*.

51. Robbins, *Forgotten Hoosiers*, 139–40.

52. Robbins, *Forgotten Hoosiers*, 3.

53. "The Story of Mattie J. Jackson," in *Six Women's Slave Narratives*, ed. Henry Louis Gates Jr. (New York: Oxford University Press, 1988), 9.

## Chapter 4. Poke Patch, Ohio

1. H. Wilson, *History of the Rise and Fall of the Slave Power in America*, 63. Western Reserve is a tract of land in northeastern Ohio, on the south shore of Lake Erie; Hickok, *The Negro in Ohio*.

2. Lincoln and Mamiya, *The Black Church*.

3. Gerber, *Black Ohio*.

4. Wilbur Siebert, "Ohio's Network of the Underground Railroad Disclosed," Section II (Draft). The Siebert Collection, Ohio Historical Society.

5. Preston, "Underground Railroad in Northwest Ohio"; Ohio Department of Natural Resources, "Ohio's Iron Age," www.dnr.state.oh.us/parks/explore/magazine/sprsum98/ironage.htm; source for iron furnace map: Amos Hawkins, "Charcoal Iron Furnaces of Lawrence County, Ohio," www.irontonfurnaces.com.

6. Malloy, "Marker Honoring Abolitionist."

7. National Forest Service, CD Rom; autobiography of John Campbell, *Semi Weekly Irontonion*, November 15, 1907; Siebert, *Mysteries of Ohio's Underground Railroad*.

8. Griffler, *Front Line of Freedom*, 93.

9. Siebert, *The Underground Railroad*.

10. Siebert, "Ohio's Network," 59.

11. Griffler, *Front Line of Freedom*; Siebert, "Ohio's Network."

12. Griffler, *Front Line of Freedom*, 93; Siebert, "Ohio's Network," 58.

13. Siebert, "Ohio's Network," 58.

14. Griffler, *Front Line of Freedom*, 93.

15. Griffler, *Front Line of Freedom*, 117.

16. Siebert, *Mysteries of Ohio's Underground Railroad*; taken from a "Letter from Gabe N. Johnson, colored, Ironton, O., Oct. 15, 1894."

17. Siebert, *Mysteries of Ohio's Underground Railroad*.

18. Personal communication.

19. J. E. K. Walker, *The History of Black Business in America*.

20. Siebert, *Mysteries of Ohio's Underground Railroad*.

21. The 150th Souvenir Book of Providence Regular Missionary Baptist Association.

22. "Poke Patch/Black Fork, Ohio," summary provided by Wayne National Forest.

23. Siebert, *Mysteries of Ohio's Underground Railroad*; "Poke Patch/Black Fork, Ohio," summary provided by Ann Cramer, National Forest Service.

24. National Forest Service, CD Rom; Siebert, *Mysteries of Ohio's Underground Railroad*; H. Mitchell, *Black Church Beginnings*.

25. Gray, "The Underground Railroad in Southern Ohio."

26. Byron W. Woodson Sr., *A President in the Family: Thomas Jefferson, Sally Hemmings and Thomas Woodson* (Westport, CT: Praeger Publishers, 2001).

27. Obituary, *Pittsburgh Commercial Gazette*, January 15, 1878; Woodson, *A President in the Family*, 91.

28. Judith P. Justus, *Down from the Mountain: The Oral History of the Hemings Family: Are They the Black Descendants of Thomas Jefferson?* (Perrysburg, OH: Jeskurtara, Inc., 1990); Griffler, *Front Line of Freedom*, 35.

29. Gray, "The Underground Railroad in Southern Ohio"; Siebert, *Mysteries of Ohio's Underground Railroad*.

30. Griffler, *Front Line of Freedom*; W. Mitchell, *The Underground Railroad*.

31. Hagedorn, *Beyond the River*.

32. Autobiography of John Campbell; Eugene B. Willard, Daniel W. Williams, George O. Newman, and Charles B. Taylor, eds., *A Standard History of the Hanging Rock Iron Region in Ohio: An Authentic Narrative of the Past, with an Extended Survey of the Industrial and Commercial Development*, vol. 1 (Lewis Publishing Co., 1916).

## Chapter 5. The Geography of Resistance

1. Bradford, *Scenes in the Life of Harriet Tubman*, 30; Loguen, *The Rev. J. W. Loguen*, 304–5.

2. Henson, *The Life of Josiah Henson*, 55.

3. Larson, *Bound for the Promised Land*; Bradford, *Harriet Tubman*, 30–31.

4. National Park Service, *Underground Railroad: Special Resource Study*.

5. Blassingame, *Slave Testimony*, 222; Pennington, *The Fugitive Blacksmith*, 15.

6. J. Lewis, *Religious Life of Fugitive Slaves*.

7. Henson, *"Uncle Tom's" Story*, 78.

8. Glasco, *WPA History*; Drew, *A North-side View of Slavery*, 24.

9. See, for example, Knabenshue, "The Underground Railroad"; Herbert, "National Park Service"; Ripley, "The Underground Railroad."

10. L. Coffin, *Reminiscences of Levi Coffin*, 16, 554; Smedley, *History of the Underground Railroad*, 355–56.

11. Allegheny Portage Railroad NHS, National Park Service, National Underground Railroad Network to Freedom Application; Still, *The Underground Railroad*.

12. Addington, *Jim Baker*, 111; Bradford, *Harriet Tubman*; Conrad, *General Harriet Tubman*; Spicer, "The Underground Railroad in Southern Illinois," testimony of James Wilson, January 1896, 9, n. 6; Siebert, *The Underground Railroad*, 70.

13. Griffler, *Front Line of Freedom*; Franklin and Schweninger, *Runaway Slaves*. See, for example, narratives of William Wells Brown, Josiah Henson, and J. W. C. Pennington.

14. Crane, "Slavery on the Edge of Freedom"; Davis, *Frontier Illinois*, 159–60; Thornbrough, *The Negro in Indiana before 1900*.

15. Ayers, *In the Presence of Mine Enemies*.

16. Douglass, "The Present Condition and Future Prospects of the Negro People"; Vincent, *Southern Seed*, xiii.

17. Siebert, *The Underground Railroad*, 32; Du Bois, ed., *Economic Co-Operation*, 27.

18. Pennington, *The Fugitive Blacksmith*, 14.

19. Glasco, *WPA History*.

20. Still, *The Underground Railroad*.

21. Delany, *North Star*, June 16, 1848.

22. Loguen, *The Reverend J. W. Loguen*.

23. Williams, *Sunshine and Shadow*; Drew, *A North-side View of Slavery*, 61.

24. Bolster, *Black Jacks*, 190–91.

25. Arnold Gragston interview, WPA Slave Narrative Project, Florida Narratives (Washington, DC: Federal Writers' Project for the Work Projects Administration for the State of Florida, 1941), vol. 3, 148–50; Berlin, Favreau, and Miller, eds., *Remembering Slavery*, 304.

26. Henson, *The Life of Josiah Henson*, 50.

27. Cecelski, *The Waterman's Song*; Jacobs, *Incidents in the Life of a Slavegirl*; Hodges and Brown, eds., *"Pretends to Be Free."*

28. *Maryland Gazette*, August 2, 1759, and June 10, 1762.

29. Pennington, *The Fugitive Blacksmith*.

30. Grobman and Kunkelman, eds., *Woven with Words*.

31. Blockson, *The Underground Railroad in Pennsylvania*, 85.

32. Hopewell Furnace, National Register Nomination, National Trust for Historic Preservation, National Park Service, www.preservationnation.org/magazine/story-of-the-week/2010/hopewell-furnace.html; Darrin Youker, "'Freedom' on an Iron Plantation: Was Pennsylvania's Hopewell Furnace Ahead of its Time?" in *Preservation, National Trust for Historic Preservation*, February 8, 2010, National Park Service, www.nps.gov/hofu/historyculture/african-americans.htm.

33. Homan, "The Underground Railroad."

34. As quoted in McCarthy and Stauffer, eds., *Prophets of Protest*, 167–68.

35. Court Records of Mary Oliver et al. vs Daniel Kaufman, November Court of 1847, Cumberland Co., Papers No. 32, 33, 34, 35, in File Box Nov. 1847, Jan 1848, indexed in Appearance Docket Book No. 23, 1846–47, Office of the Prothonotary, Cumberland County Court House, Carlisle, Pennsylvania; *Records of the District Courts of the United States*, United States Circuit Court for the Eastern District of Pennsylvania, Oliver, et al., vs Stephen Weakley, et al. Case October 14, 1849;

testimony of George Cole, 1848, as cited in Tritt, "The Underground Railroad at Boiling Springs," 111–17.

36. J. E. Walker, "Negro Labor," 467.

37. Levine, ed., *Martin R. Delany*, 98.

38. Sprague, ed., *His Promised Land*; Hagedorn, *Beyond the River.*

39. Welch, *William Paul Quinn.*

40. Elise Lemire, *Black Walden: Slavery and Its Aftermath in Concord, Massachusetts* (Philadelphia: University of Pennsylvania Press, 2009).

41. H. Smith, *History of Essex County.*

42. H. Smith, *History of Essex County*; H. Bell, ed., *Minutes of the Proceedings*, 29–30.

43. H. Smith, *History of Essex County*; Christian, "North Elba Journal"; Dyson, "Gerrit Smith's Effort," 358. See Special Report of the U.S. Commissioner of Education on the Schools of the District of Columbia, 1871, 367; *The African Repository and Colonial Journal*, X (Washington, DC: The American Colonization Society, February 1834), 312.

44. Brown-Kubisch, *The Queens Bush Settlement*, 125.

45. Vincent, *Southern Seed.*

## Chapter 6. Rethinking African American Migration

1. Harding, *There Is a River*, 116.

2. Cha-Jua, *America's First Black Town*, ix.

3. Harding, *There Is a River.*

4. Aptheker, "Maroons within the Present Limits of the United States."

5. "The Underground Railway" and "Knights of Liberty," *The Freeman* (Indianapolis), February 24, 1900; G. Early, ed., *Ain't Nothing But a Place.* See Vincent, *Southern Seed*; Cha-Jua, *America's First Black Town*; and J. E. K. Walker, *Free Frank*, for discussions of pre–Civil War Black migration. See Franklin and Schweninger, *Runaway Slaves*; Chadwick, *Traveling the Underground Railroad*, 5; Simpson, *Under the North Star*, 9; Winks, *The Blacks in Canada*, 233.

6. Wilkerson, *The Warmth of Other Suns*, 10.

7. In *The Making of African America*, historian Ira Berlin does not include the passage of Blacks moving out of slavery by their own volition among the four migrations.

8. Tadman, *Speculators and Slaves.*

9. *BAP*, vol. 3; H. Bell, ed., *Minutes of the Proceedings.*

10. Vincent, *Southern Seed*, 33.

11. Crow, *The Black Experience in Revolutionary North Carolina*, 29, discusses badges saying "free" worn on the shoulder for free Blacks.

12. Whitman, *Challenging Slavery in the Chesapeake*; Gordon-Reed, *The Hemingses of Monticello*; Freehling, *The Reintegration of American History.*

13. Woodson, *A Century of Negro Migration*, 9–10.

14. Weeks, *Southern Quakers and Slavery*, 229–30. Friends, when capitalized, refers to the Society of Friends also known as the Quakers.

15. Greensborough *Patriot*, September 6, 1826.

16. Hamm et al., "Moral Choices."

17. Greensborough *Patriot*, September 6, 1826.

18. Hilty, *Toward Freedom for All*, 182.

19. H. Bell, ed., *Minutes of the Proceedings*, 10.

20. H. Bell, ed., *Minutes of the Proceedings*, 5.

21. J. Wilson, ed., *Classical Black Nationalism*; Horton and Horton, *Free People of Color*.

22. Dillon, "The Failure of the American Abolitionists"; Finne, "The Antislavery Movement"; *BAP*, vol. 5, 54, n. 2, 56, n. 10, 204.

23. Peterson, *"Doers of the Word."*

24. Foner and Walker, eds., *Proceedings*, 58, 60.

25. H. Bell, "The Negro Emigration Movement."

26. Brauer, "The Slavery Problem"; Walter B. Hill Jr., "Living with the Hydra: The Documentation of Slavery and the Slave Trade in Federal Records," *Prologue Magazine* 32, no. 4 (Winter 2000), The National Archives, www.archives.gov.

27. Free bond posted by Jeremiah Sheppard, Hardeman County, Tennessee, Deed Book C, 328–29, Golconda Circuit Clerk's Office, Pope County, Illinois.

28. Berlin, *Slaves Without Masters*, 169; free bond posted by Jeremiah Sheppard.

29. *BAP*, vol. 5, 128.

30. Cha-Jua, *America's First Black Town*, 3.

31. *BAP*, vol. 3, 256–57.

32. Douglass, "The Present Condition and Future Prospects of the Negro People," 216.

33. Douglass. "The Present Condition and Future Prospects of the Negro People," 217.

34. Foner and Walker, eds., *Proceedings*. See also H. Bell, ed., *Minutes of the Proceedings*.

35. *Minutes of the National Convention of Colored Citizens Held at Buffalo* (New York: Piercy & Reed, 1843), reprinted in H. Bell, ed., *Minutes of the Proceedings*, 35–36.

36. Foner and Walker, eds., *Proceedings*.

37. Foner and Walker, eds., *Proceedings*, 60.

38. Hepburn, *Crossing the Border*.

39. Pease and Pease, *Black Utopia*, 23.

40. Singleton, "Following the Trail of the Fathers"; "'Mother' Baltimore No More," *St. Louis Globe Democrat*, November 30, 1882, 8; "'Mother' Baltimore's Burial," *St. Louis Globe Democrat*, December 4, 1882, 8–10; "Priscilla Baltimore v. John Baltimore: Bill for Divorce," St. Clair County Circuit Court Chancery Case Files, Case no. 0864, Box no. 05, Carbondale, Illinois Regional Archives Depository, Morris Library, 1856; S. Early, *Life and Labors of Rev. Jordan W. Early*. Her work as a ladies' nurse

to the wives of prominent St. Louisans commonly earned her as much as $150 a visit (Yancey and Galloy, "Mother Baltimore's Freedom Village," 4).

41. Shackel, *New Philadelphia.*

42. Walker, *Free Frank,* 162. See table 14, Free Frank Family Members Purchased, 1817–1857.

43. Walker, *Free Frank.*

44. Walker, *Free Frank,* 159.

45. Summary derived from Walker, *Free Frank.*

46. *Narrative of Moses Grandy,* as cited in Nichols, "Who Read the Slave Narratives?"

47. Nichols, "Who Read the Slave Narratives?" 151.

48. Charles H. Nichols, *Many Thousand Gone: The Ex-Slaves' Account of Their Bondage and Freedom* (Bloomington: Indiana University Press, 1963).

49. Walker, *Free Frank,* 1.

50. Allen, *The Life, Experience, and Gospel Labours of the Rt. Rev. Richard Allen.*

51. Quarles, *Black Abolitionists.*

52. Sterling, ed., *We Are Sisters.*

53. Quarles, *Black Abolitionists,* 60–61; Hine, Brown, and Terborg-Penn, eds., *Black Women in America.*

54. Quarles, *Black Abolitionists,* 59.

55. Aptheker, *To Be Free,* 35.

56. Griffler, *Front Line of Freedom,* 45.

57. This amounts to approximately $1,666,667 in 2012 dollars. See www.davemanuel.com/inflation-calculator.php? Aptheker, *To Be Free,* 35.

58. Dollar conversion for the $1,000 bond required by the Black Codes equates to approximately $27,027,778 in 2012 dollars. The cost per person per year was converted using the conversion factor applicable for each year of purchase based on the chart referenced below. Based on the Consumer Price Index (CPI), dollars converted from each applicable base year to an estimate in 2008 by dividing the year's dollar amount by the conversion factor for that year rounded to whole dollars. Because the Bureau of Labor Statistics came into existence in 1913, all figures prior to that date are estimates. Sahr, "Inflation Conversion," oregonstate.edu/cla/polisci/faculty-research/sahr/sahr.htm.

59. Walker, *Free Frank,* 163.

60. Dillon, "The Failure of the American Abolitionists," 172.

61. $500 in 1804 equivalent to $9,804 in 2012 dollars; Middleton, *The Black Laws.*

62. Woodson, *The Negro in Our History*; Drew, *A North-side View of Slavery*; H. Bell, ed., *Minutes of the Proceedings.*

63. Logan, "*We Are Coming*"; Carby, *Reconstructing Womanhood.*

64. Dillon, "The Failure of the American Abolitionists"; *BAP,* vol. 5, 263, n. 4; *BAP,* vol. 4, 102.

65. "An Appeal to Christians Throughout the World," Frances Ellen Watkins Harper, January 1860, as cited in *BAP,* vol. 5, 54.

66. Douglass, "The Present Condition and Future Prospects of the Negro People," 255.

67. WGBH, PBS On-Line, "Judgment Day: Bleeding Kansas," *Africa in America*, www.pbs.org/wgbh/aia/part4/4p2952.html.

68. $50 is equivalent to $1,282,315 in 2012 dollar values; $120 is equivalent to $3,077,158 in 2012 dollar values; McDougall, *Fugitive Slaves (1619–1865)*; Litwack and Meier, eds., *Black Leaders of the Nineteenth Century*, 129.

69. *Western Citizen*, December 24, 1850, 2, col. 1, as cited in Gliozzo, "John Jones," 182.

70. Ford, "Henry David Thoreau."

71. Payne, *Recollections*, 66.

72. Middleton, *The Black Laws*, 202.

73. Middleton, *The Black Laws*; Child, *Isaac T. Hopper*; Welch, *William Paul Quinn*.

74. Welch, *William Paul Quinn*, 23.

75. Welch, *William Paul Quinn*, 138; Pease and Pease, *They Who Would Be Free*, 217.

76. *BAP*, vol. 4, 51, n. 2.

77. Walker, *Free Frank*, 148.

78. Douglass, "The Present Condition and Future Prospects of the Negro People"; Vincent, *Southern Seed*, xiii.

79. Ford, "Henry David Thoreau," 369; quoted in Thornbrough, *The Negro in Indiana before 1900*, 54; Freehling, *The Reintegration of American History*, 264.

80. Still, *The Underground Railroad*, 757; Everett, *History of Slavery*; Preston, "The Fugitive Slave Acts in Ohio," 429; Bradford, *Harriet Tubman*.

81. Winks, *The Blacks in Canada*.

82. Pease and Pease, "Organized Negro Communities"; Simpson, *Under the North Star*.

83. Delany, "Political Destiny of the Colored Race," 230.

84. C. H. Johnson, "Mary Ann Shadd."

85. Hodges, *The Black Loyalist Directory*, xii.

86. Minutes of the National Convention of Colored Citizens Held at Buffalo, on the 15th, 16th, 17th, 18th and 19th of August 1843, 32–35; *BAP*, vol. 5, 82–83; *BAP*, vol. 4.

87. Lincoln and Mamiya, *The Black Church*, 58, 74; Winks, *The Blacks in Canada*, 355–56; Woodson, *A Century of Negro Migration*, 36.

## Chapter 7. Family, Church, Community

1. Carter Goodwin Woodson, *Free Negro Heads of Families in the United States in 1830* (Washington, DC: The Association for the Study of Negro Life and History, 1925), 13; Evans, *Journal*.

2. Larson, *Bound for the Promised Land*, xvii.

3. Schor, *Henry Highland Garnet*; Still, *The Underground Railroad*; Prince, *A Shadow on the Household.*

4. Prince, *A Shadow on the Household.*

5. Smedley, *History of the Underground Railroad.*

6. Blockson, *The Underground Railroad in Pennsylvania*; Sterling, *Martin Robison Delany.*

7. Glasco, *WPA Narrative.*

8. H. Brown, *Homespun Heroines*; Glasco, *WPA History*, 96.

9. H. Brown, *Homespun Heroines*; Glasco, *WPA History.*

10. Dickson, *Manual*, 7.

11. Joshua Giddings, James G. Birney, Calvin Fairbank, Harriet Beecher, and her brother, Henry Ward Beecher, in addition to many other noted men and women visited the home. "The Underground Railway—Review of the System by which Many Thousands of Slaves Were Liberated," *The Freeman* (Indianapolis), 1.

12. "Moses Dickson: The Great Negro Organizer and Fraternal Society Leader," *St. Louis Star*, April 1902, in G. Early, ed., *Ain't Nothing But a Place*, 282.

13. Death of John Jones, *The Inter Ocean*, May 22, 1879; *BAP*, vol. 5, 263, n. 4.

14. Walker, *Free Frank*, 149; Shackel, *New Philadelphia.*

15. Vincent, *Southern Seed.*

16. Du Bois, ed., *Economic Co-Operation*, 27.

17. Cockrum, *History of the Underground Railroad.*

18. Douglass, "My Escape from Slavery," 127; Crane, "Slavery on the Edge of Freedom."

19. Rose, "The All-Negro Town"; James G. Birney to Lewis Tappan, February 27, 1837, in *Letters of James Gillespie Birney, 1831–1857*, ed. Dwight L. Dumond, 2 vols. (New York: Appleton-Century Co., 1938), vol. 1, 376.

20. Richard R. Wright Jr., "The Economic Condition of Negroes in the North: Rural Communities in Indiana," *Southern Workman* 37 (March 1908): 158–68; Peters, *The Underground Railroad in Floyd County, Indiana.*

21. Rose, "The All-Negro Town."

22. Frances Ellen Watkins Harper to Jane E. Hitchcock Jones, September 21, 1860, as cited in *BAP*, vol. 5, 81–82.

23. Delany to Douglass, January 16, 1849, *North Star*, February 16, 1849.

24. Vincent, *Southern Seed.*

25. Payne, *History of the African Methodist Episcopal Church*, 84.

26. Payne, *History of the African Methodist Episcopal Church*, 84.

27. As a point of clarification, the first floor of many historic Black churches is referred to as the basement even though it is above ground. This fact often confuses Underground Railroad scholars, who often look for a subsurface feature and discredit the story when no "basement" is evident. Generally, the sanctuary is up one or two flights of stairs.

28. Lincoln and Mamiya, *The Black Church*, 202; Child, *Isaac T. Hopper*, 208–9; Carol V. R. George, *Segregated Sabbaths: Richard Allen and the Emergence of In-*

*dependent Black Churches 1760–1840* (New York: Oxford University Press, 1973), 3–4; Wesley, *Richard Allen*, 159; Newman, *Freedom's Prophet*.

29. Newman, *Freedom's Prophet*.

30. Glasco, *WPA History*; Still, *The Underground Railroad*.

31. Glasco, *WPA History*, 231–32; Switala, *Underground Railroad in Pennsylvania*; History of Bethel African Methodist Episcopal Church, www.bethelpittsburgh.org/about-us.php.

32. Howe, *What Hath God Wrought*.

33. Payne, *History of the African Methodist Episcopal Church*, 45.

34. Hinks, *To Awaken My Afflicted Brethren*, 38, 63, 79; Payne, ed., *The Semi-Centenary*, 24; George, *Segregated Sabbaths*, 131; Lincoln and Mamiya, *The Black Church*, 52; Gomez, *Exchanging Our Country Marks*; Harding, *There Is a River*; David, ed., *Black Defiance*; C. Walker, *A Rock in a Weary Land*, 20–21; Charles Spencer Smith, *History of the African Methodist Episcopal Church* (Philadelphia: Book Concern of the A.M.E. Church, 1922).

35. George, "Widening the Circle"; Moore, *Cincinnati*; L. Coffin, *Reminiscences of Levi Coffin*; Writers' Program of the Work Projects Administration in the State of Ohio, comp., *Cincinnati*.

36. National Register of Historic Places Inventory—Nomination Form.

37. National Register Inventory, Bethel AME, Reading.

38. Still, *The Underground Railroad*, 43–44.

39. Still, *The Underground Railroad*, 43–44.

40. Blockson, *The Underground Railroad in Pennsylvania*.

41. *Christian Recorder*, January 14, 1875; Mathews, "Charles Colcock Jones"; McPherson, *The Negro's Civil War*, 206–7; Montgomery, *Under Their Own Vine and Fig Tree*, 30.

42. Mitchell, *Black Church Beginnings*; Lincoln and Mamiya, *The Black Church*.

43. *Frederick Douglass' Paper*, May 11, 1855.

44. Compare Quinn, "The Origin, Horrors, and Results of Slavery," 628–30, with D. Walker, *Walker's Appeal*, 40–43; or 46–49.

45. Finnie, "The Antislavery Movement"; McCarthy and Stauffer, eds., *Prophets of Protest*.

46. D. Walker, *Walker's Appeal*.

47. Johnson, Smith, and the WGBH Series Research Team, *Africa in America*.

48. Charles Spencer Smith and Daniel Alexander Payne, *History of the African Methodist Episcopal Church: Being a Volume Supplemental a History of the African Methodist Episcopal Church by Daniel Alexander Payne* (Philadelphia: Book Concern of the A.M.E. Church, 1922), 421.

49. Douglass, *Narrative of the Life of Frederick Douglass*, 82.

50. Haviland, *A Woman's Life Work*, 115–16, 128–29, 161; Wilbur H. Siebert, "Mysteries of Ohio's Underground Railroad," Section II (Draft), Siebert Collection, Ohio Historical Society, 4.

51. Haviland, *A Woman's Life Work*, 161.

52. L. Coffin, *Reminiscences of Levi Coffin*, 107, 324.

53. African Methodist Episcopal Zion Church Branch Militant.

54. *BAP*, vol. 4, 195; S. Early, *Life and Labors of Reverend Jordan W. Early*, 37; Gibson, *History*.

55. S. Early, *Life and Labors of Reverend Jordan W. Early*, 5–6.

56. Mitchell, *Black Church Beginnings*, 114; Horton and Horton, *Black Bostonians*.

57. *The Christian Recorder*, July 28, 1866; George, *Segregated Sabbaths*, 28, quoted in Allen, *The Life, Experience, and Gospel Labours of the Rt. Rev. Richard Allen*.

58. Payne, *History of the African Methodist Episcopal Church*; Brown-Kubisch, *Queen's Bush Settlement*, 86–87, 152–53.

59. Welch, *William Paul Quinn*, 6; Quinn, "The Origin, Horrors, and Results of Slavery."

60. Welch, *William Paul Quinn*; Trusty, *Underground Railroad*; Richard Gilbert Johnson, "A Social History of Bethel A.M.E. Church, Reading, Pa,: First Twenty-five Years, 1834 to 1859" (master's thesis, Morgan State University, 1981); *Christian Recorder*, Bishop Quinn's Tour West on a Visit to the Churches, August 16, 1862.

61. Thornbrough, *The Negro in Indiana before 1900*, 44.

62. Cord, "Black Rural Settlements," 101; Coy Robbins, "Location of A.M.E. Churches, 1840–1845," provided by Indiana Underground Railroad scholar, Dona Stokes-Lucas.

63. Cord, "Black Rural Settlements," 101; Robbins, "Location of A.M.E. Churches, 1840–1845"; Siebert, "Routes through Indiana and Michigan in 1848," in *The Underground Railroad*, 138.

64. Trusty, *Underground Railroad*, 352.

65. Barton, "It Takes a Village."

66. National Register of Historic Form; J. Morgan, *Morgan's History*, 73.

## Chapter 8. Faith and Fraternity

1. Swift, *Black Prophets of Justice*; Clara Merritt De Boer, *Be Jubilant My Feet: African American Abolitionists in the American Missionary Association 1839–1861* (New York: Garland Publishing, Inc., 1994).

2. Sprague, ed., *His Promised Land*.

3. Bell, ed., *Minutes of the Proceedings*.

4. Bell, ed., *Minutes of the Proceedings*, 13.

5. Cromwell, *The Negro in American History*, 34; "Address and Constitution of the Phoenix Society of New York and of the Auxiliary Ward Associations," in *Early Negro Writing 1760–1837*, ed. Dorothy Porter (Baltimore: Black Classic Press, 1995), 614–36; Wilder, *In the Company of Black Men*.

6. *BAP*, vols. 3 and 5; "Missionary Convention," *Colored American*, September 4, 1841; Swift, Black Prophets of Justice.

7. Calarco, *People of the Underground Railroad*.

8. According to Benjamin Quarles, of the 3,200 operatives Siebert identifies, he designates 143 names as Negroes. In addition to Ray, Siebert misidentifies African Americans James J. G. Bias, Frederick Douglass, George T. Downing, Robert Morris, Robert Purvis, Stephen Smith, and William Whipper as White operatives. Siebert also omitted the names of several African Americans from membership lists of Vigilance Committees in Boston and Philadelphia and did not include the New York Vigilance Committee at all. *Black Abolitionists*, 145; Siebert, *The Underground Railroad*, appendix E. Similarly, Emma Trusty indicates that for Cumberland County, New Jersey, five of the seven operatives Siebert identifies as White were actually people of color. *Underground Railroad*, 15. As research continues delving into African American participation in local Underground Railroad operations, more entries will be corrected and many new names added to the growing list.

9. Sorin, *The New York Abolitionists*; Siebert, *The Underground Railroad*; W. W. Brown, *Rising Son*.

10. Carolyn Smardz Frost, *I've Got a Home in Glory Land: A Lost Tale of the Underground Railroad* (New York: Farrar, Straus and Giroux, 2007).

11. Bearse, *Reminiscences of Fugitive-Slave Law Days in Boston*, 8; Stowe, *Uncle Tom's Cabin*; Stowe, *A Key to Uncle Tom's Cabin*.

12. M. N. Work, "The Life of Charles B. Ray," *Journal of Negro History* 4, no. 4 (October 1919): 361–71.

13. *BAP*; David, ed., *Black Defiance*; Finkelman, ed., *Free Blacks*; H. Bell, "The Negro Emigration Movement," 141.

14. Brandt, *The Town That Started the Civil War*.

15. Du Bois, *John Brown*; Jean Libby, ed., *John Brown Mysteries* (Missoula, MT: Pictorial Histories Publishing Company, 1999).

16. Schor, *Henry Highland Garnet*, 90.

17. Sanborn, ed., *The Life and Letters of John Brown*; Du Bois, ed., *Economic Co-Operation*, 30–31; Siebert, *The Underground Railroad*, 73–75.

18. Hannah Geffert, "Regional Black Involvement in John Brown's Raid on Harpers Ferry," in *Prophets of Protest: Reconsidering the History of American Abolitionism*, ed. Timothy Patrick McCarthy and John Stauffer (New York: The New Press, 2006), 166–67, n. 2, 342.

19. Du Bois, *John Brown*, 243–44; Lumpkin, "The General Plan Was Freedom."

20. Frost, *I've Got a Home in Glory Land*; Libby, Geffert, and Kenyatta, *Allies for Freedom*; Du Bois, ed., *Economic Co-Operation*, 29; Hinton, *John Brown and His Men*, 80, 128.

21. Richard Newman, Patricia Rael, and Phillip Lapsansky, eds., *Pamphlets of Protest: An Anthology of Early African American Protest Literature, 1790–1860* (New York: Routledge, 2001).

22. See appendix.

23. LaRoche and Palmer, "The Look of Eagles."

24. S. Early, *Life and Labors of Reverend Jordan W. Early*, 51–52.

25. A. C. Robbins, *Prince Hall Masonry in Ontario 1852–1933*, 21.

26. Robbins, *Prince Hall Masonry in Ontario 1852–1933*; Simpson, *Under the North Star.*

27. Muraskin, *Middle-Class Blacks*, 53, n. 32; Victor Ullman, *Martin R. Delany: The Beginnings of Black Nationalism* (Boston: Beacon Press, 1971).

28. Sterling, *Martin Robison Delany*, 138; Blockson, *Hippocrene Guide to the Underground Railroad.*

29. Henson, *The Life of Josiah Henson*, 65.

30. Bethel, *The Roots of African-American Identity*, 66, no citation given to support her assertion.

31. *Freemasonry among the Blacks, December 10, 1831.* From the National Journal FREEMASONRY AMONG THE BLACKS. Addressed, "Dear Sir" and signed only "A.B."

32. Potter, *The Impending Crisis*; Freehling, "Why the U.S. Fugitive Slave Phenomenon Was Crucial."

33. Conrad, *General Harriet Tubman*; Conrad, *Harriet Tubman*; Larson, *Bound for the Promised Land.*

34. Champion, *Black Methodism*, 102.

35. Berlin, *Generations of Captivity*; Works Progress Administration, "Kansas."

36. *BAP*, vol. 5.

37. Levine, ed., *Martin R. Delany*, 385.

38. *BAP*, vol. 5.

39. Forstchen, "The 28th United States Colored Troops"; Libby and Allies for Freedom, "Hiram and Willis Revels, Lewis Leary and John Copeland"; *The Christian Recorder*, March 10, 1866.

40. De Boer, "The Role of Afro-Americans," 232.

41. Siebert, *The Underground Railroad*, xiii; Potter, *The Impending Crisis*; Freehling, "Why the U.S. Fugitive Slave Phenomenon Was Crucial"; *Inaugural Addresses of the Presidents of the United States* (Washington, DC: U.S. Government Printing Office, 1989).

42. *BAP*, vol. 5, 256.

43. As cited in Blackett, *Beating against the Barriers*, 80–81; *BAP*, vol. 5, 395.

44. Douglass, "What the Black Man Wants," 209.

45. Gibson, *History.*

46. Graham, ed., *Complete Poems of Frances E. W. Harper.*

## Chapter 9: Destination Freedom

1. Milton Meltzer, *The Black Americans: A History in Their Own Words 1619–1983* (New York: HarperCollins, 1987), 62.

2. Jules David Prown, "Mind in Matter: An Introduction to Material Culture Theory and Method," in *Material Life in America 1600–1860*, ed. Robert Blair St. George (Boston: Northeastern University Press, 1988), 17–37.

3. Groth, "Forging Freedom," 251.

4. See the work of Christopher Barton at Timbuctoo in New Jersey as an example; Barton, "It Takes a Village"; Barton, "Antebellum African-American Settlements."

5. Shackel, *Memory in Black and White.*

6. P. Lewis, "Common Landscapes as Historic Documents."

7. Fruehling and Smith, "Subterranean Hideaways."

8. Jeffrey, *Abolitionists Remember.*

9. Berry and Blassingame, *Long Memory*, 33.

10. Gordon-Reed, *The Hemingses of Monticello*, 291.

11. Berlin, *The Making of African America*, 117.

12. Berry and Blassingame, *Long Memory*, 33.

13. Loguen, *The Rev. J. W. Loguen*, 304–5.

# BIBLIOGRAPHY


*Acts of the General Assembly of the State of Georgia, 1829*. Milledgeville, 1830.

Adams, H. G., ed. *God's Image in Ebony: Being a Series of Biographical Sketches, Facts, Anecdotes, Etc., Demonstrative of the Mental Powers and Intellectual Capacities of the Negro Race*. London: Partridge and Oakey, 1854.

Addington, Thomas. *Jim Baker: A Thrilling Episode of Ante-Bellum Days: A True Story of the Oppressed Race among Friends and Foes*. Winchester, IN: A. C. Beeson and Sons, The Journal, 1898.

*African Repository and Colonial Journal*, X. Washington, DC: The American Colonization Society, 1834.

Allen, Richard. *The Life, Experience, and Gospel Labours of the Rt. Rev. Richard Allen. To Which Is Annexed the Rise and Progress of the African Methodist Episcopal Church in the United States of America. Containing a Narrative of the Yellow Fever in the Year of Our Lord 1793: With an Address to the People of Colour in the United States*. Philadelphia: Martin & Boden, Printers, 1833.

"Alton and the Underground Railroad." www.altonweb.com/history/civilwar/railroad.htm.

Annable, Edward L. *Pope County Illinois, Forgotten Records*. Cypress, IL: Ed Annable Publishing Company, 2000.

Aptheker, Herbert. "The Quakers and Negro Slavery." *Journal of Negro History* 25, no. 3 (1940): 331–62.

———. *"One Continual Cry": David Walker's Appeal to the Colored Citizens of the World (1829–1830)—Its Setting and Its Meaning*. New York: Humanities Press for AIMS, 1965.

———. *To Be Free: Pioneering Studies in Afro-American History*. New York: Carol Publishing Group, 1991. First published in 1948.

———. "Maroons Within the Present Limits of the United States." In *Maroon Societies: Rebel Slave Communities in the Americas*, 3rd ed., edited by Richard Price, 151–67. Baltimore: Johns Hopkins University Press, 1996.

Arnett, Rev. Benjamin W. *In Memoriam. Funeral Services in Respect to the Memory of Rev. William Paul Quinn Late Senior Bishop of the African M.E. Church.* Toledo, OH: Warren Chapel, March 9, 1873.

Asukile, Thabiti. "The All-Embracing Black Nationalist Theories of *David Walker's Appeal.*" *Black Scholar* 29, no. 4 (1999): 16–24.

Ayers, Edward L. *In the Presence of Mine Enemies: War in the Heart of America, 1859–1863.* New York: W. W. Norton, 2003.

Bacon, Margaret H. "One Great Bundle of Humanity: Frances Ellen Watkins Harper (1825–1911)." *Pennsylvania Magazine of History and Biography* 113, no. 1 (January 1989): 21–44.

Baldwin, Lewis V. *"Invisible" Strands in African Methodism: A History of the African Union Methodist Protestant and Union American Methodist Episcopal Churches, 1805–1980.* Metuchen, NJ: American Theological Library Association and Scarecrow Press, Inc., 1983.

———. *Peter Spencer and the African Union Methodist Tradition.* Lanham, MD: University Press of America, 1987.

Bartlett, John. *Bartlett's Familiar Quotations.* 15th and 125th Anniversary ed. Ed. Emily Morison Beck. Boston: Little, Brown and Company, 1980.

Barton, Christopher P. "Antebellum African-American Settlements in Southern New Jersey," *The African Diaspora Archaeology Network*, December 2009 Newsletter. www.diaspora.uiuc.edu/news1209/news1209-4.pdf.

———. "It Takes a Village: Archaeology and Identity at Timbuctoo." Unpublished manuscript.

Beard, Augustus Field. *A Crusade of Brotherhood: A History of the AMA.* Boston: Pilgrim Press, 1909.

Bearden, Jim, and Linda Jean Butler. *Shadd: The Life and Times of Mary Shadd Cary.* Toronto: New Canada Press, Ltd., 1977.

Bearse, Austin. *Reminiscences of Fugitive-Slave Law Days in Boston.* Boston: Printed by Warren Richardson, 1880; reprint, New York: Arno Press and The New York Times, 1969.

Beckly, Rev. M. W. "The African Methodist Episcopal Church." In *History of Madison County Illinois.* Edwardsville: W. R. Brinks and Co., 1882.

Bell, Derrick. *Race, Racism and American Law.* Boston: Little, Brown and Company, n.d.

Bell, Howard H. "Free Negroes of the North, 1830–1835: A Study in National Cooperation." *Journal of Negro Education* 26, no. 4 (1957): 447–55.

———. "The Negro Emigration Movement, 1849–1854: A Phase of Negro Nationalism." *Phylon Quarterly* 20, no. 2 (1959): 132–42.

———, ed. *Minutes of the Proceedings of the National Negro Conventions 1830–1864.* New York: Arno Press and The New York Times, 1969.

Berlin, Ira. "Foreword." www.freeafricanamericans.com/foreword.htm.

———. *Slaves Without Masters: The Free Negro in the Antebellum South.* New York: The New Press, 1974.

———. *Generations of Captivity: A History of African-American Slavery*. Cambridge: Harvard University Press, 2003.

———. *The Making of African America: The Four Great Migrations*. New York: Viking Adult, 2010.

Berlin, Ira, Marc Favreau, and Steven F. Miller, eds. *Remembering Slavery: African Americans Talk about Their Experiences of Slavery and Emancipation*. New York: The New Press, 1998.

Berry, Mary Frances, and John W. Blassingame. *Long Memory: The Black Experience in America*. New York: Oxford University Press, 1982.

Bethel, Elizabeth Rauh. *The Roots of African-American Identity: Memory and History in Free Antebellum Communities*. New York: St. Martin's Press, 1997.

Bezís-Selfa, John. *Forging America: Ironworkers, Adventurers, and the Industrious Revolution*. Ithaca: Cornell University Press, 2004.

Billington, Monroe Lee, and Roger D. Hardaway. *African Americans on the Western Frontier*. Niwot: University of Colorado Press, 1998.

Blackett, R. J. M. *Beating against the Barriers: Biographical Essays in Nineteenth-Century Afro-American History*. Baton Rouge: Louisiana State University Press, 1986.

Blassingame, John W., ed. *Slave Testimony: Two Centuries of Letters, Speeches, Interviews, and Autobiographies*. Baton Rouge: Louisiana State University Press, 1977.

———. *The Frederick Douglass Papers Series One: Speeches, Debates, and Interviews Volume 1: 1841–46*. New Haven: Yale University Press, 1979.

Blassingame, John W., and Mae G. Henderson, eds. *Antislavery Newspapers and Periodicals*. 5 vols. Vol. 1. Boston: G. K. Hall & Co., 1980.

Blight, David W., ed. *Race and Reunion: The Civil War in American Memory*. Boston: Belknap Press, 2001.

———. *Passages to Freedom: The Underground Railroad in History and Memory*. Washington, DC: Smithsonian, 2004.

———. *Slave No More: Two Men Who Escaped to Freedom, Including Their Own Narratives of Emancipation*. New York: Houghton Mifflin Harcourt, 2007.

Blockson, Charles L. "A Black Underground Resistance to Slavery, 1833–1860." *Pennsylvania Heritage* 4, no. 1 (1977): 29–33.

———. *The Underground Railroad in Pennsylvania*. Jacksonville: Flame International, Inc., 1981.

———. "Escape from Slavery: The Underground Railroad." *National Geographic Magazine* 166, no. 1 (1984): 3–39.

———. *The Underground Railroad*. Baltimore: Black Classics Press, 1994.

———. *Hippocrene Guide to the Underground Railroad*. New York: Hippocrene Books, 1994.

Bolster, W. Jeffrey. *Black Jacks: African American Seamen in the Age of Sail*. Cambridge: Harvard University Press, 1997.

*Book of Meetings; Containing an Account of the Times and Places of Holding the Meetings of The Society of Friends in America*. New York: Samuel S. & William Wood, 1858.

Bordewich, Fergus M. "Digging into a Historic Rivalry." *Smithsonian Magazine* 4 (February 2004). www.smithsonianmag.si.edu/smithsonian/issues04/feb04/pdf/buchanan.pdf.

———. *Bound for Canaan: The Underground Railroad and the War for the Soul of America*. New York: HarperCollins Publishers Inc., 2005.

Bracey, John H., Jr., August Meier, and Elliott Rudwick, eds. *Blacks in the Abolitionist Movement*. Belmont, CA: Wadsworth Publishing Co., 1971.

———, eds. *Free Blacks in America, 1800–1860*. Belmont, CA: Wadsworth Publishing Co., 1971.

Bradford, Sarah. *Scenes in the Life of Harriet Tubman*. Auburn, NY: W. J. Moses, 1869.

———. *Harriet Tubman: The Moses of Her People*. New York: George R. Lockwood and Son, 1886; reprint, Bedford, MA: Applewood Books, 1993.

Brandt, Nat. *The Town That Started the Civil War*. Syracuse: Syracuse University Press, 1990.

Brauer, Kinley J. "The Slavery Problem in the Diplomacy of the Civil War." In *Race and U.S. Foreign Policy in the Ages of Territorial and Market Expansion, 1840–1900*, edited by Michael L. Krenn, 117–47. New York: Garland Publishing, Inc., 1998.

Brawley, Benjamin. *A Social History of the American Negro*. New York: Macmillan Company, 1921; reprint, Minneola: Dover Publications, Inc., 2001.

———. *Negro Builders and Heroes*. Chapel Hill: University of North Carolina Press, 1937.

Breen, T. H., and Stephen Innes. *"Myne Owne Ground": Race and Freedom on Virginia's Eastern Shore*. New York: Oxford University Press, 1980.

"Brief History of the African Methodist Episcopal Church." www.bethelameannarbor.org/history.htm.

Brown, Hallie Quinn. *Homespun Heroines and Other Women of Distinction*. New York: Oxford University Press, 1988.

Brown, William H. *Historical Sketch of the Early Movement in Illinois for the Legalization of Slavery*. Chicago: Chicago Historical Society, 1876.

Brown, William Wells. *The Travels of William Wells Brown, An American Slave, Written by Himself*. London: Charles Gilpin, 1849.

———. *Rising Son; or, The Antecedents and Advancement of the Colored Race*. Boston: A. G. Brown & Co., 1874; reprint, New York: Negro Universities Press, 1970.

———. *The Black Man; His Antecedents, His Genius, and His Achievements*. 4th ed. Miami: Mnemosyne Pub. Inc., 1969.

Brown-Kubisch, Linda. *Queen's Bush Settlement: Black Pioneers 1839–1865*. Toronto: Natural Heritage Books, 2004.

Buchanan, Thomas C. *Black Life on the Mississippi: Slaves, Free Blacks and the Western Steamboat World*. Chapel Hill: University of North Carolina Press, 2004.

Buckmaster, Henrietta. *Let My People Go: The Story of the Underground Railroad and the Growth of the Abolition Movement*. New York: Harper and Brothers,

1941; reprint, Boston: Beacon Press, 1959; Southern Classics Edition, Columbia: University of South Carolina Press, 1992.

———. *Flight to Freedom: The Story of the Underground Railroad*. New York: Thomas Y. Crowell Company, 1958.

Butler, Marvin Benjamin. *My Story of the Civil War and the Underground Railroad, 1834–1914*. Huntington, IN: United Brethren Publishing, 1914.

Calarco, Tom. *People of the Underground Railroad: A Biographical Dictionary*. New York: Greenwood Press, 2008.

Carby, Hazel V. *Reconstructing Womanhood: The Emergence of the Afro-American Woman Novelist*. New York: Oxford University Press, 1987.

Cassidy, John Thomas. "The Issue of Freedom in Illinois under Gov. Edward Coles, 1822–1826." *Journal of the Illinois State Historical Society* 57 (1964): 284–88.

Catterall, Helen Tunnicliff, ed. *Judicial Cases Concerning American Slavery and the Negro Volumes I–V*. Washington, DC: Carnegie Institution of Washington, 1926; reprint, New York: Octagon Books, Inc., 1968.

Cecelski, David S. *The Waterman's Song: Slavery and Freedom in Maritime North Carolina*. Chapel Hill: University of North Carolina Press, 2000.

*Cemeteries and Tombstone Inscriptions of Madison County, Illinois*. Madison County Genealogical Society, 1992.

Cha-Jua, Sundiata Keitha. *America's First Black Town: Brooklyn, Illinois 1830–1915*. Urbana: University of Illinois Press, 2000.

Chadwick, Bruce. *Traveling the Underground Railroad*. Secaucus: Carol Publishing Group, 1999.

Champion, Lovelace. *Black Methodism: Basic Beliefs*. Nashville: AMEC Sunday School Union Legacy Publishing, 1995.

Chapman, Abraham. *Black Voices: An Anthology of African American Literature*. New York: Signet Classic, 2001.

Cheek, William, and Aimee Lee. *John Mercer Langston and the Fight for Black Freedom, 1829–65*. Urbana: University of Illinois Press, 1989.

Child, L. Maria. *Isaac T. Hopper: A True Life*. Boston: John P. Jewett and Company, 1854.

Christian, Nicole M. "North Elba Journal; Recalling Timbuctoo, A Slice of Black History," *The New York Times*, February 19, 2002.

Christianson, Scott. *Freeing Charles: The Struggle to Free a Slave on the Eve of the Civil War.* Champaign: University of Illinois Press, 2010.

*Cincinnati Enquirer*. "Ohio Civil War History Sought: Researchers Look for Railroad Site," June 18, 2001. www.enquirer.com/editions/2001/06/18/loc_ohio_civil_war.html.

Cobb, Thomas R. R. *An Inquiry into the Law of Negro Slavery in the United States of America. To Which Is Prefixed, an Historical Sketch of Slavery*. Philadelphia: T. & J. W. Johnson and Co., 1858; reprint, Athens: University of Georgia Pres, 1999.

Cockrum, Col. William M. *History of the Underground Railroad as It Was Conducted by the Anti-Slavery League*. Oakland City, IN: J. W. Cockrum Printing Company, 1915; reprint, New York: Negro Universities Press, 1969.

Coffin, Addison. *Life and Travels of Addison Coffin.* Cleveland: William G. Hubbard, 1897.

Coffin, Levi. *Reminiscences of Levi Coffin, the Reputed President of the Underground Railroad; Being a Brief History of the Labors of a Lifetime in Behalf of the Slave, with the Stories of Numerous Fugitives, Who Gained Their Freedom through His Instrumentality, and Many Other Incidents.* Cincinnati: Western Tract Society, 1879.

Conrad, Earl. *Harriet Tubman: Negro Soldier and Abolitionist.* New York: International Publishers Co., 1942.

———. *General Harriet Tubman.* Washington, DC: Associated Publishers, 1943.

Cooley, Verna. "Illinois and the Underground Railroad to Canada." *Transactions of the Illinois State Historical Society* (1917): 76–98.

Coon, Diane Perrine. *Southeastern Indiana's Underground Railroad Routes and Operations.* Louisville: State of Indiana Department of Natural Resources and NPS, 2001. www.statelib.lib.in.us/www/ihb/ugrr/ugrrbooks.html.

Cord, Xenia E. "Indiana Applications to the Cherokee Restitution Appropriation of 1906: A Little-Known Source for Black Genealogy." In *Indiana's African-American Heritage: Essays from Black History News & Notes*, edited by Wilma L. Gibbs, 215–32. Indianapolis: Indiana Historical Society, 1993.

———. "Black Rural Settlements in Indiana before 1860." In *Indiana's African-American Heritage: Essays from Black History News & Notes*, edited by Wilma L. Gibbs, 99–110. Indianapolis: Indiana Historical Society, 1993.

Cox, George H., Jr. "The Peace and Social Concerns of Wrightsborough Friends: Part III, The Taint of Slavery." *The Southern Friend, Journal of the North Carolina Friends Historical Society* 12, no. 1 (Spring 1990): 1–10.

Craft, William, and Ellen Craft. *Running a Thousand Miles for Freedom: The Escape of William and Ellen Craft from Slavery.* Baton Rouge: Louisiana State University Press, 1999.

Crane, John Michael, Jr. "Slavery on the Edge of Freedom: The Lower Ohio River Valley in the Antebellum and Civil War Era." Ph.D. dissertation, Vanderbilt University, 2009.

Cromwell, John W. *The Negro in American History.* Washington, DC: The American Negro Academy, 1914.

Crouchett, Lawrence. "Early Black Studies Movements." *Journal of Black Studies* 2, no. 2 (1971): 189–200.

Crow, Jeffery. *The Black Experience in Revolutionary North Carolina.* Raleigh: North Carolina Department of Cultural Resources, 1977.

Curry, Leon P. *The Free Black in Urban America, 1800–1850: The Shadow of the Dream.* Chicago: University of Chicago Press, 1981.

D. A. Spaulding Papers. Springfield: Illinois State Library, 1851.

David, Jay, ed. *Black Defiance: Black Profiles in Courage.* New York: William Morrow & Company, 1972.

Davis, David Brion. "The Emergence of Immediatism in British and American Antislavery Thought." In *Antislavery*, edited by Paul Finkelman, 83–104. New York:

Garland Publishing, Inc., 1989. Original publication, *Mississippi Valley Historical Review* 49 (1962): 209–310.

Davis, Harry E. *A History of Freemasonry among Negroes in America.* Published under the Auspices of the United Supreme Council Ancient and Accepted Scottish Rite of Freemasonry, Northern Jurisdiction, U.S.A. (Prince Hall Affiliation) Incorporated, 1946.

Davis, James E. *Frontier Illinois.* Bloomington: Indiana University Press, 1998.

De Boer, Clara Merritt. "The Role of Afro-Americans in the Origin and Work of the American Missionary Association." Ph.D. dissertation, Rutgers University, 1973.

———. *The Role of Afro-Americans in the Origin and Work of the American Missionary Association: 1839–1877.* New Brunswick, NJ: Rutgers University Press, 1973.

Deagan, Kathleen. *Fort Mosé: Colonial America's Black Fortress of Freedom.* Gainesville: University Press of Florida, 1994.

Dearinger, Lowell A. "Miller Grove: Pope County's Early Negro Community Led a Pattern of Life Which Has Disappeared." *Outdoor Illinois* (November 1965): 7–12.

Delany, Martin R. *North Star*, June 16, 1848.

———. "Political Destiny of the Colored Race on the American Continent." In *Proceedings of the National Emigration Convention of Colored People, Held at Cleveland, Ohio, August 24, 1854.* Pittsburgh, PA: A. A. Anderson, Printer, 1854; reprint, *Pamphlets of Protest: An Anthology of Early African American Protest Literature, 1790–1860*, edited by Richard Newman, Patricia Rael, and Phillip Lapsansky, 226–39. New York: Routledge, 2001.

Demczuk, Bernard. "Unionville: Race, Time, Place and Memory in Talbot County, Maryland, 1634–1892." Ph.D. dissertation, The George Washington University, 2008.

Demos, John. "The Antislavery Movement and the Problem of Violent 'Means.'" In *Antislavery*, edited by Paul Finkelman, 115–35. New York: Garland Publishing, Inc., 1989.

DeRamus, Betty. *Forbidden Fruit: Love Stories from the Underground Railroad.* New York: Atria Books, 2005.

Dickson, Moses. *Manual of the International Order of Twelve Knights and Daughters of Tabor.* St. Louis: A. R. Fleming & Co., 1891.

Dillon, Merton L. "The Failure of the American Abolitionists." In *Antislavery*, edited by Paul Finkelman, 165–77. New York: Garland Publishing, Inc., 1989.

Dingman, Jason Carl. Book review, *Southern Seed, Northern Soil. International Labor and Working-Class History* 6, no. 1 (2003): 216–18.

Dodson, Howard, and Sylviane A. Diouf. *In Motion: The African-American Migration Experience.* New York: Schomburg Center, 2005.

"Don A. Spaulding Was Early Surveyor." *Alton Evening Telegraph, Granite City Press-Record, Edwardsville Intelligencer*, Tuesday, September, n.d.

Douglass, Frederick. *Narrative of the Life of Frederick Douglass an American Slave.* Boston, 1845; reprint, New York: Penguin Group, Inc., 1982.

———. "What the Black Man Wants." Paper presented at the Annual Meeting of the Massachusetts Anti-Slavery Society, Boston, 1865.

———. "My Escape from Slavery." *The Century Illustrated Magazine* 23, n.s. 1 (November 1881): 125–31.

———. *Life and Times of Frederick Douglass*. Reprint, New York: Bonanza Books, 1962. Revised edition published in 1892.

———. "The Present Condition and Future Prospects of the Negro People." In *Frederick Douglass: Selected Speeches and Writings*, edited by Philip S. Foner, 250–59. Chicago: Lawrence Hill Books, 1999.

Drake, Thomas E. *Quakers and Slavery in America*. New Haven: Yale University Press, 1950.

Drew, Benjamin. *A North-side View of Slavery. The Refugee: or The Narratives of Fugitive Slaves in Canada. Related by Themselves, with an Account of the History and Condition of the Colored Population of Upper Canada*. Boston: John P. Jewett and Co., 1856.

Du Bois, W. E. B. *John Brown*. Philadelphia: George W. Jacobs & Co., 1909; reprint, with new introduction and edited by David Roediger, New York: Modern Library, 2001.

———. *The Negro*. New York: Henry Holt and Company, 1915; reprint, Philadelphia: University of Pennsylvania Press, 2001.

———, ed. *Economic Co-Operation among Negro Americans. Report of a Study Made by Atlanta University, under the Patronage of the Carnegie Institution of Washington, D.C., Together with the Proceedings of the 12th Conference for the Study of the Negro Problems, Held at Atlanta University, on Tuesday, May the 28th, 1907*. docsouth.unc.edu/church/Du Bois07/Du Bois.html#dub24.

Dungy, Katherine. "A Friend in Deed: Quakers and Manumission in Perquimans County, North Carolina 1775–1800." *The Southern Friend: Journal of the North Carolina Friends Historical Society* 24, no. 1 (Spring 2002): 5–36.

Dunn, Craig L. *Iron Men, Iron Will: The Nineteenth Indiana Regiment of the Iron Brigade*. Indianapolis: Guild Press of Indiana, Inc., 1995.

Dunphy, John J. *Abolitionism and the Civil War in Southwestern Illinois*. Charleston: The History Press, 2011.

Dyson, Zita. "Gerrit Smith's Effort in Behalf of the Negroes in New York." *Journal of Negro History* 3, no. 4 (October 1918): 354–59.

Early, Gerald, ed. *Ain't Nothing But a Place: An Anthology of African American Writings about St. Louis*. St. Louis: Missouri Historical Society Press, 1998.

Early, Sarah J. W. *Life and Labors of Reverend Jordan W. Early: One of the Pioneers of African Methodism in the West and the South*. Nashville: Publishing House of the A.M.E. Church Sunday School Union, 1894. 216.239.37.104/search?q=cache:QpOAVANXkU4J:docsouth.unc.edu/neh/early/early.html+%22priscilla+baltimore%22&hl=en&ie=UTF-8.

Eaton, Clement. "A Dangerous Pamphlet in the Old South." *Journal of Southern History* 2 (August 1936): 323–34.

Ernst, John. *A Nation Within a Nation: Organizing African-American Communities Before the Civil War*. Lanham, MD: Ivan R. Dee, 2011.

Evans, David. *Journal: 1838–1890*. Chester County Historical Society.

Everett, Susanne. *History of Slavery*. Wigston, UK: Magna Books, 1978; reprint, Edison, NJ: Chartwell Books, Inc., 1996.

Fee, John G. *Autobiography of John G. Fee*. Chicago: National Christian Association, 1891. docsouth.unc.edu/fee/menu.html.

Fields, Barbara. "Ideology and Race in American History." In *Region, Race, and Reconstruction*, edited by J. Morgan Kousser and James M. McPherson, 143–77. New York: Oxford University Press, 1982.

Fifth Census of the United States, Illinois, 1830.

Final Decree, Peter Singleton, decd. November 19, 1850, recorded December 31, 1850. Deed Book E, 52–53. Circuit Clerk's Office, Pope County Courthouse, Golconda, IL.

Finkelman, Paul, ed. *Free Blacks in a Slave Society*. 18 vols. Vol. 17, *Articles on American Slavery*. New York: Garland Publishing, Inc., 1989.

———. *Slavery and the Founders: Race and Liberty in the Age of Jefferson*. 2nd ed. New York: M. E. Sharpe, Inc., 2001.

Finnie, Gordon E. "The Antislavery Movement in the Upper South before 1840." In *Antislavery*, edited by Paul Finkelman, 203–26. New York: Garland Publishing, Inc., 1989. Original publication, *Journal of Southern History* (1969): 319–42.

Fleming, John E. "History and the Black Community." In *The State of Afro-American History: Past, Present, and Future*, edited by Darlene Clark Hine, 197–203. Baton Rouge: Louisiana State University Press, 1989.

Foner, Philip S., ed. *Frederick Douglass: Selected Speeches and Writings*. Chicago: Lawrence Hill Books, 1999.

Foner, Philip S., and George E. Walker, eds. *Proceedings of the Black State Conventions, 1840–1865*. Vol. 2: New Jersey, Connecticut, Maryland, Illinois, Massachusetts, California, New England, Kansas, Louisiana, Virginia, Missouri, South Carolina. Philadelphia: Temple University Press, 1980.

Ford, Nick Aaron. "Henry David Thoreau, Abolitionist." *New England Quarterly* 19, no. 3 (1946): 359–71.

Forstchen, William Robert. "The 28th United States Colored Troops: Indiana's African-Americans Go to War." Ph.D. dissertation, Purdue University, 1994.

Franklin, John Hope. *The Free Negro in North Carolina 1790–1860*. New York: Russell and Russell, 1969. First published in 1943.

———. "Slaves Virtually Free in Ante-bellum North Carolina." *Journal of Negro History* 28, no. 3 (July 1946): 284–310.

Franklin, John Hope, and Alfred A. Moss Jr. *From Slavery to Freedom: A History of African Americans*. 8th ed. Boston: McGraw Hill, 2000.

Franklin, John Hope, and Loren Schweninger. *Runaway Slaves: Rebels on the Plantation*. New York: Oxford University Press, 1999.

Freehling, William W. *The Reintegration of American History: Slavery and the Civil War*. New York: Oxford University Press, 1994.

———. "Why the U.S. Fugitive Slave Phenomenon Was Crucial." Paper presented at the Fifth Annual Gilda Lehrman Center International Conference, Yale University, December 2002.

Freeman, Douglas Southall. *George Washington: A Biography*. Vol. 5. New York: Charles Scribner's Sons, 1952.

Friedman, Lawrence. *Gregarious Saints: Self and Community in American Abolitionism, 1830–1870*. New York: Cambridge University Press, 1982.

Friends of Freedom Society, Ohio Underground Railroad Association. www.ohioundergroundrailroad.org/AboutUs.htm.

Fruehling, Byron D., and Robert H. Smith. "Subterranean Hideaways of the Underground Railroad in Ohio: An Architectural, Archaeological and Historical Critique of Local Traditions." *Ohio History* 102 (1993): 98–117.

Fuller, Elizabeth L. "Miller Grove: African American Identities in a Southern Illinois Farming Community." Paper presented at the Society for Historical Archaeology, St. Louis, January 7–11, 2004.

Gara, Larry. *The Liberty Line: The Legend of the Underground Railroad*. Lexington: University of Kentucky Press, 1996. First published in 1961.

———. "Friends and the Underground Railroad." *Quaker History* 51, no. 1 (1962): 3–19.

———. "The Underground Railroad in Illinois." *Journal of the Illinois State Historical Society* 56 (1963): 508–28.

Gates, Paul Wallace. *The Illinois Central Railroad and Its Colonization Work*. Cambridge: Harvard University Press, 1934.

George, Carol. "Widening the Circle: The Black Church and the Abolitionist Crusade, 1830–1861." In *African American Religion: Interpretative Essays*, edited by Timothy J. Fulop and Albert J. Raboteau, 153–73. New York: Routledge, 1997.

Gerber, David A. *Black Ohio and the Color Line 1860–1915*. Urbana: University of Illinois Press, 1976.

Gibbs, Wilma L., ed. *Indiana's African-American Heritage: Essays from Black History News & Notes*. Indianapolis: Indiana Historical Society, 1993.

Gibson, W. H. *History of the United Brothers of Friendship and Sisters of the Mysterious Ten*. Louisville: Bradley & Gilbert Company, 1897; reprint, Freeport, NY: Books for Libraries Press, 1971.

Giffert, Hannah N. "John Brown and His Black Allies: An Ignored Alliance." *Pennsylvania Magazine of History and Biography* 126, no. 4 (October 2002): 591–610.

Ginsburg, Rebecca. "Escaping through a Black Landscape." In *Cabin, Quarter, Plantation: Architecture and Landscape of North American Slavery*, edited by Clifton Ellis and Rebecca Ginsburg, 51–66. New Haven: Yale University Press, 2010.

Glasco, Laurence Admiral. *WPA History of the Negro in Pittsburgh*. Pittsburgh: University of Pittsburgh Press, 2004.

Glatthar, Joseph T. *Forged in Battle: The Civil War Alliance of Black Soldiers and White Officers*. New York: Free Press, 1990; reprint, Meridian Books, 1991.

Gliozzo, Charles A. "John Jones: A Study of a Black Chicagoan." *Illinois Historical Journal* 80, no. 3 (Autumn 1987): 177–88.

Goers, Carol Sue. "Rocky Fork," *Today's AdVantage*, Wednesday, April 27, 1988.

Gomez, Michael A. *Exchanging Our Country Marks: The Transformation of African Identities in the Colonial and Antebellum South*. Chapel Hill: University of North Carolina Press, 1998.

Goodspeed, Weston A., Leroy Goodspeed, and Charles Goodspeed. *History of Lawrence, Orange and Washington Counties Indiana from the Earliest Time to the Present; Together with Interesting Biographical Sketches, Reminiscences, Notes, etc.* Chicago: Goodspeed Bros. and Company, 1884.

Gordon-Reed, Annette. *Thomas Jefferson and Sally Hemings: An American Controversy*. Charlottesville: University of Virginia Press, 1998.

———. *The Hemingses of Monticello: An American Family*. New York: W. W. Norton and Co., 2009.

Graham, Maryemma, ed. *Complete Poems of Frances E. W. Harper*. New York: Oxford University Press, 1988.

Gray, Beverly. "The Underground Railroad in Southern Ohio." www.angelfire.com/oh/chillicothe/ugrr.html.

Greene, Lorenzo Johnston. *The Negro in Colonial New England*. New York: Atheneum, 1968.

Griffler, Keith P. *Front Line of Freedom: African Americans and the Forging of the Underground Railroad in the Ohio Valley*. Lexington: University of Kentucky Press, 2004.

Grobman, Laurie, and Gary Kunkelman, eds. *Woven with Words: A Collection of African American History in Berks County, Pennsylvania*. Reading, PA: Penn State Berks, 2006.

Groth, Edward Michael. "Forging Freedom in the Mid-Hudson Valley: The End of Slavery and the Formation of a Free African-American Community in Dutchess County, New York, 1770–1850." Ph.D. dissertation, State University of New York at Binghamton, 1994.

Hagedorn, Ann. *Beyond the River: The Untold Story of the Heroes of the Underground Railroad*. New York: Simon & Schuster, 2001.

Hamm, Thomas D., David Dittmer, Chenda Fruchter, Ann Giordano, Janice Mathews, and Ellen Swain. "Moral Choices: Two Indiana Quaker Communities and the Abolitionist Movement." *Indiana Magazine of History* 84, no. 2 (June 1991): 117–54.

Handy, James A. *Scraps of African Methodist Episcopal History*. Philadelphia: AME Concern, 1902; reprint, Dallas: Davis & Davis Associates, 1984.

Harding, Vincent. *There Is a River: The Black Struggle for Freedom in America*. San Diego: Harcourt Brace and Company, 1981.

Harris, N. Dwight. *The History of Negro Servitude in Illinois and of the Slavery Agitation in That State 1719–1864*. New York: Haskell House Publisher Ltd., 1969.

Harrold, Stanley. *Subversives: Antislavery Community in Washington, D.C., 1828–1865*. Baton Rouge: Louisiana State University Press, 2003.

Hatch, Nathan O. "The Second Great Awakening and Rise of Evangelicalism." In *The Democratization of American Christianity*. New Haven: Yale University Press, 1989. xroads.virginia.edu/~MA95/finseth/evangel.html.

Hatcher, Susan Tucker. "North Carolina Quakers: Bona Fide Abolitionists." *The Southern Friend: Journal of the North Carolina Friends Historical Society* 1, no. 2 (Autumn 1979): 81–94.

Haviland, Laura S. *A Woman's Life Work: Including Thirty Years Service on the Underground Railroad and in the War*. Grand Rapids: S. B. Shaw, 1881.

Hawkins, Amos. "Charcoal Iron Furnaces of Lawrence County, Ohio." Available: www.irontonfurnaces.com/.

Henderson, Donald H. "The Negro Migration of 1916–1918: Previous Negro Movements." *Journal of Negro History* 6, no. 4 (October 1921): 393–400.

Henry, Thomas W. *Autobiography of Rev. Thomas W. Henry of the A.M.E. Church*. Baltimore: s.n., 1872.

Henson, Josiah. *The Life of Josiah Henson, Formerly a Slave, Now an Inhabitant of Canada, as Narrated by Himself*. Boston: Arthur D. Phelps, 1849.

———. *"Uncle Tom's" Story of His Life from 1789 to 1876*. Ed. John Lobb. London: Christian Age, 1877.

Hepburn, Sharon. *Crossing the Border: A Free Black Community in Canada*. Champaign: University of Illinois Press, 2007.

*Herald Enterprise*. "Silver Trowel Lodge, Bethany Chapter, O.E.S. Install Officers," January 16, 1930.

Herbert, Bertram. "National Park Service, National Historic Landmark Underground Railroad Archeological Initiative," 1997.

Hershberg, Theodore. "Free Blacks in Antebellum Philadelphia: A Study of Ex-Slaves, Freeborn, and Socioeconomic Decline." In *Philadelphia: Work, Space, Family, and Group Experience in the Nineteenth Century*, edited by Theodore Hershberg, 368–91. New York: Oxford University Press, 1981.

Heuman, Gad, ed. *Out of the House of Bondage*. London: Frank Cass and Co., Ltd., 1986.

Hickok, Charles Thomas. "The Negro in Ohio, 1802–1870." Ph.D. dissertation, Western Reserve University. Cleveland: Williams Publishing and Electric Co., 1896; New York: AMS Press, 1975.

Higginbotham, A. Leon, Jr. *In the Matter of Color: Race and the American Legal Process: The Colonial Period*. New York: Oxford University Press, 1978.

Hilty, Hiram H. *Toward Freedom for All: North Carolina Quakers and Slavery*. Richmond, IN: Friends United Press, 1984.

Hine, Darlene Clark, Elsa Barkley Brown, and Rosalyn Terborg-Penn, eds. *Black Women in America: An Historical Encyclopedia, Vol. 1 A–L*. Bloomington: Indiana University Press, 1993.

Hinks, Peter P. *To Awaken My Afflicted Brethren: David Walker and the Problem of Antebellum Slave Resistance*. University Park: Pennsylvania State University Press, 1997.

Hinton, Richard J. *John Brown and His Men*. New York: Funk and Wagnalls Co., 1894.

*History of Madison County Illinois, Illustrated, with Biographical Sketches of Many Prominent Men and Pioneers*. Edwardsville, IL: W. R. Brinks & Co., 1882.

Hodges, Graham Russell. *The Black Loyalist Directory: African Americans in Exile after the American Revolution*. New York: Garland Publishing, Inc., 1996.

———. *Slavery and Freedom in the Rural North: African Americans in Monmouth County, New Jersey, 1665–1865*. Madison, WI: Madison House, 1997.

———. Book review, *Southern Seed Northern Soil. Journal of American History* 88, no. 1 (June 2001).

———. *David Ruggles: A Radical Black Abolitionist and the Underground Railroad in New York City*. Chapel Hill: University of North Carolina Press, 2010.

Hodges, Graham Russell, and Alan Edward Brown, eds. *"Pretends to Be Free" Runaway Slave Advertisements from Colonial and Revolutionary New York and New Jersey*. New York: Garland Publishing, Inc., 1994.

Hoffman, Judy. *God's Portion: Godfrey, Illinois 1817–1865*. Nashville: Cold Tree Press, 2005.

Hofstadter, Richard. *The American Political Tradition*. New York, 1948.

Hogarth, George. *African Methodist Episcopal Church Magazine* 2, no. 1 (June 1844).

Homan, Wayne E. "The Underground Railroad." *Historical Review of Berks County* (Fall 1958): 112.

Hooper, Isaac T. *The Narrative of Thomas Cooper*. New York: Isaac Hooper, 1832.

Hoosier National Forest. "The Underground Railroad and African American Heritage." www.fs.fed.us/r9/hoosier/docs/history/ur_research.htm.

———. *Cultural Resource Reconnaissance Report No. 09-12-04-170*. U.S. Department of Agriculture, National Forest Service.

Horton, James Oliver, and Lois E. Horton. *Black Bostonians: Family Life and Community Struggle in the Antebellum North*. New York: Holmes and Meier Publishers, Inc., 1979.

———. *Free People of Color: Inside the African American Community*. Washington, DC: Smithsonian Institution Press, 1993.

Howe, Daniel Walker. *What Hath God Wrought: The Transformation of America 1815–1848*. New York: Oxford University Press, 2007.

Hudson, J. Blaine. *Fugitive Slaves and the Underground Railroad in the Kentucky Borderland*. Jefferson, NC: McFarland & Company, Inc., 2002.

———. *Encyclopedia of the Underground Railroad*. Jefferson, NC: McFarland & Company, 2006.

Humez, Jean M. *Harriet Tubman: The Life and the Life Stories*. Madison: University of Wisconsin Press, 2003.

Illinois Anti-Slavery Convention [1838]. *Proceedings of the Illinois Anti-Slavery Convention: Held at Upper Alton on the Twenty-sixth, Twenty-seventh, and Twenty-eighth October, 1837*. Alton, IL: Parks and Breath, The Illinois Historical Digitization Projects, Northern Illinois University Libraries. lincoln.lib.niu.edu/cgibin/getobject_?c.105:1./lib35/artfl1/databases/sources/IMAG/.

Indiana State Historical Bureau. www.statelib.lib.in.us/www/ihb/ugrr/ugrrbooks.html.

———. "National Heritage Area: Bleeding Kansas, The Enduring Struggle for Freedom." www.bleedingkansas.com.

Institute for Advanced Technology in the Humanities, University of Virginia. "Uncle Tom's Cabin & American Culture," manuscript of Uncle Tom's Cabin. www.iath.virginia.edu/utc/index2f.html.

Jacobs, Harriet. *Incidents in the Life of a Slavegirl*. New York: Penguin Classics, 2000.

Jefferson, Paul, ed. *The Travels of William Wells Brown*. New York: Markus Wiener Publishing, Inc., 1991.

Jeffrey, Julie Roy. *Abolitionists Remember: Antislavery Autobiographies and the Unfinished Work of Emancipation*. Chapel Hill: University of North Carolina Press, 2008.

Jenifer, John T. *Centennial Retrospect History of the African Methodist Episcopal Church*. Nashville: A.M.E. Sunday School Union, 1916.

Johnson, Charles, Patricia Smith, and the WGBH Series Research Team. *Africa in America: America's Journey through Slavery*. New York: Harcourt Brace and Co., 1998.

Johnson, Charlotte. "Underground Railroad Network to Freedom Application, Camp Warren Levis, Godfrey, IL." 2000.

Johnson, Clifton H. "Mary Ann Shadd: Crusader for the Freedom of Man." *Crisis* 78, no. 3 (1971): 89–90.

Johnson, H. U. *From Dixie to Canada: Romances and Realities of the Underground Railroad*. Orwell, OH: H. U. Johnson, 1896.

Jones, Absalom. *A Thanksgiving Sermon, Preached January 1, 1808, on Account of the Abolition of the African Slave Trade on That Day, By the Congress of the United States*. Philadelphia: Fry and Kammerer, 1808.

Jones, James Pickett. "The Illinois Negro Law of 1853: Racism in a Free State." *Illinois Quarterly* 40, no. 2 (1977): 5–22.

Jones, Norrece T., Jr. *Born a Child of Freedom, Yet a Slave*. Hanover, NH: Wesleyan University Press, 1990.

Jordan, Ervin L., Jr. *Black Confederates and Afro-Yankees in Civil War Virginia*. Charlottesville: University of Virginia Press, 1995.

Jordan, Winthrop D. *White Over Black: American Attitudes Toward the Negro, 1550–1812*. Chapel Hill: University of North Carolina Press, 1968.

Kashatus, William C. *Just over the Line: Chester County and the Underground Railroad*. University Park: Pennsylvania State University Press, 2002.

Katz, William Loren. *Black Indians: A Hidden Heritage.* New York: Atheneum, 1986.

———. *The Black West.* New York: Simon & Schuster, 1987.

Knabenshue, S. S. "The Underground Railroad." In *Ohio Archaeological and Historical Publications*, 396–403. Columbus: Fred J. Heer, 1905.

Krieger, Angie R. Initial Report of Phase I Survey of the Lick Creek African American Settlement Orange County, Indiana 1817–1911. *Cultural Resource Reconnaissance Report No. 09-12-04-170.* U.S. Department of Agriculture, National Forest Service, Hoosier National Forest, n.d.

Kroupa, Daniel Richard. "Slave Revolts and North Carolina Quaker Migration." Master's thesis, Michigan State University, 1997.

"Land Transfer Records, Edwardsville, IL." Edwardsville: Madison County Courthouse.

LaRoche, Cheryl J. "On the Edge of Freedom: Free Black Communities and the Underground Railroad." Ph.D. dissertation, University of Maryland, 2004.

———. "The Balance Principle: Slavery, Freedom and the Geography of Statehood." In *Cabin, Quarter, Plantation: Architecture and Landscapes of North American Slavery*, edited by Clifton Ellis and Rebecca Ginsburg, 233–62. New Haven: Yale University Press, 2010.

LaRoche, Cheryl J., and Ronald D. Palmer. "The Look of Eagles: Notes Toward a Biographical Chronology of William Paul Quinn, Senior Bishop of the AME Church, 1788–1873." Unpublished manuscript, 2009.

Larson, Kate Clifford. *Bound for the Promised Land: Harriet Tubman: Portrait of an American Hero.* New York: Ballantine Books, 2004.

Leighty, George. "Old Rocky Fork: Hundreds Look on 'Settlement' as Their Home," *Alton Evening Telegraph*, September 28, 1962.

Lesick, Lawrence Thomas. *The Lane Rebels: Evangelicalism and Antislavery in Antebellum America.* Metuchen, NJ: The Scarecrow Press, Inc., 1980.

Levine, Robert S., ed. *Martin R. Delany: A Documentary Reader.* Chapel Hill: University of North Carolina Press, 2003.

Lewis, James K. *Religious Life of Fugitive Slaves and Rise of Coloured Baptist Churches, 1820–1865, in What Is Now Known as Ontario.* New York: Arno Press, 1980. Original publication, master's thesis, McMaster Divinity College, April 1965.

Lewis, Pierce. "Common Landscapes as Historic Documents." In *History From Things: Essays on Material Culture*, edited by Steven Lubar and W. David Kingery, 115–39. Washington, DC: Smithsonian Institution Press, 1993.

Lewis Tappan Antislavery Library Catalogue, Lewis Tappan Collection, Catalogues of Anti-Slavery Books and Pamphlets 101-3, 1851. Folders 12–14. Moorland-Spingarn Research Center, Manuscript Division, Howard University.

Libby, Jean. *From Slavery to Salvation: The Autobiography of Rev. Thomas W. Henry of the A.M.E. Church.* Jackson: University Press of Mississippi, 1994.

Libby, Jean, and Allies for Freedom. "Hiram and Willis Revels, Lewis Leary and John Copeland." In *John Brown Mysteries*, edited by Jean Libby, 72–75. Missoula, MT: Pictorial Histories Publishing Company, 1999.

Libby, Jean, Hannah Geffert, and Jimica Akinloye Kenyatta. "Hiram Revels Related to Men in John Brown's Army." *Allies for Freedom*. www.alliesforfreedom.org/allies.htm.

Lincoln, C. Eric, and Lawrence H. Mamiya. *The Black Church in the African American Experience*. Durham: Duke University Press, 1990.

Little, Barbara J. "Archaeology, History, and Material Culture: Grounding Abstractions and Other Imponderables." *International Journal of Historical Archaeology* 1, no. 2 (1997): 179–87.

Litwack, Leon F. *North of Slavery: The Negro in the Free States 1790–1860*. Chicago: University of Chicago Press, 1961.

Litwack, Leon F., and August Meier, eds., *Black Leaders of the Nineteenth Century*. Champaign: University of Illinois Press, 1991.

Lockley, Timothy James, ed. *Maroon Communities in South Carolina: A Documentary Record*. Columbia: University of South Carolina Press, 2008.

Logan, Shirley Wilson. *"We Are Coming": The Persuasive Discourse of Nineteenth-Century Black Women*. Carbondale: Southern Illinois University Press, 1999.

Loguen, Rev. Jermain W. *The Rev. J. W. Loguen as a Slave and a Freeman. A Narrative of a Real Life*. Syracuse: J. G. K. Truair & Co., 1859; reprint, New York: Negro Universities Press, 1968.

Lovejoy, Paul E., and David V. Trotman. "Introduction: Ethnicity and the African Diaspora." In *Transatlantic Dimensions of Ethnicity in the African Diaspora*, edited by Paul E. Lovejoy and David V. Trotman, 1–8. London: Continuum, 2003.

Lu, Marlene K. *Walkin' the Wabash*. Indianapolis: Indiana Department of Natural Resources, Division of Historic Preservation and Archaeology, 2001.

Lumpkin, Katherine DuPre. "'The General Plan Was Freedom': A Negro Secret Order on the Underground Railroad." *Phylon Quarterly* 28, no. 1 (1967): 63–77.

Lundy, Benjamin. *The Poetical Works of Elizabeth Margaret Chandler: With a Memoir of Her Life and Character*. Philadelphia: T. E. Chapman, 1845.

"Lyman Beecher." In *An American Family: The Beecher Tradition*. newman.baruch.cuny.edu/digital/2001/beecher/lyman.htm.

Mabee, Carleton. *Black Freedom: The Nonviolent Abolitionists from 1830 through the Civil War*. London: Macmillan Company, 1970.

Malloy, David E. "Marker Honoring Abolitionist to be Displayed." *Herald-Dispatch*, September 18, 2003. www.herald-dispatch.com/2003/September/18/LNlist6.htm.

Mason, Matthew. *Slavery and Politics in the Early American Republic*. Chapel Hill: University of North Carolina Press, 2008.

Mathews, Donald G. "Charles Colcock Jones and the Southern Evangelical Crusade to Form a Biracial Community." *Journal of Southern History* 41, no. 3 (August 1975): 299–320.

May, Samuel. *The Fugitive Slave Law and Its Victims*. Freeport, NY: Books for Libraries Press, 1970.

Mayer, Henry. *All on Fire: William Lloyd Garrison and the Abolition of Slavery*. New York: St. Martin's Press, 1998.

McCarthy, Timothy Patrick, and John Stauffer, eds. *Prophets of Protest: Reconsidering the History of American Abolitionism*. New York: The New Press, 2006.

McDaniel, Donna, and Vanessa Julye. *Fit for Freedom, Not for Friendship: Quakers, African Americans, and the Myth of Racial Justice*. Philadelphia: Quaker Press, 2009.

McDougall, Marion Gleason. *Fugitive Slaves (1619–1865)*. New York: Bergman Publishers, 1891.

McGraw, Marie Tyler, and Kira R. Badamo. *Underground Railroad Resources in the United States Theme Study*. Washington, DC: National Park Service, 2000.

McManamon, Francis P. "America's National Archaeological Heritage." *The Bulletin* 114 (1998): i.

McNerney, Michael J. "A Thematic Study of Rural Historic Farmsteads, Pope County, Illinois." Harrisburg, IL: Prepared for U.S. Department of Agriculture, Forest Service, Shawnee National Forest, American Resources Group, Ltd., 1987.

McPherson, James M. *The Abolitionist Legacy: From Reconstruction to the NAACP*. Princeton: Princeton University Press, 1975.

———. *The Negro's Civil War: How American Blacks Felt and Acted during the War for the Union*. New York: Random House, 2008.

Meaders, Daniel. "Kidnapping Blacks in Philadelphia: Isaac Hooper's Tales of Oppression." *Journal of Negro History* 8, no. 2 (1995): 47–65.

Melton, J. Gordon. *A Will to Choose: The Origins of African American Methodism*. Lanham, MD: Rowan and Littlefield Publishers, Inc., 2007.

Meltzer, Milton. *The Black Americans: A History in Their Own Words 1619–1983*. New York: HarperCollins, 1987.

Middleton, Stephen. *The Black Laws in the Old Northwest: A Documentary History*. Westport: Greenwood Press, 1993.

———. "The Fugitive Slave Crisis in Cincinnati: Resistance, Enforcement, and Black Refugees, 1850–1860." *Journal of Negro History* 72, nos. 1–2 (Winter–Spring 1987): 20–32.

*Millennium Trail Initiative*. www.coax.net/people/lwf/pr_mt.htm.

Millennium Trails Program. www.dot.gov/mtp/.

"Miller Grove Research Activities." Shawnee National Forest, U.S. Forest Service, 2001.

Mills, Randy, Mark Coomer, Leslie Conway Coomer, and Sandy McBeth. *Report to Indiana Department of Natural Resources, Division of Historic Preservation and Archaeology, 402 W. Washington Street, W274, Indianapolis, Indiana 46204-2748 Concerning Underground Railroad Activity in Southwestern Indiana*, 2001.

Mitchell, Henry H. *Black Church Beginnings: The Long-Hidden Realities of the First Years*. Grand Rapids: Wm. B. Eerdmans Publishing Company, 2004.

Mitchell, William M. *The Underground Railroad: From Slavery to Freedom*. London: William Tweedie, 1860.

Montgomery, William E. *Under Their Own Vine and Fig Tree: The African-American Church in the South*. Baton Rouge: Louisiana State University Press, 1994.

Moore, Gail Ruffin. *Cincinnati: America Is Woven of Many Strands*. Charleston: Acadia Publishing, 2007.

Morgan, Joseph H. *Morgan's History of the New Jersey Conference of the A.M.E. Church, from 1872 to 1887, and of the several churches, as far as possible, from date of organization with biographical sketches of members of the conference*. Camden: S. Chew, Printer, 1887.

Morgan, Philip D. "Rethinking Early American Slavery." In *Inequality in Early America*, edited by Carla Gardina and Sharon V. Salinger Pestana, 239–66. Hanover, NH: University Press of New England, 1999.

Morris, Harvey. *The Underground Railroad*. Salem, 1924; reprint, Salem, IN: Washington County Historical Society, 1993.

Morrison, Tara. "The UGRR Archeology Initiative." *CRM* (1998): 46–47.

Moses, Wilson Jeremiah, ed. *Classical Black Nationalism: From the American Revolution to Marcus Garvey*. New York: New York University Press, 1996.

Muelder, Hermann R. *Fighters for Freedom: The History of Anti-Slavery Activities of Men and Women Associated with Knox College*. New York: Columbia University Press, 1959.

Muelder, Owen W. *The Underground Railroad in Western Illinois*. Jefferson, NC: McFarland & Co., Inc., 2008.

Muller, Nancy Ladd. "The House of the Black Burghardts: An Investigation of Gender, and Class at the W. E. B. Du Bois Boyhood Homesite." In *Those of Little Note: Race, Gender and Class in Historical Archaeology*, edited by Elizabeth M. Scott, 81–94. Tucson: University of Arizona Press, 1994.

Mullin, Gerald W. *Flight and Rebellion: Slave Resistance in Eighteenth-Century Virginia*. New York: Oxford University Press, 1972.

Muraskin, William A. *Middle-Class Blacks in a White Society: Prince Hall Freemasonry in America*. Berkeley: University of California Press, 1975.

Nash, Gary B. *Forging Freedom: The Formation of Philadelphia's Black Community 1720–1840*. Cambridge: Harvard University Press, 1988.

National Forest Service. "Miller Grove: An Early African American Community in Pope County." www.fs.fed.us/r9/shawnee/heritage/elizabeth/millergrove2000.htm; www.fs.fed.us/r9/hoosier/docs/history/lick_creek.htm.

———. Wayne National Forest and Paynes Crossing, Recent History. www.fs.fed.us/r9/wayne/heritage/Research_History/index.shtml.

National Park Service. *Underground Railroad Special Resource Study*. Denver Service Center: U.S. Department of the Interior, 1995.

———. "National Underground Railroad Network to Freedom Program." 209.10.16.21/TEMPLATE/FrontEnd/program.cfm.

———. *The Underground Railroad: Official National Park Handbook*. Washington, DC: U.S. Department of the Interior, 1998.

———. *Exploring a Common Past: Researching and Interpreting the Underground Railroad*. Washington, DC: U.S. Department of the Interior, 2000.

———. "Aboard the Underground Railroad: A National Register Travel Itinerary." www.cr.nps.gov/nr/travel/underground/.

———. "List of Sites, Aboard the Underground Railroad." www.cr.nps.gov/nr/travel/underground/states.htm.

National Register, History and Education, National Park Service. *Underground Railroad Resources in the United States: Theme Study*. Washington, DC: U.S. Department of the Interior, 2000.

National Register of Historic Places Inventory—Nomination Form. "Bethel African Methodist Episcopal Church," 119 North Tenth Street, Reading, PA, January 1979.

National Register of Historic Places Registration Form. Bethel African Methodist Episcopal Church, Sheppards Mill Road, Springtown, Cumberland, NJ, October 1999.

National Underground Railroad Freedom Center. www.freedomcenter.org.

"National Underground Railroad Freedom Center Act: Report to Accompany H.R. 2919." U.S. Congress, Committee on Energy and Natural Resources, 2000. purl.access.gpo.gov/GPO/LPS8362.

"National Underground Railroad Network to Freedom Act of 1998," Public Law 105-203, 105th Congress, 2nd Sess. National Underground Railroad Network to Freedom Program, 209.10.16.21/TEMPLATE/FrontEnd/program.cfm?textfield=illinois.

"New Philadelphia, Illinois: Dr. Juliet E. K. Walker Commemorates Free Frank McWorter." www.newphiladelphiaillinois.org.

Newman, Richard S. "Protest in Black and White: The Formation and Transformation of an African American Political Community during the Early Republic." In *Beyond the Founders: New Approaches to the Political History of the Early American Republic*, edited by Jeffrey S. Palsey, Andrew W. Robertson, and David Waldstretcher, 180–204. Chapel Hill: University of North Carolina Press, 2004.

———. *Freedom's Prophet: Bishop Richard Allen, the AME Church, and the Founding Black Fathers*. New York: New York University Press, 2008.

Nichols, Charles. "Who Read the Slave Narratives?" *Phylon Quarterly* 20, no. 2 (1959): 149–62.

O'Hair, Mary C. *Slavery: The Underground Railroad Movement and Some History as Related to Wabash County, Indiana*. Wabash, IN: Wabash County Historical Museum, 1965.

Ohio Department of Natural Resources. "Ohio's Iron Age." www.dnr.state.oh.us/parks/explore/magazine/sprsum98/ironage.htm.

150th Souvenir Book of Providence Regular Missionary Baptist Association, 1984.

Paige, John C. "NPS Study to Preserve and Interpret the UGRR." *CRM* (1998): 39–40.

Payne, Daniel Alexander, ed. *The Semi-Centenary and the Retrospection of the A.M.E. Church in the United States of America*. Baltimore: Sherwood & Co., 1866.

———. *Recollections of Seventy Years*. Nashville: A.M.E. Sunday School Union, 1888; reprint with a new preface by Benjamin Quarles, New York: Aron Press and The New York Times, 1969.

———. *History of the African Methodist Episcopal Church*. Nashville: A.M.E. Sunday School Union, 1891.

Paynter, Robert. "Afro-Americans in the Massachusetts Historical Landscape." In *Politics of the Past*, edited by P. Gathercole and D. Lowenthal, 49–62. London: Unwin Hyman, 1990.

Pease, Jane H., and William H. Pease. *They Who Would Be Free: Blacks' Search for Freedom, 1830–1861. New York:* Atheneum, 1974.

Pease, William H. and Jane H. Pease. "Organized Negro Communities: A North American Experiment." *Journal of Negro History* 47, no. 1 (January 1962): 19–34.

———. *Black Utopia: Negro Communal Experiments in America.* Madison: The State Historical Society of Wisconsin, 1964.

———. "Confrontation and Abolition in the 1850s." *Journal of American History* 58, no. 4 (1972): 923–37.

Pennington, James W. C. *The Fugitive Blacksmith or Events in the History of James W. C. Pennington.* 3rd ed. London: Charles Gilpin, 1850; reprinted in Arna Bontemps. *Great Slave Narratives.* Boston: Beacon Press, 1969.

Peters, Pamela R. *The Underground Railroad in Floyd County, Indiana.* Jefferson, NC: McFarland & Co., Inc., 2001.

Peterson, Carla L. *"Doers of the Word": African-American Women Speakers and Writers in the North (1830–1880).* New Brunswick, NJ: Rutgers University Press, 1995.

Pickard, Kate E. *The Kidnapped and the Ransomed: Recollections of Peter Still and His Wife "Vina," after Forty Years of Slavery.* Syracuse: William T. Hamilton, 1856.

Pierce, Rick. "Proposal for Crosstown Highway Is Seen as Boon for Godfrey Area," *St. Louis Post-Dispatch*, February 17, 2003.

Pirtle, Carol. *Escape Betwixt Two Suns: A True Tale of the Underground Railroad in Illinois.* Carbondale: Southern Illinois University Press, 2000.

*Pope County History and Families.* "History of Rural Pope County Blacks," vol. 2, n.d.

Porter, Dorothy, ed. *Early Negro Writing 1760–1837.* Baltimore: Black Classic Press, 1995.

Potter, David M. *The Impending Crisis: America before the Civil War, 1848–1861.* New York: Harper and Row, 1976.

Preston, E. Delorus, Jr. "The Underground Railroad in Northwest Ohio." *Journal of Negro History* 17, no. 4 (1932): 409–36.

———. "The Genesis of the Underground Railroad." *Journal of Negro History* 18, no. 2 (1933): 144–70.

Preston, Emmett D. "The Fugitive Slave Acts in Ohio." *Journal of Negro History* 28, no. 4 (October 1943): 422–77.

Price, Richard, ed. *Maroon Societies: Rebel Slave Communities in the Americas.* 3rd ed. Baltimore: Johns Hopkins University Press, 1996.

Prince, Bryan. *A Shadow on the Household: One Enslaved Family's Incredible Struggle for Freedom.* New York: Random House, 2009.

*Proceedings of the National Convention of People of Color and Their Friends, Held in Troy, N.Y., on the 6th, 7th, 8th and 9th October.* Troy, NY: Steam Press of J. C. Kneeland and Co., 1847; reprint, *Pamphlets of Protest: An Anthology of Early African American Protest Literature, 1790–1860*, edited by Richard Newman, Patricia Rael, and Phillip Lapsansky, 166–77. New York: Routledge, 2001.

*Proceedings of the Thirty-Third Annual Encampment of the Depart of Illinois, G.A.R., Held at Danville, May 16, 17 and 18, 1899.* Chicago: M. Umbdenstock and Co., 1899.

*Provincial Freeman*. Toronto, Canada West, December 23, 1854.

Pulis, John W., ed. *Moving On: Black Loyalists in the Afro-Atlantic World*. New York: Garland Publishing, Inc., 1999.

Quarles, Benjamin. *Black Abolitionists*. New York: Oxford University Press, 1969.

———. "The War as a Black Declaration of Independence." In *Slavery and Freedom*, edited by Ira Berlin and Ronald Hoffman, 284–301. Charlottesville: University of Virginia Press, 1983.

Quinn, Rev. W. Paul. "The Origin, Horrors, and Results of Slavery, Faithfully and Minutely Described, In a Series of Facts, and Its Advocates Pathetically Addressed" (1834). In *Early Negro Writing 1760–1837*, edited by Dorothy Porter, 614–36. Baltimore: Black Classic Press, 1995.

Raboteau, Albert J. *Canaan Land: A Religious History of African Americans*. New York: Oxford University Press, 1999.

Rael, Patrick, ed. *African-American Activism before the Civil War*. New York: Routledge, 1999.

———. *Black Identity and Black Protest in the Antebellum North*. Chapel Hill: University of North Carolina Press, 2002.

Raines, Edgar F. *Abolitionists and Anti-Slavery Men in Southern Illinois, 1850–1863*. Unpublished manuscript, 1969.

Rawick, George P. *From Sundown to Sunup: The Making of the Black Community*. Westport: Greenwood Press, 1972.

Reed, Harry. *Platform for Change: The Foundations of the Northern Free Black Community, 1775–1865*. East Lansing: Michigan State University Press, 1994.

Rhodes, Jane. *Mary Ann Shadd Cary: The Black Press and Protest in the Nineteenth Century*. Bloomington: Indiana University Press, 1998.

Ripley, C. Peter, ed. *The Black Abolitionist Papers*. 5 vols. Chapel Hill: University of North Carolina Press, 1992.

———. "The Underground Railroad." In *The Underground Railroad*, 45–75. U.S. Department of the Interior, National Park Service, 1998.

Rivers, Larry Eugene. *Slavery in Florida: Territorial Days to Emancipation*. 2nd ed. Gainesville: University Press of Florida, 2009.

Robbins, Arlie C. *Prince Hall Masonry in Ontario 1852–1933*. Authorized by Most Worshipful Prince Hall Grand Lodge Free and Accepted Masons of the Province of Ontario and Jurisdiction, 1980.

Robbins, Coy D. *Forgotten Hoosiers: African Heritage in Orange County Indiana*. Bowie, MD: Heritage Books, 1994.

Romaine, Judi. "Lick Creek Settlement: Survey of Life in a Rural 19th Century Free Black Community." Unpublished manuscript, 1993.

Rose, Harold M. "The All-Negro Town: Its Evolution and Function." *Geographical Review* 55, no. 3 (July 1965): 362–81.

Sahr, Robert. "Inflation Conversion Factors for Dollars 1774 to Estimated 2019." oregonstate.edu/cla/polisci/faculty-research/sahr/sahr.htm.

Sanborn, Franklin Benjamin, ed. *The Life and Letters of John Brown: Liberator of Kansas, and Martyr of Virginia*. Boston: Roberts Brothers, 1891.

Scarlett, George C. *Laws Against Liberty*. New York: George C. Scarlett, 1937.

Schmidt, Sanford J. "Blaze Destroys Rocky Fork Again." *Telegraph*, October 18, 1988.

Schor, Joel. *Henry Highland Garnet: A Voice of Black Radicalism in the Nineteenth Century*. Westport: Greenwood Press, 1977.

Schwarz, Philip J. *Migrants Against Slavery: Virginians and the Nation*. Charlottesville: University of Virginia Press, 2001.

Shackel, Paul A. *Memory in Black and White: Race, Commemoration, and the Post-Bellum Landscape*. Walnut Creek, CA: AltaMira Press, 2003.

———. *New Philadelphia: An Archaeology of Race in the Heartland*. Berkeley: University of California Press, 2011.

Shadd, Adrienne L., Afua Cooper, and Karolyn Smartz Frost. *The Underground Railroad: Next Stop, Toronto!* Toronto: National Heritage Books, 2002.

Shawnee National Forest. "Buried History at Miller Grove." African American Heritage of the Shawnee National Forest, Attachment A, Supporting Correspondence, Proposal Number: R9-08-99-Bcucp-01. Summary: Historic Black College and University Comprehensive Program, Heritage Program, 1999.

———. "Shawnee National Forest Miller Grove Historically Black College Project." On file, Murphysboro Ranger Station, IL, NFS, n.d.

Sheridan, Richard B., ed. *Freedom's Crucible: The Underground Railroad in Lawrence and Douglas County, Kansas, 1854–1865: A Reader*. Lawrence: University of Kansas Press, 1998.

Sieber, Ellen, and Cheryl Ann Munson. *Looking at History: Indiana's Hoosier National Forest Region 1600 to 1950*. U.S. Department of Agriculture, National Forest Service, 1992.

Siebert, Wilbur. "The Underground Railroad in Ohio." In *Ohio Archaeological and Historical Publications* 4, 1895.

———. *The Underground Railroad from Slavery to Freedom*. Gloucester: Peter Smith, 1898.

———. *Mysteries of Ohio's Underground Railroad*. Columbus: Long's College Book Company, 1951.

Simmons, Rev. William J. *Men of Mark: Eminent, Progressive and Rising*. Cleveland: Geo. M. Rewell & Co., 1887.

Simon, Paul. *Freedom's Champion Elijah Lovejoy*. Carbondale: Southern Illinois University Press, 1994.

Simpson, Donald G. *Under the North Star: Black Communities in Upper Canada*. Ed. Paul E. Lovejoy. Trenton: Africa World Press, Inc., 2005.

Singleton, George A. *The Romance of African Methodism: A Study of the African Methodist Episcopal Church*. New York: Exposition Press, 1952.

———. "Following the Trail of the Fathers: Priscilla Baltimore." *A.M.E. Church Review* 79 (April 1964): 3–5.

Slaughter, Thomas P. *Bloody Dawn: The Christiana Riot and Racial Violence in the Antebellum North*. New York: Oxford University Press, 1991.

Smedley, Robert Clemens. *History of the Underground Railroad in Chester and the Neighboring Counties of Pennsylvania*. Lancaster, PA: Office of the Journal, 1883.

Smith, Charles Spencer. *A History of the African Methodist Episcopal Church: Being a Volume Supplemental to a History of the African Methodist Episcopal Church, by Daniel Alexander Payne, D.D., LL.D., Late One of Its Bishops, Chronicling the Principal Events in the Advance of the African Methodist Episcopal Church From 1856 to 1922*. Philadelphia: Book Concern of the AME Church, 1922.

Smith, Elbert B. *The Death of Slavery: The United States, 1837–65*. Chicago: University of Chicago Press, 1967.

Smith, H. Perry. *History of Essex County, with biographical sketches of some its prominent men and pioneers*. Syracuse: D. Mason & Co., 1885.

Soderlund, Jean R. *Quakers & Slavery*. Princeton: Princeton University Press, 1985.

Sorin, Gerald. *The New York Abolitionists: A Case Study of Political Radicalism*. Westport: Greenwood Press, 1971.

Spicer, Carl L. "The Underground Railroad in Southern Illinois." Unpublished manuscript, The William H. Siebert Underground Railroad Collection, Ohio Historical Society, n.d.

Sprague, Stuart Seely, ed. *His Promised Land: An Autobiography of John P. Parker, Former Slave and Conductor on the Underground Railroad*. New York: W. W. Norton and Co., 1996.

Starling, Marion Wilson. *The Slave Narrative: Its Place in American History*. Washington, DC: Howard University Press, 1988.

Sterling, Dorothy, ed. *We Are Sisters: Black Women in the Nineteenth Century*. New York: W. W. Norton and Co., 1984.

———. *Martin Robison Delany: The Making of an Afro-American 1812–1885*. New York: Da Capo Press, 1996.

Stewart, James Brewer. *Wendell Phillips: Liberty's Hero*. Baton Rouge: Louisiana State University Press, 1986.

Still, William. *The Underground Railroad*. Philadelphia: Porter and Coates, 1872; reprint, Salem, NH: Ayer Company, Publishers, Inc., 1992.

Stout, Owen. *History of Orange County, Indiana: A Reproduction of the Original History of Lawrence, Orange and Washington Counties, 1884*. Paoli, IN: Stout's Print Shop, 1965.

Stowe, Harriet Beecher. *Uncle Tom's Cabin or Life among the Lowly*. Boston: John P. Jewett & Co., 1852.

———. *A Key to Uncle Tom's Cabin; Presenting the Original Facts and Documents upon Which the Story Is Founded Together with Corroborative Statements Verifying the Truth of the Work*. Boston: John P. Jewett & Co., 1853.

Stuckey, Sterling, ed. *The Ideological Origins of Black Nationalism*. Boston: Beacon Press, 1972.

Sumler-Lewis, Janice. "The Forten-Purvis Women of Philadelphia and the American Anti-Slavery Crusade." *Journal of Negro History* 66, no. 4 (Winter 1981–82): 281–88.

Swift, David E. "Black Presbyterian Attacks on Racism: Samuel Cornish, Theodore Wright, and Their Contemporaries." In *Black Apostles at Home and Abroad: Afro-Americans and the Christian Mission from the Revolution to Reconstruction*, edited by David W. Wills and Richard Newman, 43–84. Boston: G. K. Hall and Co., 1982.

———. *Black Prophets of Justice: Activist Clergy Before the Civil War*. Baton Rouge: Louisiana State University Press, 1989.

Switala, William J. *Underground Railroad in Pennsylvania*. Mechanicsburg, PA: Stackpole Books, 2001.

———. *Underground Railroad in Delaware, Maryland, and West Virginia*. Mechanicsburg, PA: Stackpole Books, 2004.

———. *Underground Railroad in New York and New Jersey*. Mechanicsburg, PA: Stackpole Books, 2006.

Tadman, Michael. *Speculators and Slaves: Masters, Traders, and Slaves in the Old South*. Madison: University of Wisconsin Press, 1989.

Tanner, Benjamin T. *An Apology for African Methodism*. Baltimore, s.n., 1867.

Tate, Gayle T. "Free Black Resistance in the Antebellum Era, 1830–1860." *Journal of Black Studies* 28, no. 6 (1998): 764–82.

Taylor, Clarence. *The Black Churches of Brooklyn*. New York: Columbia University Press, 1994.

tenBroek, Jacobus. *The Antislavery Origins of the 14th Amendment*. Berkeley: University of California Press, 1951.

"The Gist Settlement." hometown.aol.com/ugrrinfo/page36.html.

"The National Underground Railroad Network to Freedom Act," 105th Congress, 1st Sess., May 15, 1997.

"The Schism of 1861: Presbyterian Church History, Lesson 7. The North-South Schism of 1861." www.americanpresbyterianchurch.org/the_north-south_schism_of_1861.htm.

"The Underground Railroad: From Slavery to Freedom on the National Forests." On file, Shawnee National Forest, 2000.

Thompson, Bob. "Civil War, Take 2: Hollywood Captured the Blood of Battle but Shrank Away from Slavery's Reality." *Washington Post*, December 24, 2003, C-1, 8.

Thoreau, Henry David. *The Variorum Civil Disobedience*. New York: Twayne Publishers, Inc., 1967.

Thornbrough, Emma Lou. *The Negro in Indiana before 1900: A Study in Minority*. Bloomington: Indiana University Press, 1985.

Thornton, Rosemary. "New Bethel Church in Godfrey Withstands Arsonists, Vandals, Time," *Alton Area Post*, February 8, 1999, AA-5.

Tillery, Tyrone. "The Inevitability of the Douglass-Garrison Conflict." *Phylon Quarterly* 32 (1976): 137–49.

Timmermiere, Irene. "History of New Bethel A.M.E. Church Rocky Fork." Rededication program of New Bethel Rocky Fork AME Church, May 18, 1975.

Titcomb, Jason M. "Rocky Fork: A Sanctuary for Freedom." *Illinois Antiquity* 40, no. 3 (2005): 12–13.

Tregillis, Helen Cox. *River Roads to Freedom: Fugitive Slave Notices and Sheriff Notices Found in Illinois Sources*. Bowie, MD: Heritage Books, 1988.

Tritt, Richard L. "The Underground Railroad at Boiling Springs." In *At a Place Called the Boiling Springs*, edited by Richard L. Tritt and Randy Watts, 111–17. Boiling Springs, PA: Boiling Springs Sesquicentennial Committee, 1995.

Trusty, Emma Marie. *Underground Railroad: Ties That Bound Unveiled*. Philadelphia: Amed Literary, 1999.

Turner, Glennette Tilley. *The Underground Railroad in Illinois*. Glen Ellyn, IL: Newman Educational Publishing, 2001.

Turner, Henry M. "African M. E. General Conference," *Georgia Weekly Telegraph*, May 15, 1868.

Twelvetrees, Harper, ed. *The Story of the Life of John Anderson, the Fugitive Slave*. London: William Tweedie, 1863.

UGRR Network to Freedom Program. *Network to Freedom Database*, National Park Service. www.cr.nps.gov/ugrr/network_d.htm.

Upton, William H., and Thomas M. Reed. *Negro Masonry: Being a Critical Examination of Objections to the Legitimacy of the Masons Existing Among the Negroes of America*. M. W. Grand Lodge of F. and A. Masons of Washington, 1989.

"U.S. Secretary of Agriculture Recognizes Wayne National Forest." *U.S.D.A. Forest Service News*, May 31, 2001.

Ustinova, Anastasia. "An Underground Railroad Theory Being Questioned." *Grand Forks Herald Co.*, February 20, 2004.

Vincent, Stephen A. *Southern Seed, Northern Soil: African-American Farm Communities in the Midwest, 1765–1900*. Bloomington: Indiana University Press, 1999.

Walker, Clarence E. *A Rock in a Weary Land: The African Methodist Episcopal Church During the Civil War*. Baton Rouge: Louisiana State University Press, 1982.

Walker, David. *Appeal to the Colored Citizens of the World* (1829, 1830). In *Pamphlets of Protest: An Anthology of Early African American Protest Literature, 1790–1860*, edited by Richard Newman, Patrick Rael, and Phillip Lapsansky, 90–109. New York: Routledge, 2001.

———. *Walker's Appeal, in Four Articles; Together with a Preamble, to the Coloured Citizens of the World, but in Particular, and Very Expressly, to Those of the United States of America, Written in Boston, State of Massachusetts, September 28, 1829*. Electronic Edition, Documenting the American South. docsouth.unc.edu/nc/walker/walker.html.

Walker, Joseph E. "Negro Labor in the Charcoal Iron Industry of Southeastern Pennsylvania." *Pennsylvania Magazine of History and Biography* 93, no. 4 (October 1969): 466–86.

———. *Hopewell Village: The Dynamics of a Nineteenth Century Ironmaking Community*. Philadelphia: University of Pennsylvania Press, 1974.

Walker, Juliet E. K. "'Free' Frank and New Philadelphia: Slave and Freedman, Frontiersman and Town Founder." Ph.D. dissertation, University of Chicago, 1976.

———. *Free Frank: A Black Pioneer on the Antebellum Frontier*. Lexington: University Press of Kentucky, 1983.

———. *The History of Black Business in America: Capitalism, Race, Entrepreneurship*. New York: Twayne Publishers, 1998.

Walls, Bishop William Jacob. *The African Methodist Episcopal Zion Church: Reality of the Black Church*. Charlotte: A.M.E. Zion Publishing House, 1974.

Warranty Deed, Bedford and Abigail Miller to School Directors of District No. 1 Township 12 R East, Book Y of Deeds. Circuit Court, Pope County, IL.

Wasser, Elsie M., comp. "1845 Census Madison County, IL." 1985.

Wayne National Forest. "U.S. Secretary of Agriculture Veneman to Recognize Wayne NF," U.S. Department of Agriculture, May 31, 2001.

Weeks, Samuel. *Southern Quakers and Slavery*. Baltimore: Johns Hopkins Press, 1896.

Weik, Terrance M. *The Archaeology of Antislavery Resistance*. Gainesville: University Press of Florida, 2012.

Welch, Elaine. *William Paul Quinn: A Militant Churchman*. Chicago: Quinn Chapel, 1933.

Wellman, Judith. "Documenting the Underground Railroad: Some Considerations." Paper presented at the Organization of American Historians, Toronto, April 1999.

Wepler, William R., Robert McCullough, Dot McCullough, and Sarah Arthur. "The Roberts Site Initial Investigation of an Antebellum Biracial Community, Orange County, Indiana." U.S. Department of Agriculture, National Forest Service, Hoosier National Forest, 2001.

Wesley, Charles H. *Neglected History: Essays in Negro History by a College President*. Washington, DC: Association for the Study of Negro Life and History, 1969.

———. *Richard Allen: Apostle of Freedom*. Washington, DC: Associated Publishers, 1969.

"Western Reserve, Ohio, Facts and Statistics." reference.allrefer.com/gazetteer/W/W02473-western-reserve.html.

WGBH, PBS On-Line. "Judgment Day: Bleeding Kansas." *Africa in America*. www.pbs.org/wgbh/aia/part4/4p2952.html.

———. Judgment in America: Part IV-1831–1865. "The Compromise of 1850 and the Fugitive Slave Act." In *Africa in America*. www.pbs.org/wgbh/aia/part4/4p2951.html.

Whitman, T. Stephen. *Challenging Slavery in the Chesapeake: Black and White Resistance to Human Bondage, 1775–1865*. Baltimore: Maryland Historical Society, 2007.

Wilder, Craig Steven. *In the Company of Black Men: The African Influence on African American Culture in New York City*. New York: New York University Press, 2001.

Wilkerson, Isabel. *The Warmth of Other Suns: The Epic Story of America's Great Migration*. New York: Random House, 2010.

Willard, Eugene B., Daniel W. Williams, George O. Newman, and Charles B. Taylor, eds. *A Standard History of the Hanging Rock Iron Region in Ohio: An Authentic Narrative of the Past, with an Extended Survey of the Industrial and Commercial Development*, vol. 1. St. Louis: Lewis Publishing Co., 1916.

Williams, Isaac D. *Sunshine and Shadow of Slave Life. Reminiscences as told by Isaac D. Williams to "Tege."* Saginaw: Evening News Printing and Binding House, 1885.

Wills, David W., and Richard Newman, eds. *Black Apostles at Home and Abroad: Afro-Americans and the Christian Mission from the Revolution to Reconstruction*. Boston: G. K. Hall and Co., 1982.

———. "Woman and Domesticity in the AME Tradition: The Influence of Daniel Alexander Payne." In *Black Apostles at Home and Abroad: Afro-Americans and the Christian Mission from the Revolution to Reconstruction*, edited by David W. Wills and Richard Newman, 133–46. Boston: G. K. Hall and Co., 1982.

Wilson, Henry. *History of the Rise and Fall of the Slave Power in America*. Vol. 2. Boston: Houghton, Mifflin and Company, 1872; reprint, New York: Negro Universities Press, 1969.

Wilson, Jeremiah Moses, ed. *Classical Black Nationalism: From the American Revolution to Marcus Garvey*. New York: New York University Press, 1996.

Winks, Robin W. *The Blacks in Canada: A History*. 2nd ed. Montreal: McGill-Queen's University Press, 1997.

Withrow, W. H. "The Underground Railroad." Royal Society of Canada, 1902.

Woods, Clyde. *Development Arrested: Race, Power, and the Blues in the Mississippi Delta*. London: Verso, 1998.

Woodson, Carter G. "Eighteenth Century Slaves as Advertised by Their Masters." *Journal of Negro History* 1, no. 2 (1916): 163–216.

———. *A Century of Negro Migration*. Washington, DC: The Association for the Study of Negro Life and History, 1918; reprint, New York: Russell and Russell, 1969.

———. *The Negro in Our History*. Washington, DC: Associated Publishers, 1922.

Woodson, Carter G., and Charles H. Wesley. *The Story of the Negro Retold*. 4th ed. Washington, DC: Associated Publishers, 1935.

Works Progress Administration. "Kansas, a Guide to the Sunflower State." Kansas Department of Education, 1939.

———. "WPA Slave Narrative Project, Florida Narratives, Volume 3." Washington, DC: Federal Writers' Project for the Work Projects Administration for the State of Florida, 1941.

Wright, Donald R. *African Americans in the Early Republic 1789–1831*. Arlington Heights, IL: Harlan Davidson, Inc., 1993.

Wright, Giles R. *Afro-Americans in New Jersey: A Short History*. Trenton: New Jersey Historical Commission, 1988.

Wright, Richard R. *Centennial Encyclopaedia of the African Methodist Episcopal Church Containing Principally the Biographies of the Men and Women, Both Ministers and Laymen, Whose Labors During a Hundred Years, Helped Make the A. M. E. Church What It Is; Also Short Historical Sketches of Annual Conferences, Educational Institutions, General Departments, Missionary Societies of the A. M. E. Church, and General Information About African Methodism and the Christian Church in General; Being a Literary Contribution to the Celebration of the One Hundredth Anniversary of the Formation of the African Methodist Episcopal Church Denomination by Richard Allen and Others, at Philadelphia, Penna., in*

*1816*. Philadelphia: Book Concern of the A.M.E. Church, 1916. docsouth.unc.edu/church/wright/wright.html.

Writers' Program of the Work Projects Administration in the State of Ohio, comp. *Cincinnati: A Guide to the Queen City and its Neighbors*. Cincinnati: Wiesen-Hart Press, 1943.

Wyatt-Brown, Bertram. "The Abolitionists' Postal Campaign of 1835." *Journal of Negro History* 50, no. 4 (October 1965): 227–38.

———. *Lewis Tappan and the Evangelical War against Slavery*. Baton Rouge: Louisiana State University Press, 1997.

Yancey, Miranda L., and Joseph M. Galloy. "Mother Baltimore's Freedom Village and the Development of Brooklyn, Illinois." Illinois State Archaeological Survey, University of Illinois at Urbana-Champaign. Paper presented at the Midwest Archaeological Conference, October 15–19, 2008.

Yannessa, Mary Ann. *Levi Coffin, Quaker: Breaking the Bonds of Slavery in Ohio and Indiana*. Richmond, IN: Friends United Press, 2001.

## Interviews

Johnson, Charlotte. Committee member, Committee on Black Pioneers, Alton Museum of History and Art, Alton, IL. Interview with author. Tape recording. Wood Station, IL, June 2000, June 2002, June 2003.

Kennedy, Clementine. Interview with author. Tape recording. Alton, IL, June 2000.

Matlock, John, Jr. Interview with author. Tape recording. Rocky Fork, IL, June 2000.

McClure, Wilbur. Telephone interview with author. Vienna, IL, July 31, 2003.

Ransom, Terry. UGRR-Illinois expert, Civil Rights Division of the Illinois Department of Transportation. Interview with author. Springfield, IL, June 2000.

Townsend, Charles B., III. Interview with author. Tape recording. Alton, IL, June 2000.

Wadleigh, George. Interview with author. Rocky Fork, IL, September 2, 2000.

# INDEX

Page numbers in *italics* indicate illustrations or maps.

CHERYL JANIFER LAROCHE is a lecturer in American studies at the University of Maryland.

The University of Illinois Press
is a founding member of the
Association of American University Presses.

---

Composed in 10/13 Sabon
by Lisa Connery
at the University of Illinois Press
Manufactured by Sheridan Books, Inc.

University of Illinois Press
1325 South Oak Street
Champaign, IL 61820-6903
www.press.uillinois.edu